On the Banks of the Yaryn

Middlebury Studies in Russian Language and Literature

Thomas R. Beyer, Jr.
General Editor

Vol. 28

PETER LANG
New York • Washington, D.C./Baltimore • Bern
Frankfurt am Main • Berlin • Brussels • Vienna • Oxford

Aleksandr Kondratiev

On the Banks of the Yaryn

A Demonological Novel

TRANSLATED AND WITH INTRODUCTION,
NOTES, AND APPENDIX BY

Valentina G. Brougher

PETER LANG
New York • Washington, D.C./Baltimore • Bern
Frankfurt am Main • Berlin • Brussels • Vienna • Oxford

Library of Congress Cataloging-in-Publication Data
A. K. (Aleksandr Kondratiev), b. 1876.
[Na beregakh Yaryni. English]
On the banks of the Yaryn: a demonological novel /
Alexandr Kondratiev; translated and with introduction,
notes, and appendix by Valentina G. Brougher.
p. cm. — (Middlebury studies in Russian language and literature; v. 28)
Includes bibliographical references.
I. Brougher, Valentina G. II. Title. III. Series.
PG3467.K547N313   891.73'42—dc21   2003000414
ISBN 0-8204-6746-4
ISSN 0888-8752

Bibliographic information published by **Die Deutsche Bibliothek.**
Die Deutsche Bibliothek lists this publication in the "Deutsche
Nationalbibliografie"; detailed bibliographic data is available
on the Internet at http://dnb.ddb.de/.

The paper in this book meets the guidelines for permanence and durability
of the Committee on Production Guidelines for Book Longevity
of the Council of Library Resources.

© 2004 Peter Lang Publishing, Inc., New York
275 Seventh Avenue, 28th Floor, New York, NY 10001
www.peterlangusa.com

Printed in Germany

Contents

Acknowledgments

I discovered the existence of Aleksandr Kondratiev's novel, *На берегах Ярыни* (*On the Banks of the Yaryn*), by pure chance. Researching the demonic in recent Russian prose at the University of Illinois Summer Research Lab on Russia and Eastern Europe, I came across several references to Kondratiev's work. To my good fortune, a post-Soviet collection of the writer's prose, which included the novel, was available in the stacks. After beginning to read *На берегах Ярыни* I could not put it down, and the decision to locate the 1930 original version and work on an English translation formed in my mind the very next day. Thus, my first thank you is to the University of Illinois for the use its facilities and special holdings, leading me to discover Kondratiev's fascinating novel.

A number of people helped in various ways in the early stages of the project and I offer them my sincere thanks. When the microfiche copy of the novel arrived from the University of Berkeley just as I was leaving for a conference in Russia, my colleague George Mihaychuk generously arranged for a copy to be made in my absence. Galina Pyadusova, St. Petersburg State University, helped me meet Boris Zabirokhin, whose etchings of folk demonic beings in an art gallery at the Alexander Nevsky Monastery had caught my eye. Frank Miller, Columbia University, carried back for me several of the artist's illustrations when he returned from a Russian trip.

I would like to express my gratitude to a number of my students whose enthusiasm for Russian language and folklore made the task of translating Kondratiev's novel a wonderful distraction from the daily routine. Jason Mulvihill, Daniel Krebs, and Wells Bennett worked with me on the first rough draft through the

Georgetown Research Opportunities Program (GUROP) sponsored by the Office of the Provost. They juggled dictionaries, tested their knowledge of Russian and English, worked magic with the computer, and never lost their sense of humor. Ashley Ailey and Michael Phillips read the draft and offered some helpful comments.

During the whole process my colleague, Valery Petrochenkov, always found the time to respond to my questions about Kondratiev's syntax and sometimes puzzling lexicon. With his poetic sensibility and vast knowledge of Russian literature, he unfailingly helped me to resolve whatever questions arose.

I am enormously indebted to two people whose friendship, forbearance, and wisdom encouraged me to pursue the project to completion. David Harris, Professor Emeritus of Linguistics at Georgetown University, carefully read through the first third of the translation and offered detailed commentary and imaginative solutions to some challenging stylistic problems. His generosity of spirit and mind meant that I could always count on his help and expertise as I continued to work on the translation. Holly Stephens, my colleague at Georgetown with whom I teach a course on Slavic folklore, offered moral support and a sympathetic ear whenever I needed to vent my frustrations with the volume. She spent many hours reading through the first version of the manuscript, offering helpful suggestions and sage advice.

My dear friend, Helen Wolff, provided invaluable assistance by generously giving of her time and reading through the manuscript as I was getting ready to mail it to a potential publisher. Curtis Murphy, a graduate student in Russian studies, read through the manuscript after changes had been made in response to the publisher's suggestions and worked with me to eliminate any remaining inconsistencies. Of course, any errors or infelicities of style that still remain are ultimately mine.

I could not have completed this volume without the professionalism and good humor of Helen Sullivan and Julia Gauchman of the Slavic Library, University of Illinois at Urbana-Champaign. They assisted me with research on Russian/Ukrainian folklore and never dismissed my questions, no matter how ridiculous they must have sounded at times ("I've consulted all the basic sources, but no luck. Do you know where can I find out something about 'chicken name days?'").

My profound thanks to Heidi Burns, Senior Editor, Peter Lang

Publishing, Inc., whose courtesy and efficiency made the often difficult task of placing a manuscript with a publisher relatively stress-free; and Thomas R. Beyer, Jr., General Editor of the Middlebury Series in Slavic Languages and Literatures, who suggested ways of making the volume more accessible for the nonspecialist while at the same time providing information for the student of Russian literature and culture. He was always available to answer my questions on the phone, and I am grateful to him for his advice and guidance. I would also like to express my gratitude to Lisa Dillon, Production Manager at Peter Lang, for her professionalism and collegiality throughout the production process; and to the Graduate School of Georgetown University for providing subvention funds.

Last but not least, my love and deep gratitude to my husband, Jack, and my son, John, for their unfailing support of my work and their enthusiasm for Kondratiev's *On the Banks of the Yaryn*. Many a day John sat at the computer, taking dictation and learning about *rusalka*s; and Jack patiently read through parts of the manuscript a number of times and offered creative solutions to some difficult matters of style, nobly trying to keep his sense of humor as I lost mine. It is to the presence of these two wonderful men in my life that I dedicate this volume.

A Few Notes to the Reader

The reader may find it helpful to refer to the list of characters given at the beginning of the novel and to the descriptions of demonic spirits and practitioners of magic supplied in the appendix.

In order to make the text of Kondratiev's novel more appealing to a broad audience, I use a transliteration system intended to be easy on English-oriented eyes; I hope the Slavic scholar will forgive me for any inconsistencies or phonetic inaccuracies that such an approach entails. I ignore the "soft sign" (ь) at the end of nouns (Волынь becomes Volyn) but render it as an "i" when it is found internally in the word (Кондратьев becomes Kondratiev). In the footnotes to the introduction and the bibliography at the end of the appendix, I follow the Library of Congress system of transliteration for those who might wish to pursue their own research on Kondratiev and Russian/Ukrainian folklore.

My translation does not reflect the rich variety of diminutives that Kondratiev uses for many of his characters. The reader who knows Russian appreciates that these diminutives signal affection, closeness, and intimacy or condescension, scorn and ridicule. The reader who does not know Russian, however, would find the use of some six-eight different names for a single character confusing, making it difficult to follow the life and fortune of that character in the novel. I have, therefore, selected one name (sometimes a diminutive form) and a common diminutive of that name so that the reader has to keep track of only two names for a character, a pair that should connect relatively easily in the English-oriented eyes and mind, e. g., Aksyutka—Aksyutochka and Gorpina—Gorpinka.

I have chosen not translate into English the folk names for the spirits of water, field, marsh, and forest. Although *vodyanoi* might be translated as "water spirit" and *leshy* as "spirit of the forest," it would not be such an easy matter with names such as *rusalka:* "water imp" or "mermaid" strikes me as a misleading and inadequate choice which would lead to contamination of the *rusalka's* image with features specific to somewhat similar, but not identical, beings in other cultures. An additional reason for using the original names of the spirits of native Slavic mythology is that many are part of today's lexicon. Most Russians are comfortable referring to a *domovoi* (house spirit) or a *leshy*, and students of Russian culture should understand such references as well.

In the text the reader will encounter *leshy* and "the Leshy," *domovoi* and "the Domovoi," etc. The italicized word, let us take *leshy*, simply means generically "a spirit of the forest," whereas "the Leshy" is the actual name of a particular forest spirit whose life and adventures constitute an important part of the novel. In other words, *leshy* (italicized but not capitalized) is simply a lexical item—like house, fish, bush, river—whereas "the Leshy" (capitalized but not italicized) signals the name Kondratiev has given to a primary or secondary character in the novel.

Please note that when a plural form is needed of the Russian word for a spirit of the water, forest or field, a non-italicized "s" is added to indicate that an English plural ending has been added to the Russian singular form, i.e., *rusalka, rusalka*s (*leshy, lesh*ies is the only exception). The same approach is used for possessives: *rusalka*'s, *leshy*'s, etc.

Introduction

The name of Aleksandr Alekseevich Kondratiev (1876–1967) was unknown to Russian readers and critics for many decades until a thick volume of his prose, *Сны* (*Dreams*), was published in 100,000 copies in St. Petersburg in 1993. Kondratiev in fact was born in St. Petersburg, where he published poetry, prose, essays, and criticism until the revolution. He left Russia in 1918, never to return. However, with the new freedoms brought by the collapse of the Soviet Union, the pre-revolutionary capital of Russia was able to reclaim one of its many forgotten talents. The literary "rehabilitation" of Kondratiev, which the well-known literary critic Gleb Struve could only dream about in 1969, had become a reality some twenty-five years later.[1]

The 1993 volume of Kondratiev's prose included not only a novel, a novella (*повесть*), and stories from his St. Petersburg period, but also a work that had never before appeared in Russia, *На берегах Ярыни* (*On the Banks of the Yaryn*), with the subtitle *Демонологический роман* (*A Demonological Novel*). This novel was published in 1930 by a Russian emigre press in Berlin, Медный всадник (The Bronze Horseman), where Kondratiev had mailed it from Poland. The editor of the press, S. Krechetov, to whom the writer had mailed some of his prose and articles in 1925 (perhaps other years as well),[2] was so impressed with Kondratiev's demonological novel that he wrote an enthusiastic introduction to the volume. *On the Banks of the Yaryn* quickly earned the praise of emigre critics in Europe but, as might be

---

1. Gleb Struve, "Александр Кондратьев. По неизданным письмам," *Annali*, Instituto Universitario Orientale. Napoli. Sezione Slava Vol. XII, 1969: 8.
2. Ibid., 9.

expected, was passed over in silence by the Soviet critical world. Not only had the author left the Soviet Union, but the characters and thematics of the work hardly fit Stalin's call for fiction to model the achievements of the first five-year plan.

In 1990, a few years before the novel's appearance in Russia, a ground-breaking study of *On the Banks of the Yaryn* by the renowned critic, semiotician, and linguist Vladimir Toporov was published in Italy. In his *Неомифологизм в русской литературе начала XX века. Роман А. А. Кондратьева "На берегах Ярыни"* (*Neomythologisation in Russian Literature at the Beginning of the XX Century. A. A. Kondratiev's Novel On the Banks of the Yaryn*), Toporov described the novel as "one of the crowning achievements of 'neomythologisation' in Russian literature in the first decades of the 20th century."[3] He urged scholars to make the forgotten but "remarkable" novel part of the history of Russian literature and to use it in their research on the spiritual culture of the Russian people.

The son of a government functionary, Kondratiev graduated in 1897 from the Eighth Petersburg Gymnasium. Its director at the time was the poet, critic, and scholar of classical antiquity, Innonkenty F. Annensky. Annensky also taught classes in classical mythology, and Kondratiev's early interest in Egyptian, Greek and Roman mythology is largely due to Annensky's influence.

Kondratiev's student years (1897–1902) at St. Petersburg University played an important role in developing his interest in Slavic mythology. At the turn of the century, the University's School (*Факультет*) of Philology was "one of the most important centers [in Russia] for the study of mythology, ritual, and poetry based on folklore materials."[4] The School's focus reflected the interest in Slavic folklore, folk art and music that from the middle of the 19th century exercised such a profound influence on the creative arts in Russia.[5] Although he was a student in the

---

3. Vladimir N. Toporov. *Неомифологизм в русской литературе начала XX века. Роман А. А. Кондратьева "На берегах Ярыни."* Trento: Edizioni di Michael Yevzlin, 1990, 132.

4. Ibid., 15.

5. This interest in the life of the folk (*народ*) influenced the creativity of Pyotr Tchaikovsky, Nikolai Rimski-Korsakov, Modest Mussorgsky, and Igor Stravinsky in music, and V. Vasnetsov, Ivan Bilibin, Nikolai Rerikh, and others in art. Students and scholars of folklore roamed villages to record

University's Law Department, Kondratiev, too, became increasingly interested in native Slavic mythology. University life also brought him in contact with many aspiring poets, including Sergei Gorodetsky and Aleksandr Blok, whose use of imagery taken from fairy-tales, demonology and mythology influenced Kondratiev's own creativity.[6]

In his early years as a writer Kondratiev held readings in his home in which poets of different schools and tastes took part. Kondratiev also attended various literary evenings, where he would meet not only Blok but such prominent literary figures of Russian symbolism as Vyacheslav Ivanov, Valery Bryusov, Konstantin Balmont, Fedor Sologub, and Anna Akhmatova. Kondratiev, however, never became a symbolist himself; although drawn to the symbolists' depiction of the demonic and the otherwordly, he traveled on the periphery of the symbolist movement. His artistic tastes and socio-political orientation gravitated more toward the traditional and the conservative. In 1906 he joined a literary circle, "Evenings at Sluchevsky's" *(Вечера Случевского),* which had come into being in 1898 (and existed until 1917). The group, organized with the goal of "gathering to read new poetic works as well as to exchange ideas about phenomena of contemporary literary life,"[7] was generally opposed to the "new" poetry of the symbolists.

An important signpost in Kondratiev's literary biography was his participation in a 1906 competition administered by the journal *The Golden Fleece (Золотое руно).*[8] The challenge was to depict Satan in either a work of literature or visual art. The literature jury included Blok, Bryusov, and Ivanov. Although the jury's task was a very difficult one—in literature there were some one-hundred submissions (in the art division, about fifty),[9] and members of the jury were not clear themselves about what image they had in mind for the "Prince of Darkness"—

---

folk beliefs, superstitions, traditions, rituals, folk narratives and songs as well as designs on dresses, huts, home utensils, etc. See Toporov's study as well as Solomon Volkov, *St. Petersburg. A Cultural History* (New York: Simon & Schuster, 1995).

6. Ibid., 15-25.

7. A. A. Kondrat'ev. "Письма Б. А. Садовскому," edited and annotated by N. A. Bogomolov and S. V. Shumikhin. *De Visu,* No. 1/2 (14), 1994: 29.

8. Oleg Sedov, "Мир прозы А. А. Кондратьева: мифология и демонология," *Сны. Романы, повесть, рассказы.* Санкт-Петербург: Северо-Запад, 1993, 5-8.

9. Toporov, 145.

prizes were awarded to three competitors: Mikhail Kuzmin, Aleksei Remizov, and Aleksandr Kondratiev. What is especially interesting is that although Kondratiev won the prize for his sonnet about Lucifer, what Blok found especially appealing was the short story *"В пещере"* (In a Cave), which Kondratiev had also submitted to the jury.

The narrative of "In a Cave" is presented from the viewpoint of a forgotten petty demon. Kondratiev's story suggests that it was not Lucifer or Beelzebub who was the sovereign of the demonic forces, but a proto-mythological female deity. With Kondratiev's vast knowledge of world mythology, that deity bore the features of various female deities in mankind's rich cultural past. Kondratiev's image of Christ was also syncretical, drawing on Egyptian, Greek and Biblical imagery. In one of his notebooks Blok wrote: "Kondratiev is a remarkable man. His story about a demon and Christ is deeply symbolic. It is perfectly balanced . . . [it] doesn't force the mystery, but is mysterious and deep."[10]

Given his interest in the "forces of darkness," it is not surprising that Kondratiev felt a strong sense of affinity with three of his contemporaries—Aleksei Remizov, Fedor Sologub, and Valery Bryusov. Remizov, like Kondratiev, was attracted to the folkloric-mythological aspects of Russian culture and strove to recreate in his writing the world of demonic beings that inhabited the spiritual space of the Russian peasant. Although Sologub is "remembered as the chief decadent among the symbolists,"[11] the appeal of his prose and poetry for Kondratiev lay in his depiction of the forces of light and darkness and in his view that the universe was ruled by the demonic. In Bryusov, Kondratiev sensed a kindred spirit: his writing revealed an attraction for pagan beliefs, something that Kondratiev himself had been studying. The extent to which Kondratiev's friendship with these writers had a fertile impact on his own writing is a subject for scholarly debate. In any case, professional and social contact with Remizov, Sologub, and Bryusov strengthened Kondratiev's own interest in pagan beliefs and the demonic/unclean force and influenced his choice of themes and imagery.[12]

---

10. Ibid., 8.
11. *The Cambridge History of Russian Literature*, Revised Edition. Ed. Charles A. Moser. Cambridge: Cambridge University Press, 1992, 406.
12. See Toporov for a discussion of the possible influence of fellow writers on Kondrat'ev's development as a writer.

Kondratiev published eight books of prose and poetry before the revolution (some of the stories and poems had first appeared in newspapers and journals) which serve as testimony of his serious interest in ancient, classical mythology as well as Slavic/Russian folk beliefs. In general, his poetry (*Стихотворения/Poems*; St. Petersburg, 1905;*Стихи. Книга вторая. Черная Венера/Poems. Book Two. Black Venus*; St. Petersburg, 1909) met with a lukewarm reception. It was thought to be "good," "correct" but "timid"—traditional in form and execution at a time when poets were searching for new ways to express their personal, religious, and philosophical musings as well as the privileged view of the world they believed their poetic vision afforded them. His prose, on the other hand, earned positive, even enthusiastic comments. Kondratiev displayed exceptional erudition in his portrayal of the mythology and demonology of different epochs and nations; this erudition, coupled with a talent for interpreting and evoking the world of his mythological and folkloric beings, brought him words of praise from such poets and writers as Annensky, Blok and Bryusov.

Kondratiev's first short story, "*Домовой*" (The House Spirit), which Kondratiev later incorporated into his demonological novel, was published in the newspaper *Россия (Russia)* in 1901.[13] His first novel, *Сатиресса. Мифологический роман (The Satyr. A Mythological Novel)* appeared in 1907 (and was republished in 1914). In reviewing the work, Annensky wrote: "If you want to leave at least for a time the psychology of silk skirts, prayer-books, and the morgue, take a look at Kondratiev's book—you'll smell resin and the sea."[14] *Белый козёл (White Goat)*, Kondratiev's first collection of short stories on mythological themes, was published in 1908, and *Улыбка Ашеры (Ishtar's Smile)*, his second collection of short stories, in 1911. The latter was singled out for praise by Bryusov.

In 1912 Kondratiev published a volume that was a labor of love for him: *Граф А. К. Толстой. Материалы для истории жизни и творчества (Count A. K. Tolstoy. Materials for a History of His Life and Creativity)*. Kondratiev wrote in a letter that he "had been raised on [A. K. Tolstoy] and heard his Russian epic tales *(былины)*

---

13. Sedov, 16.
14. *Русские писатели, 1800-1917. Биографический словарь.* Главный редактор П. А. Николаев. Москва: Научное изд. "Большая российская энциклопедия,"1994, 48.

when [he] could not even read."[15] Tolstoy also had quite a good knowledge of studies in the occult, as Toporov has pointed out,[16] and Kondratiev—as many artists, musicians, philosophers and men of letters at the turn of the century—shared Tolstoy's fascination with the occult, i.e., with the invisible, the mystical, and the fantastic that, through the centuries, people incorporated into their interpretations of the world around them.

The last book of Kondratiev's to be published in Russia was a play, *Елена. Драматический эпизод из эпохи Троянской войны.* (*Helen. A Dramatic Episode from the Time of the Trojan War.* 1917).

It is of some interest to note that Kondratiev's writing was an avocation which brought him very little money; in fact, a number of times he contributed his own funds, and that of his relatives, to offset the publication costs of his books. Upon graduation from the university in 1902, he supported himself by working as a secretary in the Ministry of Transportation; then, from 1908 until the end of 1917, he carried out various secretarial duties in the Office of the State Duma. His correspondence (1911–1917) with B. A. Sadovsky, a poet who lived in Moscow and for a time caught the attention of the reading public, serves as a revealing look into Kondratiev's personal life and professional interests as well as an illuminating source of his thoughts on Russia's political fortunes. Since there are relatively few published materials on Kondratiev,[17] what he writes in these letters helps to fill out our image of a man whose life combined the world of government service and the world of the literary arts.

In his letters to Sadovsky, Kondratiev shares facts, observations, and not a few rumors about St. Petersburg literary life: various intrigues and scandals, Sologub's suicide attempts, Bryusov's health, Nikolai Gumilyov's travels, philosophical disputes between Dmitry Merezhkovsky, Vasily Rozanov and Vyacheslav Ivanov, and the like. Although his comments about literary life provide testimony of the social circles in which he moved, they are disappointingly brief, as if he had only a superficial interest in this world or some unspoken reservations about sharing the details.

---

15. "Письма Садовскому," *De Visu* (letter of 4 January 1912), 5.

16. Toporov, 133.

17. See Toporov (187-232) for information on Kondrat'ev's letters to various literary figures on deposit in several Russian archives as well as long excerpts from these letters.

Kondratiev does write with passion and at length, however, about the evolving political life of Russia. "We live in an epoch that from a romantic point of view is no less interesting than the second half of the 18th century, don't you think?" he observes to Sadovsky in February1914.[18] At first he refuses to believe all the rumors about Rasputin as well as about German influence at court that "the mob" is so ready to believe,[19] but soon he becomes less dogmatic. As the war with Germany progresses, several things begin to distress him deeply. He senses a lack of patriotism among the people, particularly the young, and laments the absence of the kind of patriotic fervor that had permeated the land during the 1812 war with Napoleon.[20] He decries how easily and in what great numbers Russian soldiers surrender to the Germans.[21] He also predicts that a "terrible revolution awaits [the Russians] after the war, particularly if it is not successful."[22] When the revolution does come, he writes at the end of 1917: "I am hanging between heaven and earth in an undefinable mood . . . I have not taken an oath to anyone and do not plan to do so."[23] One suspects that as for many of his contemporaries, the old Russia he knew was changing too quickly for him and the political situation was chaotic and confusing. It appears that he felt lost and in limbo.

In 1918 Kondratiev left Petrograd, which was under Bolshevik control, and joined his wife and children in the Crimea. A year later, in 1919, Kondratiev moved his family from the Crimea to his mother-in-law's large estate near Rovno (Rivne in Ukrainian), the Volyn Province (in north-western Ukraine, which had become part of Poland after World War I), where he remained until 1939.[24]

In those post-Petersburg years, he became immersed in studying even more seriously the paganism and demonology of the Eastern Slavs. According to Oleg Sedov in his informative introduction to the 1993 collection of the writer's prose,[25] Kondratiev's reading included A. N. Afanasiev's *Поэтические воззрения славян*

---

18. Kondrat'ev, "Письма Б. А. Садовскому" (letter of 3 February, 1914), 14.
19. Ibid. (letters of 5 November, 1914, and 5 December, 1914), 8 and 22, respectively.
20. Ibid. (letter of 22 November 1914), 20.
21. Ibid. (letter of 5 December 1914), 21.
22. Ibid. (letter of 22 November 1914), 20.
23. Ibid. (letter of 5 December 1917), 26-27.
24. Struve, 4.
25. Sedov, 14.

на природу (*The Slavs' Poetic Views of Nature*, 1865–1869), S. V. Maksimov's *Нечистая, неведомая, и крестная сила* (*The Unclean, Mysterious Force and the Power of the Cross*, 1903), I. P. Sakharov's *Сказания русского народа* (*Legends of the Russian People*, 1885), and books by D. K. Zelenin, A. A. Potebnya, A. N. Veselovsky, V. F. Miller, and E. V. Anichkov. Since these studies appeared in the second half of the 19th century and at the beginning of the twentieth, we have to assume that Kondratiev had first read most, if not all, of these volumes while still in St. Petersburg.

Kondratiev's reading was reinforced and made the more vivid by the fact that people in the area in which he now lived and wrote still actively believed in witches and various demonic beings. To some extent he even adopted their mind set. In a letter to Remizov written in 1912 from his mother-in-law's estate—which he visited many times before settling there more permanently in 1919—he wrote that he saw a "witch, wanted to get acquainted with her but changed [my mind]. . . . She could put the evil eye on [me]."[26]

Kondratiev's life on the estate near Rovno led to the writing of articles on Slavic mythology (published in local newspapers and Warsaw, and occasionally in Berlin and Paris)[27] and a collection of sixty-nine "masterfully composed"[28] sonnets, *Славянские боги* (*Slavic Gods*, 1936).[29] In this period between the Civil War in Russia and World War II he also produced *On the Banks of the Yaryn*. The novel was based on Slavic pagan beliefs and popular folk demonology and represented the crowning achievement of his literary life.

The choice of Yaryn *(Ярынь)* for the title illustrates Kondratiev's poetic imagination at work. Yaryn—the deep, turbid river in which and around which the various beings of folk mythology and demonology live out their lives—is really a combination of the names of two rivers, Goryn *(Горынь)* and Yarun (*Ярунь*), both of which are to be found in the Rovno area where Kondratiev worked on his novel.[30] According to a detailed analysis of the

---

26. See letter of 9 December 1912, cited in Toporov, 219.
27. See Toporov (239-241) for a comprehensive list, plus comments by Struve (5) about Kondrat'ev's connections to various journals in Europe.
28. Struve, 5.
29. See Toporov (257-298) for a reprint of the sonnets, each of which is about a pagan god or a demonic being of folk belief.
30. Ibid., 48-56.

signification of Yaryn by Toporov, which can be restated only briefly here, Goryn brings to mind a hill, an elevated place, since it shares the root with *gora (гора)*, meaning "hill, mountain." Yaryn is etymologically connected to *yar (яр)*, meaning a "steep bank" or "sloping, precipitous river bank" as well as "ravine." By creatively merging Goryn and Yarun into Yaryn, Kondratiev plays on the sum total of the meanings and associations that Yaryn possesses. Images of ravines and steep banks move the perceiver's eye downward and upward, and that motion mimics a basic principle of composition in *On the Banks of the Yaryn*: the narration alternates between descriptions of life experienced in a deep pool of the Yaryn River and the world above, on the river banks and the adjoining water-meadows, forests and swamps.

The root *yar- (яр-)*, as Toporov also points out, is likewise bound in people's minds with the idea of passion, an excess of sexuality, and spring, warmth, fertility *(ярость)*. Thus in his choice of Yaryn for the name of the river in his title, Kondratiev offers another important clue to the novel. As the reader discovers, the atmosphere in *On the Banks of the Yaryn* is indeed sexually charged: passion, jealousy, and sexual need rule both the human and the demonic worlds. This "pansexualism,"[31] however, is handled with poetic restraint, leaving much to the reader's imagination.

The general appeal of Kondratiev's novel was perceptively summarized by Krechetov in his eloquent and enthusiastic introduction to the 1930 Berlin edition, which merits mention. Krechetov praised Kondratiev's talent for bringing the demonic beings of Russian folklore to life by placing them in the context of real, everyday life *(реально-бытовая жизнь)* and endowing them with a rich emotional life.[32] That, Krechetov felt, was a unique achievement: instead of contending with hazy, symbolic images from Russian folklore, the reader was given the opportunity to enter into a world whose reality was visually rich, concrete, and palpable. Krechetov also felt very strongly that Kondratiev's novel made for especially engaging reading and would produce the same degree of emotional involvement in the reader as Nikolai Gogol's Вечера на хуторе близ Диканьки (*Evenings on a Farm*

---

31. Ibid., 92.
32. S. Krechetov, "Предисловие," *На берегах Ярыни*. Берлин: Медный Всадник, 1930, 4.

near Dikanka, 1831–32).[33] It is noteworthy that Krechetov's observations were echoed not only by one of the reviewers of the work, Vl. Tatarinov in Paris,[34] but expanded upon by Toporov some sixty years later.

Kondratiev's artistic vision in *On the Banks of the Yaryn* serves as eloquent testimony of his belief that "[t]he mythology of almost every nation and every country owes its existence not only to its priests (жрецы: priests of heathen religious cults) but to its artists and poets."[35] In his narrative Kondratiev offers his reader an encyclopedia of Russian/Ukrainian folk belief, but in the more engaging genre of a novel. The work portrays all the major unclean spirits of water, marsh, field, and forest that inhabit the folk imagination; various magical and religious rituals as well as practices and traditions dating back to pagan times; celebrations connected to the agricultural calendar that regulated people's lives; and folk stories and legends that have arisen out of the people's need to understand the world around them. This rich, diverse material is combined into a harmonious whole, in a style that speaks of the writer's especially fine talent for nature descriptions and realistic dialogue.

A reader familiar with Slavic folklore will especially appreciate the artistic craftsmanship with which Kondratiev molds each demonic spirit out of the characteristics and behaviors that typify that spirit in folk beliefs and folk narratives. Thus his *rusalka* is a pretty, young village girl who, by drowning herself because of unrequited love, condemns herself to the world of demonic spirits. The physical appearance of his *leshy,* the spirit of the forest, evokes the image of the *leshy* of folk imagination: Kondratiev's description combines anthropomorphic features with those taken from the world of nature which the *leshy* guards—the trees, shrubs, and greenery that constitute his world. Kondratiev's *leshy* is also territorial—just as his fellow spirits of the water, bog and field are—ever ready to attack anyone who encroaches on his area without permission or without the proper rituals. Kondratiev's *bolotnitsa*s are visually rich recreations of

---

33. Ibid., Krechetov, 5.

34. Vl. Tatarinov, "Александр Кондратьев. На берегах Ярыни," *Руль* (Париж), 12 February 1930. I was not able to gain access to other positive reviews: V. Brandt, *За свободу,* 13 May 1931; and A. V. Amfiteatrov, *Сегодня* (Рига), 16 February 1931. Both are listed in *Русские писатели. 1800-1917. Биографический словарь.*

35. Toporov, 257.

the female spirits of the bog, celebrated in folk beliefs and stories for their beauty and alluring singing as well as their zeal for luring men to death in the boggy waters of the swamps they inhabit. And all of these beings are particularly active when the moon is out, the "sun" of the demonic world.

Kondratiev's rich mythopoetic imagination is able not only to bring the various beings of Slavic demonology and folk belief to life but to seamlessly establish a hierarchy among them as they come in contact with each other. The *vodyanoi* or spirit of the water makes every *rusalka* his wife for a time, rules over the *utoplenniks*, or men who have drowned, and uses a sheat-fish as his horse; and the *bolotnik*, or master of the swamp, commands the *bolotnitsas* as well as countless other little demons. The *vodyanoi* and the *bolotnik* rule their own domains, but consider themselves related. And Satan, "The Prince of Darkness," with the call of his demonic tambourine, is able to summon various monstrous beings, devils, sorcerers and witches to a sabbath,[36] where he rules over the celebration and calls for deeds of evil.

In recreating the world of mythology and folk demonology Kondratiev takes great care to acknowledge the pre-Christian past as well as the pagan heritage that continues to affect people's spiritual beliefs in the novel's time frame—the 19th century, pre-revolutionary Russia. An oak wood effigy of the ancient Slavic god of thunder, Perun, lies on the river bottom and reminisces about his days of glory when he ruled the sky and people worshiped him. With the *vodyanoi* he discusses the evolution and change that rule belief in gods: just as he displaced one god in people's beliefs, in time another god came to displace him, and thus it shall ever be. Kondratiev devotes parts of several chapters to reviewing for his reader the pantheon of pagan gods that used to rule the natural world in popular belief, and the rituals and traditions that peasants subsequently followed—a combination of pagan and Christian beliefs—as they marked the passing of seasons and time.

The lives and actions of Maksim and Praskukha serve to illustrate the "dual belief"*(двоеверие)*, or amalgam of folk beliefs and Russian Orthodoxy, that rules peasant life. Maksim recognizes Gorpina, his former girlfriend, in the *rusalka* or phantom he sees in the river but agrees to follow a Christian ritual and have

---

36. Most folklorists argue that the notion of a witches' sabbath reached Russia and Ukraine through the West Slavs (particularly Poland), who adopted it themselves from Western Europe.

prayers said for her soul. Praskukha, a village magic healer, uses magical herbs to protect herself from the evil spirits that are said to roam the landscape on St. John's Eve; but she also sprinkles Aksyutka, her adopted daughter, with holy water from a corner of the hut and says "half-pagan, half-Christian" prayers over her when the latter has troubling dreams.

Another important dimension of Kondratiev's novel is that the events in the novel and the various story lines that Kondratiev weaves together for his reader capture an important assumption of Russian/Ukrainian folk belief: the world of the demonic may exist in an "otherworldly" dimension, generally invisible to the human eye, but there is no question that this world affects and operates on human life. *On the Banks of the Yaryn* abounds in situations in which the demonic and human worlds come in contact with each other. Gorpina's and Maksim's chance meeting after her death is one example; the special relationship between Savely Ipatiev and his *domovoi* or house spirit is another; and the *leshy* eating Fedot's food, drinking his vodka, and complaining about women is yet another. The constant possibility of contact between the two worlds is also suggested in the charms, spells and incantations that people use to protect themselves and in the ritualistic traditions they have learned to observe when moving through a wood, working in a field, or celebrating a holiday.

The folkloric, demonic world and the human world also come together in special "alignment" in the existence of witches and sorcerers. These people are part of the daily village life, yet they possess secrets and knowledge from the "dark world" that set them apart from others. They can be sorceresses like old Praskukha, who gathers herbs and grasses for white magic and refuses to teach Aksyutka spells for summoning demons, although she has had some dealings with the unclean force in the past. They can be young, beautiful women like Aniska, who have received secrets of black magic from the devil and can shape-shift into a cat or a pig, or fly on brooms to witches' sabbaths. Although such servants of the demonic/unclean force can also tell fortunes and cure illnesses, they are more inclined to concoct potions of bewitchment or bring down illnesses upon others. At the sabbath they bow to the "Master of Darkness," eat, get drunk, and engage in relations with a variety of semi-monstrous beings, illustrating the physical and moral ugliness, as well as the perversion, of the demonic world.

A vital philosophical question at the core of Kondratiev's novel is the whole question of evil. Kondratiev's moral vision recognizes the existence of Satan to whom the witches and sorcerers who practice malefic magic ultimately owe their souls. The fate of the novel's various human characters serve as dramatic testimony of the high price that must be paid for contact and dealings with the unclean force. Through the figure of the young Aksyutka, however, Kondratiev raises a serious and oft-debated question: to what extent is one born or fated to do evil? His answer is neither simple nor unequivocal. Aksyutka, the daughter of a human male and a *bolotnitsa* or female swamp demon, tries not to do any harm to anyone, although she hears the devil's tempting whisperings in her ears. Although sorcery attracts Aksyutka and she seems to have an innate instinct for it, her interest in the demonic is not a question of wanting to possess powers which she can use against others but rather of a longing to find her parents, especially her mother. That longing is so innate and overpowering that, after various attempts to locate them have come to nothing, she takes the only choice she feels is left to her: to align herself with the forces of "darkness" and seek their help. That choice ultimately brings out her demonic side and leads to unfortunate consequences.

On the Banks of the Yaryn opens with the Vodyanoi, master of the Yaryn waters, waiting for a recently drowned village girl, Gorpina, to wake up as moonlight dimly illuminates her body. And the novel closes with Maryska, a swamp demon, looking at the body of a drowned young girl that has come to rest on the silty river bottom. As a patch of moonlight passes over that body, Maryska recognizes her own daughter by the birthmark on her hip, the daughter she had tried but failed to find. Overcome with despair, she kisses and holds her after fourteen long years. The love of a mother for her daughter that is such a vital part of life in the human dimension also finds its reflection in the demonological world of Kondratiev's conception. This last moving scene in the novel serves as an appropriately emotional farewell to the multi-dimensional reality on and near the banks of the Yaryn.

～

A few words about the rest of Kondratiev's life are in order not only because the reader of this volume may be curious about his

fate but also because his life serves as a poignant reminder of
what happened to hundreds of thousands of people displaced by
World War II. As was mentioned earlier, Kondratiev stayed in the
Volyn Province until 1939. In December of that year he, his wife,
and daughter[37] literally "walked away" from the estate near
Rovno, and the approaching Soviet forces, with what they could
carry and headed for Warsaw. According to the information Gleb
Struve received from Kondratiev's daughter, Elena Aleksan-
drovna Andreeva,[38] they soon moved from Warsaw to a small village in the Krakow Province, where Kondratiev's wife/Elena 's
mother, died of cancer. Subsequently, Elena and her father lived
near Vienna, Austria, but in trying to get away from "the front
drawing ever nearer," they found themselves near Berlin in April
1945. "By the grace of God" they managed to get to Belgrade,
where they lived until 1950. In that year, they, as many other
Russians, were sent out of the country by the Tito government
and found a temporary refuge in a camp for displaced persons
near Trieste, Italy. Elena emigrated to the United States in 1952,
and Kondratiev moved to Switzerland, where he lived in an old
folks' home.

In his letters to A. M. Aseev in the 1950s,[39] Kondratiev wrote
about his failing memory, long walks, and bouquets of flowers—
which included "flowers mentioned in ancient Greek mythology"[40]—which he gathered for those unable to leave the home.
He lamented having had to leave behind in Volyn almost all his
research notes, books, and unfinished manuscripts and reported
that he had only one worn copy of *Slavic Gods* with him.[41] As old
and frail as he felt, he wished he could learn more about spiritu-
alism[42] and revealed that he was "still interested in theoso-
phy."[43] Interestingly, he volunteered that "from childhood I was

---

37. Evidently his son and daughter-in-law stayed behind in Volyn'. In a letter
   dated 18 September 1953 (Struve, 39) Kondrat'ev mentions receiving information from a "spirit" at a seance that his son was still alive. That he had
   his fears that his son was dead, however, is suggested in the letter to Aseev
   of March 10, 1954 (Struve, 44).
38. Struve, 6.
39. A. M. Aseev was the editor of the journal Оккультизм и йога, published in
   Belgrade in the 1930s and subsequently in Paraguay.
40. Struve (letter of 18 November 1953 to Aseev), 40.
41. Struve (letter of 18 November 1953 to Aseev), 40.
42. Struve (letter of 16 February 1954 to Aseev), 42.
43. Struve (letter of 7 July 1954 to Aseev), 47.

terribly interested in ancient religions and believed in gods. And even now I believe in their existence."[44]

In 1957, at his daughter's urging, Kondratiev emigrated from Switzerland to the United States. He lived at the Tolstoy Farm and then a nursing home nearby. He died in 1967 at the age of ninety-one and is buried at the Novo-Dievo Monastery in New York State.

A collection of his unpublished poetry, *Закат (Sunset)*, appeared posthumously in 1990.[45]

---

44. Struve (letter of 16 March 1954 to Aseev), 45.
45. For a review, see Viktor Dmitriev, "А Кондратьев. *Закат*, 'Антиквариат,' 1990," in *The New Review. Novyi zhurnal*, No. 188, 1992: 387-394.

Cast of Characters

(Compiled by the Translator)

In alphabetical order:

Aksyutka (Aksyutochka): daughter of Maryska, adopted child of Praskukha

Aniska (Anisushka): young witch and sorceress

Black-Beard: see Pyotr Ankudinich

Bolotnik: spirit of the swamp

Brown-Bear: Leshachikha's bear and companion

Domovoi: house spirit of Ipat Saveliev

Fedot: an old man and hunter

Fiery Serpent: a devil who has assumed this form for love trysts

Gorpina (Gorpinka): a young girl who drowns herself and becomes a *rusalka*

Green-Goat: see Leshy

Leshachikha (nicknamed Wart-Face): spirit of the forest and the wife of the Leshy

Leshy: Leshachikha's husband (nicknamed Green-Goat): spirit of the forest

Maksim (Maksimushka): a village fellow, loved by Gorpina and then Aniska

Marten-Soul: one of the Bolotnik's wives

Maryska: Bolotnitsa, a spirit of the swamp; one of the Bolotnik's favorite wives

Master of Darkness, Lord of Darkness, Sovereign of the Night, Black Goat, Goat of the Night, the Black One: chief demonic spirit in charge of the witches' and demons' sabbath

Parakha (Parashka): the village girl Maksim marries

Perun: the ancient god of thunder and rain; the Vodyanoi's companion on the river bottom

Pyotr Ankudinych: a drowning victim, an *utoplennik* or one of the living dead, known as Pull-by-the-Leg and Black-Beard

Praskukha: sorceress and magic healer; Aksyutka's caregiver

Senya (Senichka) Voloshkevich: a young village youth

Sheep-Mug: another *leshy* or spirit of the forest; a neighbor of Green-Goat

Stepanida (Styopka): witch and sorceress, Aniska's rival

Towhead: the *utoplennik* who replaces Pull-by-the Leg

Vodyanoi: spirit of the water; master and sovereign of the Yaryn

Wart-Face: see Leshachikha

plus: Slavic pagan gods

  other demonic beings of the swamp, water and forest

  minor (human) characters

On the Banks of the Yaryn

A Demonological Novel

I

The full moon was casting its greenish light on the watery surface of the rather wide river. A section of the river was partitioned off by a dam and turned a mill wheel. At the present moment, however, the wheel was not turning, the mill stones had been raised, and the water was flowing down freely. People were asleep.

Knowing this, old man Vodyanoi[1] surfaced from the deep pool in the river and, grasping with his frog paws the edge of the dike that divided the stream, he climbed out of the water and sat down.

Smoothing his wet, nearly bald head, whose bare spot was covered not so much by thin hair as by pale-green seaweed, and throwing away a black crayfish which had gotten tangled up in his grey beard, the Vodyanoi, with a feeling of self-satisfaction, glanced around with the look of someone confident in himself, his judgement, and his power as master.

Except for the water murmuring at the mill dam, all was quiet. Only the wild ducks quacked quietly now and then in the reeds. The old man loved these nocturnal hours of tranquility, with the moon out, when the unbearable people were sleeping, and all kinds of spirits could quietly lead their half-ghostly, as is commonly assumed, existence. Here a witch was flying somewhere on her broomstick, attending to her woman's business; here another, concealing herself from people in the form of a cat, was hastily running down the road, apparently headed for another village.

---

1 *vodyanoi (водяной):* one of the unclean spirits, master of the waters and all water riches and lord of drowned people. Kondratiev's capitalization of this spirit signals that this is a specific *vodyanoi*, a character in his own right in the novel. See appendix for a more detailed discussion of this spirit as well as others.

Over there a shapeshifter[2] could be spotted fleetingly, running after her and away from the graveyard fence in the form of a white dog.

After looking around and not seeing any *rusalkas*,[3] who usually came out at this time to catch a bit of moonlight, the Vodyanoi remembered . . . It must be that they had swum out to the water-meadows that lay between the old and new river course. There, they've probably climbed out on the bank and are playing together, awaiting the arrival, perhaps, of some careless night fisherman under the influence, or some fellow tending horses in the fields at this time of night.

The Vodyanoi remembered, too, that at the bottom of a deep pool in the river a village girl who had drowned recently lies motionless, guarded by a huge catfish. Tonight, when moonlight penetrates to the bottom and touches the drowned girl's face, she must awaken. Since almost every drowned woman becomes for a time the wife of the Vodyanoi, and this one was pretty and pleased him, the bald old man, in thinking of the girl, smugly stroked his fat belly and wet beard. Then, beginning to worry that the drowned girl could wake up in his absence, the Vodyanoi sighed and, business-like, dived into the deep.

A moonbeam, thrusting its bright shaft through the turbid green depths of the vast pool, crept slowly as a broad pale patch along the silty bottom which had snags protruding here and there, sunken tree trunks, and boulders stuck in the uneven bottom. Now it lit up the hideous face of an oak idol,[4] half sunk in silt, lying here from ancient times. The Vodyanoi considered this idol his friend and advisor. The sovereign of the river bottom loved to lie next to him and talk about ancient times and new.

The motionless, outstretched body of the drowned girl, already undressed by the *rusalkas*, was not yet stirring, since the patch of

---

2. In Slavic folklore, a demonic spirit can transform himself/herself into an animal, a human being, or an object, i.e., become a shapeshifter *(оборотень)*. The term is also applied to a person turned into an animal by a sorcerer or a sorcerer who has turned himself into an animal.

3. A *rusalka (русалка)* is a female demonic being, the spirit of an unbaptized child or, more frequently, a young woman who has died an unnatural death, usually because of unrequited love. See appendix for a more detailed discussion.

4. As will become clear, this is a reference to Perun (Перун), the ancient god of thunder and rain who lived in the sky and had absolute control over the weather. He was depicted riding across the sky in a chariot and carrying bows and arrows. A statue of Perun stood outside the palace of Vladimir I but was cast into the Dnieper River after Vladimir accepted Christianity in 988 A. D.

moon had not yet reached her pale face. A catfish lay like a motionless log near the drowned girl, his dissolute whiskers feeling the bluish-white nakedness of her thighs and belly barely glimmering in the gloom.

"Clear out, you fool! Just look at how he's spread out his long bristles! Watch those damn whiskers!" And with the heel of his strong webbed foot, the Vodyanoi poked the ribs of his old servant, who at times even served as his horse.

Turning his mighty tail right and left and raising a turbid cloud from the river bottom, the great fish flashed by and hid—that terror of ducks, geese and even little children who, at times, foolishly risk swimming close to the mill.

Waiting for the sediment to settle, the master of the river lowered himself onto a rock sticking out of the bottom which often served him as a seat, and there he became rooted and still, like a large snag.

The moonbeam was slowly moving along its usual course and would soon reach the body of the drowned girl. The Vodyanoi became lost in daydreams. Each new girl who submissively became his wife, each young *rusalka*, brought variety for a time into the old man's rather boring life. At first all of them, terribly afraid of their sovereign, submitted to his caresses with fear, quivering—like small fish tossed out on the shore—in the huge and slippery frog paws of the Vodyanoi, but later, settling down and managing to get acquainted with other *rusalkas*, they soon forgot their fear and then ceased altogether to show the old man the obedience due him.

"How will this one turn out to be? Judging by her face, she doesn't seem like an angry one," flashed through the mind of the master of the deep pool in the river.

The bright little circle of the moon finally reached the drowned girl's heavy braids flung along the bottom like black snakes. . . . Oh, how many of those braids had the old Vodyanoi seen in his life, how many had he plaited and unplaited, how many had he irately shaken in his angry strong paw! Had all of them been collected, it would have become crowded at the bottom of this full-flowing river. But the old and wise master knew full well that as they spent time in his domain, with each year the *rusalka*s became thinner, lighter, more transparent and, finally, they disappeared entirely from the bottom of the deep Yaryn. The Vodyanoi was inclined to explain their disappearance as the treacherous mischief of the winds, who could carry off the beauties who had caught their fancy to their airy kingdom. In any case, not one of those *rusalka*s whom he remembered from olden times was any longer at the river bottom.

Such was the case with the wife of the Varangian Viking, who disappeared long, long, ago; she drowned here in days of old while crossing the river during battle with the Dulebians[5] who had suddenly attacked her retinue. The *rusalka*s, recalled the old man, had then taken off her winged helmet but for a long time couldn't manage the clasps of her heavy gilded shirt of mail. Later this shirt of mail hung for a long time on the branches of submerged trees until it was carried off during the spring floods. The Varangian woman was at first recalcitrant, but then she resigned herself, and the Vodyanoi remembered her with pleasure. And he remembered as well the female slaves sacrificed to him in days of old, bound with thongs, a rock hung from the neck, and thrown over the side of a boat whose bottom moved above like the body of a large predatory fish.

"Now it's not the same. A bit of butter, a large round loaf of black bread, a scrawny goose from the fishermen in the fall, and a half-dead nag at the end of the spring thaw. . . . And that's all! Before, butchers would drown black pigs for me. Now they've stopped! People have become stingy; they don't value the lord who gives them and their cattle water to drink and allows women to rinse their dirty clothes in it, without touching their mills and boats, and to crown it all, who feeds everyone fish. . . . Stupid and ungrateful people!"

At this point the old man roused himself because he noticed that the drowned girl who had been lying motionless till now began to stir. A patch of pale blue-green moonlight brightly lit up her young face with its now raised black arrows of eyelashes and its dark flower of half-open lips. She raised herself, sat up, and began to look around in fright.

"Where am I? What's happened to me?" her lips seemed to want to ask, moving silently.

By their movement, the old man immediately understood the drowned beauty's thoughts. At the river bottom people do not

---

5. The Dulebians, one of the early Slavic tribes, first mentioned in *The Russian Primary Chronicle* in a reference to an era when the Avars dominated various Slavic groups (between about 550 A.D. and about 800 A.D.), dwelt along the (western) Bug River and later were called the Volynians.

speak, but even without words they understand each other very well.

Wanting to prove his hospitality and at the same time not give his new spouse time for any kind of independent decision making, the Vodyanoi, as he was wont to do, rushed to show his feelings for her.

But barely had he bent over his victim and begun to stroke her body with his slippery frog paws than an angry fire flashed in the wide-open eyes of the drowned girl, the lovely face became twisted in anger, one beautiful hand seized his long beard touching her full white breasts, and the other gave a sound slap to the bewildered old man.

The Vodyanoi jerked back, raising a cloud of turbid water, freed his beard and, displeased, moved away from the rebellious drowned girl.

"Just wait! You won't get away from me. You'll even ask for forgiveness," he comforted himself in his failure, knowing full well the state of indifference to which melancholy and despair sometimes brought the drowned girls.

Approaching the oak idol, the Vodyanoi lay down next to him, waiting to see what the latter would say.

"That happens," the Vodyanoi read the sympathy which flashed on the crude, slimy-green features of the oak god's savage face. "You can always expect foolish things from women. You have to be strict with them. When I lived in the sky . . ."

"Were you really in the sky? You grew, after all, in an oak forest until they cut down your tree and made a scarecrow out of you to which people bowed sometimes, burned locks of hair and inflammable sea rock, and slaughtered youths taken prisoner. . . ."

"Yes, only youths; on earth I didn't have young girls brought to me in sacrifice. But believe me, the smell and taste of their blood was also very pleasant."

"What kind of women and maidens are you talking about if you grew up in the forest and didn't have them on earth?" the Vodyanoi asked distrustfully.

"But I was in the sky, too. Sometimes a memory surfaces of how I roared with laughter, chasing cloud maidens. They tried to hide from me, assuming the form of various animals and monsters. But can you really fool a heavenly god?! You have to be strict and unyielding with women, otherwise they'll betray you," the oak idol repeated didactically.

"And did they really betray you?"

"I'm afraid so."

"With who?"

"Can you really keep track of them?! I think that there was more than one they betrayed me with. Do you know the one who now hides in the sky behind a round shield and brings the dead back to life with his light?"

The Vodyanoi nodded his head affirmatively.

"He did me a lot of evil in his time. I even cut off his ear for being too much of a nuisance to the Morning Maiden with the star on her brow. . . . Since then, always and everywhere, that hero with horns on his silver helmet has harmed me on the sly. He was too weak and cowardly for open struggle with me."

The Vodyanoi usually did not believe the oak idol's stories but did not show this too openly, fearing that his old friend and advisor would feel hurt. But now his own hurt forced the old man to pour out his accumulated feelings of hostility onto someone else.

"Brother," he said suddenly, "which god ripped out your mustache?"

The Vodyanoi hit his mark. Feeling the pain of an old hurt, the idol sighed heavily just as he had once sighed on the eve of that ill-fated day when, under the leadership of a votary of a hostile faith, people with axes broke into the forbidden enclosure, chopped down his strong legs, which stood on a thick oak trunk rooted in the ground, hurled him to the ground, removed the precious pendant from around his neck, pulled out his gold mustache and ripped out his long silver beard whose thin strands represented celestial rain drops falling to earth. The one thing which they left on him through an oversight were several gold, silver, and boar bone teeth fixed around his belt.

The oak idol sighed once more when he remembered how, showering him with blows from a whip, they dragged him by horse reins down the high hill to a steep precipice and then pushed him into the rapid waves. He remembered how he kept plunging and circling in the eddies and being carried farther and farther away from the town that had betrayed him.

For many years the overthrown god soaked entangled in the roots of the eroded shore and then, having become submerged, he rolled along the river bottom to this peaceful pool.

"Brother, who ripped out your mustache?" resounded the question in his head, repeated by the Vodyanoi.

"The same ones who forbade throwing trussed-up male and female slaves to you in the spring. The same ones who, without asking you, build dikes, erect bridges, and force your river to turn millstones."

"They pay me for that," the Vodyanoi muttered reluctantly in reply. "Whether they want to bring me sacrifices or not, year after year I take a set number of people doomed by Fate to be mine. Ever since they threw you into my river, you've never once flown thundering in the sky, as you love to talk about. . . . Enough! Isn't this true?"

"It's true. While people lifted up their hands to me and brought me sacrifices, I felt that at the same time I heard their entreaties and rode in a heavy chariot, escorting frightened devils with my fiery arrows. But since I've been deprived of prayers, I'm no longer in the sky, either."

"And who thunders there instead of you?" the Vodyanoi asked.

"And how do I know? Gods change and drive out other gods."

"And do you know that the devils you're talking about live in a swamp close by?"

"Catch me a pair and bring and show them to me," was the answer which followed.

"When I have free time, why not? But now I'm busy," the Vodyanoi said, getting to his feet.

The sovereign of the river bottom wanted to show the former oak god his might and, passing by the drowned girl sitting now in a posture of despair, he drew near the meadow bank, came up and, climbing out of the water, whistled once, and then once more.

There was no answer.

Then the Vodyanoi repeated his call.

Although his whistle was like that of a snipe, only sharper and stronger, the one who needed to, heard it.

In the pre-morning gloom amid fog rolling over the dewy grass, there swayed nearer and nearer the outline of a black-bearded man in wet clothing, with a swollen face, a melancholy-etched expression, and fixed, glassy eyes.

From the first glance it was apparent that this was a dead man, and an *utoplennik*,[6] who had no peace after death.

---

6. *utoplennik (утопленник):* literally, a "drowned man." In folk belief, anyone who drowned either as the result of suicide or too much alcohol was considered to have died an unnatural death and thus destined to become part of the "dark world."

"What do you need?" the black-bearded man asked in an indifferent tone.

"Where have you been? Why didn't you come right away?" the Vodyanoi asked, turning to him angrily. "You probably haven't gotten a beating for a long time! Just watch out!" The master of the river became agitated.

"I was here, in the meadow. I was watching children grazing horses from a distance," the *utoplennik* defended himself.

"And couldn't you lure them here?!"

"It's not my job to lure them. Send your girls for that. My job is to pull on a leg if someone is swimming at night, or to look after the *rusalka*s," the *utoplennik* answered in a confident but monotonous voice like the pre-morning rustle of grass. "I'm bored, I feel sick," he suddenly continued. "Let me go!"

"And you didn't feel sick drinking vodka? And you weren't bored getting into the water drunk? No, brother! Until you serve out your time, I won't let you go! So go on and serve! . . Do you know the swamp demons?"

"How can I not know them! Beyond the meadows the bushes begin, and after that, a stream and swamp, and they're in that swamp."

"So here's my order. Catch me a little demon as soon as you encounter one—it could be even two—and bring it to the pool."

"And what if they pull me into the bog?" the black-bearded *utoplennik* asked matter-of-factly but not without some apprehension.

"It'd serve you right," answered the Vodyanoi. "You yourself just said that you were bored here. Well then, get yourself to the swamp! Only watch out, bring me the little demons tomorrow night, or else I'll find you wherever you are!" the Vodyanoi concluded his threatening speech.

The black-bearded one turned around and vanished in the fog, the usual refuge of unclean spirits and the living dead.

Meanwhile, not seeing any unpleasant or hostile faces, the new *rusalka* took a look around, got to her feet, and with a tentative walk went along the soft, oozy bottom. It occurred to her that it would be good to walk out on the shore and hide from the repugnant Vodyanoi in the thick grass. In the turbid water she made out a path winding among the rocks and twigs of trees half-covered with silt. This path led upward in the direction of the shore.

But barely had the girl got up to knee-deep water when *rusal-kas* appeared in her path, returning to the river squealing and laughing loudly.

"Ah, a new one! Where are you going? Go back! It'll be dawn soon," they shouted, surrounding the drowned girl and blocking her way.

"Let me go! I want to go home," she begged.

"They won't be very happy to see you. At the sight of you everyone will hide, and they won't open doors for anything, no matter how much you beg! No, what's done is done! You've come to us of your own accord, so bear with it," the oldest one said to her sternly, looking more like a ghost than the others.

They were all naked, wet from the dew, with unplaited braids down which water flowed. Some had long green grass around their waists, and all wore wreaths made of wild swamp flowers. Some of them, who had recently ended up on the river bottom, looked more like living people, differing only in the chalky paleness of their bodies; those who had drowned long ago stood out with a gossamer, sometimes even translucent, appearance to their bodies.

"Cheer up! We don't live with grief all the time. Sometimes we even manage to shake it off. It's too bad you came late when we can't run around in broad daylight. But on the other hand, we go where we want at night. Don't be afraid, dear girl. If the fat-bellied Vodyanik isn't to your liking, put up with him for a while. Later on, he'll leave you alone himself. And as for songs and games, you'll find ours no worse than those of the living," said another *rusalka,* turning to the new one.

"And now it's time to go home!" shouted the third.

And arm-in-arm with their new friend, the *rusalka*s led her into the water again.

"What's your name?" asked the fourth along the way.

"Gorpina."

"Where from?"

"Zaretskoye."

"And do you know the Syuntyaevs?" the fifth questioned.

But at this point the Vodyanoi returned from his stroll and immediately began to show signs of attention to the new one again, now slapping her loudly on the hips with his webbed paw, now trying to tickle her, his frog's mouth repellingly agape in silent laughter, which made his fat ungirdled belly rock.

"Don't resist him, just put up with him," one of her new friends again advised her in a whisper. "That's how it's supposed to be—he pesters you at first and won't leave you alone. If you start chasing him off, it'll be worse. . . . He'll torment you to death."

Gorpina was forced to submit.

"That's the way," the Vodyanoi whispered in the girl's ear, releasing her all worn out, and even took a painful bite of her neck with his small but sharp teeth like those of a pike fish.

Having satisfied his attraction for the new, the Vodyanoi really did leave Gorpina in peace, and little by little she got used to her situation and surroundings.

The scales of the small and large fish shone in the light of the sun's rays weakly penetrating the depths. Sometimes the long dark shadow of a boat bottom passed by overhead. At times ducks or geese ventured across the pool of water, quickly moving their red and black feet, and whenever this happened, a huge, fat cat-fish would rise repeatedly from the bottom, trying to catch one of them.

At night Gorpina, with her friends noticeably keeping an eye on her, began to go out on dry land, to luxuriate and play in the moonlight, which cast blue-green reflections on the white bodies of the *rusalka*s. Wandering through the grainfields, the most rancorous of them made little twists out of the wheat spikes on the plots[7] of people who were their enemies when they were alive. All the *rusalka*s loved flowers, and almost every night they made themselves new wreaths. Getting up to their chests in the darkish waves of the ripening rye, some sang a favorite centuries-old song of children stolen by evil spirits before baptism. In this song, among its exclamations containing references to the straw spirit, could be heard bitter complaints about their joyless, bitter fate. Sometimes they sang in pairs, portraying a *rusalka* mother and daughter, the former talking sadly about the inevitability of the coming time when the daughter would have to "please" the Water Tsar.

Some of the underwater maidens, distinguished for their mischievous ways, entertained themselves even during the day by tangling fishnets or frightening ducks and geese. The most daring

---

7. Kondratiev uses the word *desyatina* (десятина), a land measure equivalent to 2.7 acres. Here, and in other parts of the novel, *desyatina* will be translated as "plot" for the sake of simplicity.

would select one of the darker nights and sit on the mill wheel in order to go round and round with it.

Once, strolling among the moonlit meadows and fields, the Yaryn River *rusalka*s came upon a tall shadow moving in their direction from the forest. Dark and obscure, as if overgrown with grass, the outline of a half-being howling in a thick voice moved towards them with giant steps and with hands wide open and waving. "Walked round and found, run and raid"—the frightened *rusalkas* managed to catch very fragmentary snatches of the song of this half-spectral inhabitant of the meadows.

"The Polevik!"[8] the water maidens shrieked and, some laughing loudly and some howling, they rushed away from him in the direction of the river.

Whistling and shouting, the Polevik pursued them to the very shore.

"Who is that?" Gorpina asked one of her friends when she found herself at the river bottom.

"A kind of *leshy*.[9] Only he makes mischief more in the fields and along the boundary-strips. I saw him once, during the day, in the spring. He wears a kaftan the color of winter oatmeal which changes color, now turning green, now silver. His hair stands on end like a high hat, and it's also green. And his face is like sand . . . And, well, he feels a strong attraction for our sisters. Don't let him catch you!"

After noticing that Gorpina had gotten used to the water and was feeling at home, they began to let her go even without any supervision. One night, after swimming far from her place in the pool, the young *rusalka* came upon a dug-out with a solitary fisherman in a thicket of reeds. How great was her surprise when that fisherman turned out to be Maksim, the very same fellow whose thoughtless betrayal had caused her to throw herself into the river.

Gorpina stood rooted to the spot in water up to her shoulders, face-to-face with her former beloved. But Maksim was drunk and not at all surprised to see her.

"Oh, no!" he said. "First you drowned yourself, and now you want to drag me into the water as well? . . . I'm not that kind! Do you hear?! I won't go! . . . And there was no reason for you to

8. *polevik (полевик):* the keeper and master of grain fields and meadows.
9. *leshy (леший):* the master of all forest riches, of wood flora and fauna.

throw yourself into the river. Because I fooled around a bit with another girl, she took it into her head to lose her life! No! Get this straight! I'm not going to join you!"

"Maksimushka, dear! Take me to your place," Gorpina whispered and moved forward, trying to grasp the tarred side of the dug-out.

"No! Don't try that on me! . . . You won't lure me!" the fellow shouted in response. "I really need to fill up on water when there's vodka! Here, drink. To hell with you!"

And the fellow offered his former girlfriend the unfinished bottle, which the latter took submissively with her pale, half-transparent hands.

"But don't touch me!" Maksim continued. "And don't cling to the side of the boat or I'll break your hands!" He swung his oar threateningly, which made the dug-out rock violently and almost overturn.

However, the fellow managed to regain balance and, with a few strokes of the oar, to sail pretty far from Gorpina.

The *rusalka,* who was watching after him sadly, heard the fellow as he banged and splashed with his oar, rowing toward the village and talking and swearing loudly to himself.

"What's this noise?! Who were you chatting with?" The fat, wet, balding head of the Vodyanoi surfaced near Gorpina, puffing and panting.

"There was a drunken fisherman here. He saw me and began to swear," the drowned girl attempted to explain her encounter.

"Oh yes, I can smell the vodka," the old man muttered, displeased, and continued, "And if he was drunk, why didn't you pull him into the water?"

"He threatened to break my hands with his oar."

"And what's this?!" the Vodyanoi suddenly asked menacingly, pointing to Maksim's unfinished bottle in Gorpina's hands.

"He gave me that so that I'd leave his boat alone."

"And you took it! Instead of overturning his dug-out, you took vodka from him! Took pity on him! So this is for you for that pity!"

Wrenching the bottle from Gorpina's hands, the Vodyanoi gave the girl's face a loud, sharp slap with his wet open paw.

Gorpina began to cry and hid in the reeds.

The Vodyanoi, without hurrying, looked through the vodka—visible in the transparent bottle—at the light of the narrow moon which had appeared from behind the clouds, raised this vessel to his blissfully grinning mouth, and began to pour in the precious liquid which the unclean spirits[10] of the forest, swamp, and water love and value no less than man.

Maksim repeated his story in the morning in the village, how Gorpina, who had become a *rusalka,* wanted to pull him into the water, how he beat her off with an oar and stayed alive thanks only to the fact that he threw her almost a full bottle. "While this lost soul was occupied with the vodka, I sailed away quickly. That's the only thing that saved me."

---

10.   unclean spirits: demonic, potentially harmful spirits.

II

The black-bearded *utoplennik,* who used to have the name of
Pyotr Ankudinych, or simply Pyotra, and now was known more
by the name of Pull-by-the-Leg, was very afraid of his master.
Once in the old days the Vodyanoi, pretending to be a friend of
Pyotra's from a neighboring village, led him drunk into the reeds,
where Pyotra came upon a deep place and, with curses on his
lips, drowned. Since that time, both his swollen body and his
simple soul became the sole property of the master of the river
bottom. Pyotra took this as his due and submitted to his fate.

Seeing the obedience of the black-bearded fellow and the slavish readiness on his part to please his new master, the Vodyanoi
singled out the peasant from the drowned people like him and ordered him to live near the deep pool in the river—an honor
which, unfortunately, was not bestowed on Pyotr's brothers-in-
service. All of them were settled up and down the river, and they
were strictly forbidden to come near the *rusalka*s. Only Ankudinych enjoyed this privilege since he had the secret assignment
from the Vodyanoi of keeping an eye on them and reporting every
intentional and unintentional misdeed.

Not daring to disobey his lord, the night after receiving his
order to get some small demons, Pull-by-the-Leg set out on his
journey. He glided almost silently through places inundated by
water, between thick bushes, tall mossy tussocks and blackened
tree stumps, heading for a lake half overgrown with greenery, the
former den of the *lozovik*s,[1] shapeshifters, *bolotnitsa*s,[2] demons,

---

1. *lozovik (лозовик):* a swamp spirit, related to the *leshy* and the *vodyanoi,*
   who lives in low-lying willow bushes *(лоза* means "willow").
2. *bolotnitsa (болотница):* female swamp demon, related to the *leshy* and the
   vodyanoi.

and other spirits of the swamp. He crept up rather close to the shifting bog and, hiding in the bushes, he began to watch for a small, still hornless, little swamp demon, to turn up. After waiting for some time, Pyotra was very surprised when he heard pleasant, sweetly inviting singing.

Pull-by-the-Leg took a good look and was deeply struck by the beauty of the *bolotnitsa* whom he was seeing for the first time in his life.

Sitting on a tussock with her feet lowered into the black water (so that her unsightly paws, half-swan, half-frog, could not be seen) and with her dark flowing hair crowned with large, white flowers, the bog beauty closest to Ankudinych sang about how she was languishing in her loneliness and was waiting and waiting for someone close to her on whom she could bestow the full ardor of her love, which gave her no peace. . . . The *utoplennik* got so lost in listening and looking that he forgot not only about the little demons but even about the Vodyanoi and his order. From time to time Pull-by-the-Leg heard the crunching of fallen branches and the smacking sound of someone's steps in the swamp, but did not bother turning around in the direction of this noise until a man appeared very close to him, probably a hunter who had gotten lost in the forest. That man, jumping carefully from tussock to tussock, and stopping from time to time as if stealing up on a wood grouse giving the mating call, was steadily approaching the singing *bolotnitsa*. Then he stopped at the edge of a flat meadow, which looked like a pale-green carpet, at the other end of which, in the middle of a relatively small body of water, sat the sweetly singing *bolotnitsa* on a mossy tussock.

She, too, noticed the man and began to sing even more sweetly, extending her arms—white and round as if chiseled out of chalk—invitingly toward the new arrival.

After a few moments of indecision, the man suddenly rushed forward and ran along the mossy surface of the bog swaying under him. But without even reaching the water, he unexpectedly sank and disappeared, head and all, into the treacherous depths. Only a few bubbles came up, spluttering on the black surface of the newly formed hole. The *bolotnitsa*, in pure *rusalka* style, clapped her hands and, breaking off singing, burst into loud laughter standing at her full height on the tussock.

"Just look at the joy that has taken hold of her," Black-Beard whispered, looking at the female demon dancing in delight, rhythmically moving her monstrous paws.

Out of all the bog holes and crevices, from the stumps of trees and piles of brushwood and snags, there suddenly appeared a multitude of little demons. Making wry faces and producing loud, high-pitched laughs like the squeaking of mice or the creaking of an old tree, they turned somersaults and cruelly clapped their hands in honor of the successful and beautiful *bolotnitsa*. And she, casting a victorious look at the surrounding area and, apparently enjoying her victory, suddenly froze like a huge white frog, and exactly like one, jumped headfirst into the swaying bog.

The little demons, who had been hiding during her singing, now began to run around, creating pandemonium, jumping over each other with shrieks and laughter. Some, the stronger ones, chased the weaker ones, scratched them, and pulled their ears. One of the small and weak little demons, to his grief, ran for cover in the same bush behind which sat Black-Beard. The *utoplennik* instantly gathered it up in his huge plump hand, squeezing its neck lightly so that it would not squeal or bite.

This was a child demon of a pale-green color, still very young, with little knobs instead of little horns, with a little mug resembling a cat's, a body reminiscent of a human's, and hind paws like a frog's. Little claws which had not yet reached their full size were visible on the front paws.

After looking over his quarry, Ankudinych carefully rose to his feet and set out on his return journey. It was inopportune as well as too late to catch a second little demon.

After going about a verst through a forest meadow, overgrown with alder bushes along the edges, Black-Beard suddenly heard a long, mournful sound and stopped. It seemed to him that the top of one of the spruce trees, which grew on the other side of the meadow, had begun to sway strangely. A little later the tree, gradually taking on the appearance of the Leshy and growing smaller in height as it approached, moved in the direction of Black-Beard, who was rooted to the spot in fright. . . . An instant more, assuming the size of a young birch tree, but two and a half times taller than the *utoplennik*, the Leshy stood before him, with pointed head, disheveled, overgrown with fur like wood moss and, apparently, very irate.

"What are you doing here? What brought you into my forest,

damned carrion?!" angrily squealed the forest master, nicknamed Green-Goat (he was so named because of the shape of his
beard and the color of his fur), raising a heavy club of knotted
wood at the newcomer.

Sensing that he was in a situation reminiscent of olden times,
when the mounted patrol or the forest warden himself would
catch him in the state forest with a sled full of cut wood, Pull-by-
the-Leg deemed it necessary to fall to his knees.

"Have mercy, let me go! Not of my own free will have I come
all the way here . . . It's a matter of orders to a slave!"

"Whose?" was the next threatening question.

"The Vodyanoi sent me. We are a subordinate folk. If they send
you, it means you'd better go!"

"And what's this?" the Leshy asked, pointing to the half-
strangled, barely moving little demon.

"He gave orders to . . . well . . , catch and deliver."

"Some master you have! Does he have so little of his own filth
that he sends you to steal someone else's? . . . How many times
did I command him not to befoul my forest with his demonic rot!
I told him I won't tolerate it!" Green-Goat shouted angrily.

He then snatched the little demon out of the hands of Black-
Beard and, holding it by its hind legs, hit its head so hard against
the stump that it did not even make one squeak.

"And now I'll settle accounts with you," the forest master exclaimed, raising his frightening club above Black Beard's head.

"Don't beat me, I'll do you a good turn. I mean, I'll honor you
like my own father!" Black-Beard appealed dolefully, embracing
the hard legs of the Leshy.

"Oh, you'll do me a good turn? What rubbish! Of what use are
you?! You only foul the air! Damned pest!"

"I'll bring you any *rusalka* you want. I guard them for the Vodyanoi. I'll bring a whole bunch of them. You only have to
choose!" Pull-by-the Leg, all a-tremble and overcome with fear,
tempted the Leshy.

Green-Goat fell into thought. He was not indifferent to the
beauty of the river inhabitants and more than once, hiding in the
bushes along the riverbank, he had enjoyed watching their games.

Once Black-Beard had happened to notice him there and now
used this circumstance to tempt and assuage the enraged Leshy.

"You won't trick me?" the Leshy asked pensively, after some
silence.

"May I go to hell if I deceive you!"

"It's, let's admit, the most suitable place for you. . . . Well, I'll forgive you this time. All right . . . Just watch it! . . . Bring me some *rusalkas*."

"Fine. They'll go on Saint John's Eve[3] to collect herbs in the forest. I'll tell them that ferns grow in a meadow in your pine forest. And that's where they'll run to. . ."

"What are you talking about! On Saint John's Eve I have more than enough trouble dealing with living girls. . . . Well, no matter. All right. Watch it, though; don't deceive me, or I'll find you wherever you are!" the Leshy concluded in a threatening way and, after gloomily giving the *utoplennik* a haughty look, headed for the thicket in his pine forest, growing longer and taller the closer he drew near it.

As soon as he disappeared from view, Black-Beard hurriedly jumped to his feet, grabbed the dead, little swamp demon by its paws and, without paying attention to the road, rushed headlong in the direction of Yaryn.

The moon had already waned. A fog was lifting from the river in which the aery outlines of *rusalkas* sometimes appeared one after another in the light of the dying stars. The morning hour was drawing near.

Pull-by-the-Leg breathed a sigh of relief as he submerged himself in the cool dark water. He had already made a firm decision not to fulfill the promise he had made to the Leshy.

〜

"Did you join battle with these little frogs when you were a god in the sky?" the Vodyanoi asked the oak idol, showing him the dead, little swamp demon.

The idol kept silent, seemingly gazing with his motionless eyes at the little, pale-green corpse with its paws spread out helplessly.

---

3. St. John's Eve *(Иванова ночь, Иван Купала,* or *Иван Купало): 24* June according to the (new) Gregorian calendar, and 7 July according to the (old) Julian calendar (henceforth, all dates will be cited this way); the feast of midsummer, when the day is at its longest and vegetation is at its peak. It was celebrated with bonfires, games, and the burning of a witch in effigy. The waters at this time were believed to be imbued with special powers, and ritualistic bathing, as well as the gathering of the morning dew, were part of the holiday celebrations.

He looked pensively for a long time at the dead little swamp demon, but this time did not say anything to the Vodyanoi.

They threw the little demon into the reeds where children soon found it. In the village, where they brought it, people began to say that this was the issue—which had appeared in the world before its time—of one of the local sorceresses, Aniska, who, according to rumor, carried on with the unclean force.[4] But Aniska somehow managed to defend her innocence, shifting suspicion to her rival Stepanida.

The little demon's corpse managed, however, to awaken some memories in the oak idol. A few days later, during a storm, when the master of the deep pool in the river was lying next to him on the silty bottom, listening to the distant rumble of thunder, the oak god soundlessly whispered to his neighbor:

"I remember how my sons would harness a chariot for me and how I would drive off in it to defeat, with fiery wasp-arrows, my primordial enemies—not those little frogs which you showed me the other day but foggy, grey, and hazy-black ones, twisting and twirling in dust columns along the roads, running around people's roofs, and appearing in poisonous swamp vapors. They were afraid of me and, assuming the form of large, dark balls, they rolled along fields and trails, trying to save themselves; they concealed themselves in animal burrows, but everywhere my arrows inevitably found them. . . ."

"What arrows?" the Vodyanoi asked.

"Those which illuminate your whole river bottom at night, heavenly fires after whose flash deep thunder and rumble are heard, forcing you to alter your countenance."

"You've gone too far, you old liar! I've never been afraid of anything. Someone else is making that noise," the Vodyanoi said. "As far as I can remember, you haven't moved once since the time that you were brought here by one of the spring floods."

"So be it. But nevertheless I was a god once," the idol whispered unyieldingly. "Gods are brought down, with one replacing the other. I, too, removed from the heavenly throne the one who sat there before me. But I was magnanimous and left the vanquished one power over all beasts covered with fur. Having

4. unclean force: Refers to all potentially harmful spirits but also serves as a designation of the devil.

removed my opponent, I didn't persecute him, and I didn't deprive him of the joys of life and the world."

"What was his name?" the Vodyanoi interrupted, forgetting that he had just expressed his doubts to the idol.

"Volos[5]. . . Living in the forests and fields with animals and cattle, he himself became overgrown with fur like an animal. Proud and with confidence in my own power, I didn't forbid hunters and shepherds to bow to him. The best people prayed to me and served me. They threw gold at my feet, taken on the field of battle, they burned amber before me, taken from the sea bottom (this was a voluntary tribute from the Tsar of the Sea), and in sacrifice to me they speared youths doomed by the casting of lots. . . . You can't imagine how pleasant the smell of human blood is," the idol whispered, sighing blissfully.

"You've told me that many times," the Vodyanoi answered, yawning in displeasure.

In his heart he was envious as he listened to these stories. The sovereign of the Yaryn had never had occasion to breathe in the smell of hot, scarlet blood flowing from a human body. He knew it only by taste and in a form greatly diluted by the river liquid at that.

The Vodyanoi was, moreover, a bit vain, and he did not like the fact that a piece of oak, which had come out of nowhere, apparently dared to consider itself more exalted than the master of such a vast river as the Yaryn.

---

5. Volos *(Волос* or *Велес): * in pagan times, the god of cattle and, apparently, commerce.

III

As autumn came closer, the grey days became shorter; the nights grew longer, the roads got muddier; the forest turned yellow and then grew bare; migrating birds flew off beyond the blue seas. The crops had been harvested long ago and peasant women performed an ancient ritual: with their backs straight they rolled in the middle of a harvested field, quietly singing, "Zhnivka, Zhnivka,[1] give me your strength," as if they wanted to regain their strength, if not from the goddess Zhniva, who had disappeared into the infinite distance, then at least from ancient Mother Earth, who still survived in folk beliefs. Naked girls performed their secret, nocturnal folk dances in honor of Makoviya,[2] crowned with her perpetually blooming wreath . . . Beginning with the Day of Dormition,[3] the Red Sun, the regal heavenly goddess whom the Russians call "Beautiful Lieto" and the ancient Greeks called "Beauteous Leto," "falls asleep"—she who is the mother of Dazhbog[4] and the moon goddess Lietnitsa-Dzevanna-Diana,[5] the protectress of brides and hunting.

---

1. Zhnivka is the diminutive form of Zhniva *(Жнива):* the goddess of harvested fields.

2. Makovia *(Маковия):* also known as Mokosh or Makosh, a fertility goddess, the only female goddess in the earliest pantheon.

3. Day of Dormition *(Успение):* 15 (28) August. The Orthodox feast commemorating the death ("falling asleep") of the Virgin.

4. Dazhbog *(Дажбог),* a sun god in East Slavic mythology who was considered the god who bestowed riches and all blessings of life. An idol of him, along with other pagan deities, stood on a hill in Kiev, where ritualistic sacrifices were offered. He is first mentioned under the year 980 A.D. in *The Russian Primary Chronicle.*

5. Lieto and Lietnitsa are both words that relate to "summer" or "lieto" *(лето)* in Russian. Kondratiev indicates a difference in pronunciation between the Russian and Greek by using a different vowel, Лето versus Лэто.

On Exaltation of the Cross Day[6] following the example of migrating birds, snakes went into their underground holes, hiding from the cold. They gathered in a swarm and, with their tsar leading them, slithered off in the direction of the forest. A small village boy, looking for his stray calves, saw that herd;[7] he also saw the gold crown on the head of the snake tsar but did not have a clean white linen cloth with him. If the boy had had one handy, and if he had spread it out in the snakes' path, then the snake tsar would surely have left his crown on this outspread material and stupid little Mitka would have become an omniscient healer.

On St. Nikita's Day[8] all the unclean spirits of the forest and swamp fell into a deep sleep, having hidden themselves in lairs at the bottom of bogs and in tree hollows. The Vodyanoi received his usual fall sacrifice, a headless goose, and accepted the fact that there would not be any more gifts until spring. He walked around gloomy and miserable and sighed loudly at night in the reeds, which were empty of river bird.

Next came the Festival of the Virgin's Intercession,[9] connected in days of old with the appearance of the first snow and the weddings of maidens. "Father Protector," as they used to address the holiday in the past, and still do now, "protect Mother Damp Earth[10] and youthful me!"

---

6. Festival of the Exaltation of the Cross *(Здвиженье* or *Воздвиженье):* 14 (27) September. People lost track of the real significance of this holiday although it was originally connected with worshiping the cross on which Christ had been crucified. In some places peasants believed that on this day all crawling things disappeared under ground.

7. Here the snakes are presented from the point of view of the young village boy, whose only experience is with cattle herds. Therefore he applies the word "herd" to describe the swarm of snakes.

8. St. Nikita's Day *(Никитин день):*15 (28) September. Nikita became a saint and martyr after being burnt alive by pagans for spreading the Christian faith. The holiday marked the beginning of the sale of killed geese. The Vodyanoi was considered the patron of geese and, on the eve of St. Nikita's Day, geese were thrown into waters in sacrifice to him.

9. Festival of the Virgin's Intercession *(Покров Пресвятой Богородицы):* 1(14) October. Celebrated by the Russian Orthodox Church since 1164 to mark the day when the Mother of God appeared in a Constantinople church, took off her veil, and spread it over the worshipers to protect them from visible and invisible enemies. This holiday marked the end of field work and, with more free time available to the peasants, encouraged the celebration of weddings.

10. Mother Damp Earth *(Мать-Сыра-Земля),* whom pagan believers visualized as a living woman, was associated with the fertility of nature, life-giving moisture, and the changing of the seasons.

Having parted already with the sun's affectionate caresses and the thunder-bearing heavenly inhabitants, Earth—grown weary in the course of the summer—donned white cloth and sank into sleep. The sun god grew pale and lost his powers before the coming of Winter, and the Thunder Tsar was sleeping the sleep of the dead like a fairy-tale *bogatyr*[11] killed by his brothers and thrown into an underground tsardom.

Deceived once by the *utoplennik*, Ankudinych, who did not bring him *rusalka*s on Ivan Kupala's Eve as he had promised, the Leshy greeted the coming of autumn and the winter that followed with gloomy resoluteness. On St. Yerofei's Day[12] he waged a long battle in the forest with an invisible being, broke trees, and snarled like an animal, but after receiving a heavy blow on his conical head from an invisible finger, he disappeared through the earth.

The snow and the cold, little by little, did their work. People hid in warm huts, brewed beer and *braga*,[13] killed chickens for "chicken name-day celebrations"[14] and stocked up on warm clothing. In days of old, a small but good goddess, Strigolnitsa or Ovechnitsa, later renamed Nastasia-Ovechnitsa,[15] provided the clothing. On St. Michael's Day[16] people celebrated the name day of Fire and also in due course won over the *domovoi*.[17]

Grey Winter arrived on the wings of midnight winds. The goddess had grown old after resettling with her fair-haired people[18]

---

11. *bogatyr (богатырь)*: a larger-than-life hero in Russian folk epic literature.
12. St. Erofei *(священно-мученик Ерофей* or *Иорофей)*: 4 (17) October, celebrated in memory of an Athenian bishop, Ierofei or Erofei, who became a holy martyr.
13. *braga*: a kind of home brew.
14. This is a reference to a holiday known as *kurinye svyatki (куриные святки)*, celebrated 17 September (November 1), and connected with the house spirit or *domovoi*, the protector of chickens. On that day relatives and friends gave each other gifts of chickens (see Афанасьев, vol. II, 107). The chickens were never killed, and their eggs were believed to have curative powers. On this holiday a rooster's head was also cut off and thrown on the hut's roof so that chickens would grow and multiply, and the rooster's meat was eaten at a family dinner.
15. Ovechnitsa *(Овечница)*: formed from the same root as *ovtsa (овца)*, meaning "sheep;" the pagan goddess of sheep.
16. St. Michael's Day *(Михайлов день)*; also known as Archangel Michael's Day *(Михаил-архангель)*: 8 (21) November. Celebrated in the ninth month (the year began in March in ancient times) to mark the nine orders of angels.
17. A *domovoi* is a house spirit who, since ancient times, has been viewed as a mischievous protector of a dwelling and a valuable helper of its inhabitants.
18. "Fair-haired" is historically linked to the Nordic tribes who settled in Great

in the swampy forests of Sarmatia and the cool plains of Scythia, rich in grasses. She still remembered the time when she was the goddess of sea mists and death caused by the Sea. At that time they called her Marina or Mara-Marena. Then they began to call her Tsarevna Maria Morevna[19] and finally, Winter Matryona. And it is only in these snowy plains that the Tsaritsa assumed her repelling look, similar to that of the evil witch, Loukha, the goddess of the Finnish tribes that had lived here in earlier times.

Not knowing a father's affection, her son Mraz, Khlad, or Lyod[20] (in Christian profanity renamed Lyad, in fairy-tales the name Moroz having been preserved) floated in on ice floes together with his mother, the Tsaritsa. Merciless towards humans because in ancient times they called him a murderer of people, he forced them into their huts so that their eyes would not interfere with the magical enchantments of Winter.

With a wave of his magic scepter, forests became dressed in fluffy white clothing, the Vodyanoi hid on the river bottom from terrible Khlad, the river became covered with a thick layer of ice, and swamps froze over; and on the boundless snowy plains the demons of the blizzard, who had flown in from midnight with Winter and were partly bequeathed to her by the Finnish goddess, twirled in joyful dance. These were Kureva, Krucha, Zavirukha, Purga, Buran, and Metelitsa,[21] and many other merciless elemental spirits who hate the human tribe.

~

The soul of Gorpina, the suicide, was not at peace. While the river was not yet frozen over, on cold autumn nights, when the wind sang sad songs to the trees about approaching Winter and the last leaves were still rustling and falling from the nearly bare branches, she emerged stealthily several times from the mucky river bottom to see what her relatives were doing. Pressing against the window, the drowned girl watched her brothers, sisters and parents sleeping in the hut. Once she even tapped lightly

---

Russia/Ukraine. The Russian word for "fair-haired," *rusy (русый)*, gave birth to the term *ruskii,* or Russian person.

19. Morevna *(Моревна):* daughter of the Sea, from *море,* meaning "sea."

20. Mraz is the Church Slavonic form of *moroz (мороз)* or "frost;" Khlad is the Church Slavonic form of *kholod (холод)* or "cold;" and Lyod means "ice."

21. All are names for various types of snow storms.

on the glass with her half-translucent fingers, and her younger sister, who had awakened suddenly, saw Gorpina. Sitting up in bed, the girl let out a piercing scream.

Some members of the household noticed the night guest's face in the window before she could disappear. Of course, no one dared to walk out of the hut and all trembled, not closing their eyes until dawn.

And in the morning they sprinkled "blessed poppy seeds" under the windows and at the doors and hung amulets with monkshood and madder[22] around their necks. The whole village remembered how several years ago a dead bridegroom began to appear at night to a girl called Fedosia, asking to be allowed into the hut, and how, only thanks to the experience and knowledge of the sorceress Praskukha, was she able to chase him away. Praskukha had ordered Fedosia's bed to be strewn with monkshood and fragrant madder and for the same kind of flowers to be braided into the girl's hair as she was falling sleep. This remedy worked. On the first night after this ritual, a vampire who approached the window caught the scent of plants he did not like and, gnashing his teeth, uttered:

"If not for the madder and monkshood, the girl would be mine."[23]

And after that he ran off in the direction of the cemetery. . .

Off to the side of the road, in a secluded valley hidden from human eyes by snow drifts, sat Tsaritsa Winter on her snowy throne, looking pensively at the demons of the blizzard whirling before her in rapid dance. The enchantress' thoughts carried her off into the distant past, when the power she had received over new lands, allowing her to lock the earth, swamps, and rivers in hard ice for almost half the year, had so pleased her. "Then, it amused me; then, I was so happy as soon as I was able to chase away Summer—proud of the golden blush of her cheeks—from these lands. At that time I wanted so very much to hold in my

---

22. monkshood *(тоя)*: a plant with large fragrant flowers, used since ancient times as a powerful poison; madder *(марена)*: an herb used in dyeing. In folk belief, both offer protection against evil spirits.

23. The rhyme in the Russian is lost in the translation: *Кабы не марена да не тоя (тоя)—то была бы девка моя (тоя).*

hands for as long as possible this diamond scepter, which made rivers into roads for sled travel and the people who dared to spy on me, motionless corpses. I also liked the songs of the midnight winds, the grandsons of Stribog,[24] and the singing of Purga,[25] reminiscent of funereal howling, although I do not understand her words to this day. Now, I do not prize my powers as Tsaritsa and am even content when the son of my rival, Summer—she who is decked out in a red sarafan—arrives to expel me from this land. He is very handsome on his white horse, in red mesh gloves and in a golden helmet with pearl *podveski*.[26] His well-proportioned legs shine with silver . . . I always liked the youthful face of the sun god very much, and I remember that I never entered into battle with him with any particular enthusiasm. I spared my young enemy and tried more to frighten him by turning myself into a snow dragon than to bring him harm. But am I really to blame if he himself inevitably wants to fight with me instead of dismounting from his horse and treating me like an affectionate friend who is well disposed towards him? . . . I'm so alone! . . . Couldn't I, like Summer, and like Earth, ice-bound by me, give birth each year to progeny who bring joy to my heart? . . . But oh, there is no one near me whom I might like and who himself would want to be liked by me; and the one with whom I once brought a son into the world, Lada,[27] is now no longer in any condition to reproduce. . . . And many of those, whom I used to know in my youthful days, are already long gone. Where is the sovereign of the winds now, the frightening Stribog? What country has he gone off to? Only his grandsons remain here, who either don't want to or can't tell me about their grandfather. . . . My entourage advises me to choose Vila[28] for my husband. They say he used to be the husband of ugly Loukha, who was the tsaritsa here before I came. He didn't run away with his girlfriend but stayed behind with the tribes

---

24. Stribog *(Стрибог):* the principal pagan deity associated with winds, to whom an idol was erected on top of a hill in Kiev in 980 A.D. along with other gods.
25. *Purga (пурга)* means "blizzard."
26. *podveski (подвески):* a meshlike covering that extends down from a helmet, protecting the warrior's ears and the back of his neck.
27. Lada: There are many explanations offered of the role of this goddess; she is linked with beauty, wedding ceremonies, and fertility. She may have a southern origin in the classical Leto, mother by Zeus of Apollo and Artemis.
28. Vila: a forest spirit; sometimes the *vila*s were viewed as male versions of the *rusalka*s.

which live in forest-rich Lithuania. Later they recognized him as a god, and other tribes living here also considered him the husband of Baba-Yaga.[29] After two such wives, I don't want to be the third of this Vila. I'll manage somehow without him. . . . Should I look to see what that beauty, Summer, is doing now?"

"Chill,"[30] cried the Tsaritsa, "bring me my magical diamond!"

Bowing in respect, one of the principal demons in her retinue brought her a diamond that resembled a multifaceted apple. Taking it in her hands, Marena-Winter caught a moonbeam in it and began to look closely at one of the sparkling crystal facets. And she saw a tower in a distant land beyond the clouds, above warm blue seas, the highly decorated, sloping *terem*[31] of Summer, the eternally youthful beauty. That *terem* was now full of life . . . Young, rosy-cheeked guests, each with a star on her forehead, dressed in scarlet sarafans embroidered in gold, and light-blue and dark-blue ribbons plated into their light-brown braids, gathered to congratulate the woman who had recently given birth and to wish good health to her newborn sun god. One after another they bent over the little one's crib and placed beside him the gifts they had brought with them.

The eyes of Winter blazed in vexation and wrath. For a moment, she totally regained her youth and beauty. Stomping her foot, the ice goddess stood straight up and called the leading demons of her retinue—the spirits of the cold called Lomonosa, Studita, and Opuku—to come to her. All three made a low bow to the tsaritsa and waited silently for her orders.

"Listen, my faithful servants. There again," Marena said, pointing to the eastern part of the sky, "a small god has been born, who sooner or later will come and drive us, as the wind drives clouds, away from this place to the very edge of the world. Take care to delay him as long as possible. Bind in ice even more firmly all the streams and rivers in the woods and ravines. Tell the midnight winds to struggle with all their might against their

---

29. Baba-Yaga: In pre-Christian times, the patron goddess of women, benevolent to all; in post-Christian times, a malevolent witch who lives deep in a forest in a hut on chicken legs. She is a cannibal and associated with bones and death.

30. This demon's name, "Chill" (Студит), is derived from the third person singular of the verb студить, which means "to cool or chill."

31. *terem*: from mid-16th Century to early 18th Century, secluded quarters in a Moscow palace for highborn women (see Suzanne Massie, *Land of the Firebird*, 50-51, for a detailed description).

midday brothers and prevent them from flying here, or otherwise we'll all be forced to leave these parts soon."

And the loyal, obedient servants rushed to fulfill this command.

⁓

Gorpina's body was found and buried in due course; however, her soul continued to exist in its *rusalka* state. And only in winter when, freezing from the cold, she slept beside her friends on the silty bottom of the ice-locked Yaryn, did she dream at times of lying in a wooden coffin, where it was dark, cramped and lonely. . . .

And on earth at that time trees cloaked in hoarfrost cracked from the fierce malice of Frost. Sparrows and crows fell dead from these trees, killed by his breath. In the howling of the cold wind which went through the village, the groans of the souls of the dead, hovering over the huts, were clearly audible to the experienced ear. On the occasion of the birth of the new sun god, these souls were allowed to leave the other world for three days to visit their kinfolk.

And now warming themselves in the streams of warm air quivering above the stovepipes,[32] they pleaded to be let into the houses, scratched on the windows, and tried to sneak through the door with those entering, or they waited until it was possible to fly in through the stovepipe.

The interiors of the living quarters all had a festive appearance. In the Ukrainian[33] section of the town, the dirt floors were sprinkled with yellow sand on which rushes were strewn. In the Russian[34] section, the wooden floors, as well as the tables and benches, were carefully washed. Every table was covered with a clean tablecloth, under which hay and spikes of grain were visible. Dishes in great number and variety were arranged on the tablecloth. When people sat down to have supper, the old folks did not eat in the usual way. Occasionally they would empty a spoon, particularly with *kutiya*,[35] not into their mouths but over

---

32. By the end of the nineteenth century, some huts did have a chimney, but the use of a stovepipe was more common.

33. Here Kondratiev uses an adjective derived from хохол, a jocular as well as pejorative term used by a Russian for a Ukrainian.

34. Here Kondratiev uses an adjective derived from кацап, a jocular as well as pejorative term used by a Ukrainian for a Russian.

35. *kutiya (кутья):* sweet rice served at funerals and at feasts remembering the dead.

their shoulder. These spoonfuls were intended for the souls of the dead since on this night the living and the dead were supposed to celebrate the birth of the new god together without fearing each other. . . . And for those phantoms dear to them who did not manage to catch a crumb or a piece thrown in the air to them, pots and plates with spoons left in them were not removed from the table until morning.

For three whole days the women did not sweep their huts or cottages[36] so as not to accidentally disturb an ancestor quietly huddled somewhere in a corner, invisible to the eye.

Flying out with the white steam from an unfrozen patch of water in the river, Gorpina, as a misty phantom, headed for the village of Zaretskoye. Together with other familiar and unfamiliar specters floating in the air, whom she knew and did not know, she arrived at her own cottage as if she had just left it yesterday. Her own home, which she had left behind and which was now briefly returned to her, seemed both dear and, at the same time, alien to her. She did not even try to reveal herself to her sisters and mother. "They're going to be afraid of me again and won't sleep at night," the wretched little creature thought. And sadly shrinking into a little ball, she crouched on the upper ledge of the stove.

On the fourth morning after the birth of the little god, even before nightfall, the women swept the floors clean and took the refuse out to the middle of the yard. There lay a pile of straw, prepared earlier, which an old woman—the mother of the woman of the house, or just an older woman in the house—was supposed to light with a burning splinter of wood. The flames that rose up warmed the souls of the departed who were flying back to their dark graves.

Carried by the wind, the invisible, sad phantom of the drowned Gorpina took off after the others, and again descended to the bottom of the Yaryn.

~

But the living and the young only have living things on their mind. Evening parties and get-togethers, with fortune-telling and games, were in full swing.

---

36. Kondratiev uses изба and хата (the latter heard more in Ukraine), both of which mean "hut" or "cottage." Henceforth, изба will be translated as "hut" and хата as "cottage."

It is not known when and who had taught the girls to have their fortunes told by the Gumennik,[37] a being similar to a *domovoi* or house spirit, except that he lives in a threshing barn or shed. This demon is known to be less kind than Grandfather Domovoi, and he is inclined sometimes to play dirty tricks on people who come into his domain at an inopportune time. Then he inevitably pushes a plow or a harrow under the person's feet, or he displays his strength and power in some other fashion.

During the holiday season, Matrunka and Zinka admitted to their girlfriends that they had run at night to the landowner's large threshing barn, which stood far from his other buildings, where there was an opening made in the wall for bringing in the horse-pulled threshing machine. After first asking Grandfather Gumennik to reveal the whole truth—what their married life would be like—the girls, one after another, approached the opening in the wall and, turning their backs to it, raised their dresses. Grandfather Gumennik was supposed to stroke their bodies with his soft, downy palm if the marriage would be a happy one, and with his hard palm if the girl's marriage would be unhappy. Zinka said that she didn't feel any palm, but that someone breathed on her with a breath warm like a cow's. Matrunka seemed to think that somebody gently touched her bare body with a few pieces of straw; moreover, one of them even pricked her lightly.

This evidence from the girls was interpreted by their friends as unquestionably propitious for Zinka, but as for Matrunka, opinions differed. A considerable number of the girls trying to interpret the signs, however, insisted that Matrunka must repeat her attempt at fortune-telling. But neither Matrunka nor Zinka agreed to go to the threshing barn a second time, explaining that they had had enough fear since, as they were leaving, they had even heard Grandfather Gumennik, probably before some misfortune, howling like a dog and yet not like a dog.

Matrunka and Zinka's report had the effect that not even one of the village girls went to have her fortune told at the landowner's threshing barn. The fellows, not without some confusion, passed around the story that on that night, when Zinka and Matrunka had their fortunes told, Onisim Shcherbaty, hid-

---

37. Gummenik (*Гуменник*, from *гумно*, meaning "barn" or "threshing floor"): a spirit related to the *domovoi* who lives in the barn for drying crops. He is considered a soothsayer, a foreteller.

ing in the barn to frighten them, was himself terribly frightened
since either Gumennik or some other unclean spirit, in all probability Lapun,[38] jumped on his chest in the darkness and tried to
choke him. Onisim began to shriek in an inhuman voice and lost
consciousness from fear. Falling, he hurt his head on the iron
wheel of a piece of farm machinery.

Because of this, at the evening get-togethers they began to recall and relate old legends about Gumennik's demons, like the
tale about a woman who had quarreled once with her husband
and said to him, "It would be better if I lived with 'that one'
than with you." And so once, when this woman went to the
threshing barn to get something, she unexpectedly saw a demon
in the form of a stranger. The latter walked up to the woman,
who was trembling in fear, and said to her, "You wanted to live
with me, so here I am . . ." And with outstretched hands the unclean spirit blocked his victim's exit from barn. The woman,
who found herself suddenly captured, was so frightened that she
was in no condition to resist. She came home clearly mentally
deranged and totally subject to the demon-rapist. The latter
took possession of her will to such an extent that he demanded
that the unfortunate woman come to him at all times of night
and day. At first, she would run out for "that"[39] as if she had to
go to the bathroom behind the animal shed, or she would sneak
off to the threshing barn unnoticed, but then the Gumennik got
so bold that he even began to go to her hut in invisible form.

Lying behind a partition on her bed, the possessed woman
talked with her master, answering his questions, which were inaudible to others, laughed at his jokes, and sometimes asked him
teary-eyed to leave her alone.

Not wanting to share his wife with such a being, the husband
gave her up, particularly after all the usual remedies in such
cases—for example, incense, holy water sprinkled from the icon
corner, and even prayers by the village priest—turned out to be
useless. They tried to take the woman to various monasteries
and to hermits who led a life pleasing to God, but even this was
of little use. Usually the demon even accompanied them on
these trips and, according to what the defiled woman said, one

---

38. Lapun *(Лапун):* Not listed in any of the sources consulted. This spirit's be-
    havior brings to mind the *domovoi;* the name could be connected with
    "paw" *(лапа).*
39. "that:" euphemism for the sexual act.

moment he would try to rip away the sled's cover, another moment he would swing on a branch in front of horses that had stopped moving out of fear. Only death, which soon claimed her—as predicted by one of the holy fathers—freed the unfortunate woman from the power of the demon who had attached himself to her.

This story had a particularly strong affect on the girls who came to the evening get-togethers. And for a long time afterwards, not one of them could bring herself to go alone to the barn at twilight.

⌒

The oak idol of Perun and the fat Vodyanoi were lying next to each other, half-covered in silt, at the bottom of the ice-encrusted Yaryn, and both were either deep asleep or lost in their recollections of centuries long since past.

The Vodyanoi dreamed of fulfilling his cherished fantasy: after learning of the wisdom and art of governing that the ruler of the Yaryn possessed, an embassy of beings like him—water spirits, only not so strong and bright—covered with beautiful chains of silver, gold and amber, sailed to him from afar. The embassy invited him to assume the vacated throne of the Tsar of the Seas.

At first in his dreams the Vodyanoi did not agree, assuring them that he loved his Yaryn too much, and similarly loved the *utoplennik*s and *rusalka*s who lived in it, who would be deprived not only of a wise leader but also of their benefactor, spouse and, one could say, second father. . . . But then the tearful pleas of the embassy and their declarations that without him, the Vodyanoi from the Yaryn, the whole Tsardom of the Seas would perish, had their effect, and the vain old man agreed. He allowed them to place a precious chain of large pearls and uncut diamonds on him, and he accepted the old silver crown, with emeralds and sapphires, of the underwater tsars of the Varangian Sea. Half-animal, half-fish beings with tails, who had arrived with the water ambassadors, took him in a large mother-of-pearl shell to the palace, which was straight out of fairy tales in its splendor, built of crystal among the hills and valleys of the tsardom of the deep.

There the vacated amber throne, slightly worn by his predecessors, awaited him. Sharp-snouted sturgeons and blinking-eyed belugas, poking their snoots against the windows, were visible through the crystal windows; powerful large-headed whales and all kinds of small fish swam past, flashing the varied colors of their scales and glistening with their golden fins.

A collection of tsarevnas was brought to the new ruler, daughters of the former, dethroned tsar, and it was proposed that he choose one of them for his spouse. All of them were remarkably pretty and resembled one another. Then the new Tsar of the Seas, in order not to hurt the feelings of any one of them, announced to the applause of the courtiers that he liked each of the sisters equally and that he would take them all. "How are they any worse than the *rusalka*s?" the thought flashed through the Vodyanoi's mind. This former head of the Yaryn liked this thought so much that he decided to celebrate it with a banquet.

No sooner than he issues the order, in the wink of an eye tables are groaning from the abundance of the victuals placed on them. Large silver dishes hold all that the sea produces, and all that passing seafarers send to the bottom in the form of tribute. There is no shortage of bliny or pies with *viziga*[40] and sturgeon, nor of fragrant foreign wines from beyond the sea, poured into crystal pitchers and golden goblets. A sea beast, standing on his hind flippers, is nimbly selecting food with his front flippers like an expert psaltery player; a psaltery fashioned of black wood hangs on his chest with its strings sparkling. The sea-tsarevnas, in response to their sovereign's command, dance joyously before him, and even he, having drunk his fill of foreign wines which have impassioned his heart, throws himself into the dance.

At first he dances as befits a tsar, with an air of importance, moving his feet in place and gracefully kicking one foot after the other. But he wants to dance more quickly, and the sea beast does not know how to pluck the singing strings as adroitly as people do. One of the courtiers, with a head like a sturgeon, his supple back bent respectfully, reports in a whisper to the Tsar that the youngest tsarevna plays the harp well. Then after giving the pinniped,[41] the psaltery player, a good beating, the new Tsar orders that he be sent away and demands that the tsarevna show her artistry.

---

40. *viziga* (визига): foodstuff prepared from gristle of fish of the sturgeon family.
41. A pinniped is any of a suborder of aquatic carnivorous mammals (such as a seal or walrus) with all four limbs modified into flippers.

Sitting cross-legged before the ruler, as is the custom abroad, the youthful tsarevna, sparkling in her dress embroidered with scales and smiling languidly, orders her instrument to be brought and begins to play. The Vodyanoi-tsar again throws himself into the dance. Now the dance is lively, and the dancer wearing the crown can move his feet much more quickly. But ah, one foot painfully hit against something, and the sea ruler came out of his fairy tale dreams and discovered that he was only the former, simple Vodyanoi of the Yaryn. With his toes he poked the oak idol lying next to him and, as a result, the same thing happened to the oak idol as had just happened to him: he roused the idol from his sweet slumber.

"What's wrong with you, my friend?" timidly, but not without dignity, the overthrown god silently asked the Vodyanoi.

"Oh, it's just that you eternally bring misfortune," the Vodyanoi grumbled in an angry voice, clasping his webbed feet. "I had barely touched you in my sleep, when my beautiful dream, in which I was the Tsar in an underwater palace on the bottom of the Varangian Sea, shattered and vanished into nothing. It turned out that I, like you, had my throne taken away from me."

"I, too, was a tsar in my dream, from which you so unexpectedly awakened me. I occupied my former throne behind the clouds. Putting on a shirt of feathers, I turned into an eagle and, flying above the earth, watched how people and demigods were behaving themselves. Afterwards, when I returned to my palace, my main wife, the rain-bearing regal Mokosh, wiping away tears of jealousy with the hem of her dress embroidered in oak leaves, began to chide me for chasing after, it would seem, a sea tsarevna, who had turned into a swan. I kept telling her that she was mistaken, but Mokosh (she was always very argumentative) exploded in anger, removed a shoe from her foot and threw it at me, hitting me in the side and causing me pain. And I woke up exactly at that very instant when my favorite daughter, with golden curls and rosy cheeks, ran frightened into the *gornitsa*.[42] It turns out that I was awakened by you from perhaps not as merry, but just as agreeable, a dream as yours. . . . Ah, if only it would come back! . . ."

Exhausting the subject with that exchange, and not considering it necessary to argue and continue the discussion, the two

---

42. *gornitsa (горница):* clean part of a peasant hut, usually reserved for entertaining guests

who had been talking began to doze again.

The quiet and almost soundless dialogue did not disturb Pull-by-the-Leg, sleeping not far away and also burrowed into the silt. He saw in his sleep that he was approaching the bog and dirty, little green devils were crawling out towards him, bowing from the waist.

"Greetings, Uncle Pyotr Ankudinych," they say respectfully. "You haven't visited us in a long time. All the aunties have been waiting and waiting for you. And Aunt Nastasia, who sang in your presence the last time, is even hurt. What is this, she says, they[43] don't even stop by? . . . Please Uncle, we'll walk by this opening and, over there, behind the bushes, we have a hole we can crawl through.

And swiftly parting the bushes before Black-Beard, large demons who resembled cats and dogs accompanied him, and little ones who looked like frogs jumped about, jostling one another and getting under the feet of the larger demons. Pull-by-the-Leg went down into an open black hole as he would into a cold cellar and entered a spacious *gornitsa*, illuminated by blue swamp fires, with rushes thrown on the floor to protect it from dirt. The head Bolotnik[44] caught sight of Black-Beard and rose from a chamois stool.

"Ah, Pyotr Ankudinych! Greetings! . . . I extend my hand! You've finally come to see us! I was even about to send for you, but I was afraid that your viper would get a whiff of it and not let you go. He should realize himself, I say to myself, that he is expected. And low and behold, here you are. It's nice to see you!" And the head Bolotnik even "grasped the hand" of Black-Beard for a moment. "I wanted, you see, to invite you to work for me. We need an overseer for the little devils because, the rascals, they've gotten terribly spoiled! They get into all kinds of places where it isn't permitted, and they keep disappearing. How many of them the wolves alone have devoured! And so I got the idea that the older ones should look after the youngest, and you—you should be in charge of the oldest. It's sort of like you serving as my right hand . . . And your position will be as follows: as a first order of business, one of my *bolotnitsa*s will be your wife; the living quarters you'll choose yourself. It's a bit dirty here, but

---

43. The plural "they" is used here as a sign of deference to Pyotr Ankudinych.
44. bolotnik *(болотник):* spirit of the swamp *(болото).*

you'll have a lot of little devils to run errands for you. They can help your woman cover the floor with grass, and in the summer they can milk the herd, gather berries, and get fresh eggs from birds' nests. Only one is not supposed to make a fire here. . . . Incidentally, in your river, as you know, you had the same rules about fire. . . . So, can we shake on it, Pyotr Ankudinych?"

And Black-Beard slapped in his sleep the hands of the head Bolotnik, who looked like the Vodyanoi, except that he was a brownish green color and much dirtier.

IV

The Domovoi of Ipat Saveliev, a peasant in Zaretskoye, was completely happy with the master of the hut in which he dwelled. It could even be said that they lived as two souls in total harmony with each other, if Ipat did not doubt to some extent the existence of the soul of his household protector. The Domovoi, according to his nature, was a nice fellow, although like Saveliev, he sometimes liked to laze about. Their horses stood ungroomed whole weeks on end; their neighbor, the witch Aniska, taking advantage of the carelessness of the guardian of Ipat's property, would sometimes make her way into the shed and milk the cows.

One dark February night, Cow Death[1] almost got into the peasant's yard, clearly with bad intentions. Fortunately, one of Saveliev's dogs, sensing misfortune, began to bark loudly, and the sleepy-eyed Domovoi managed to run out in time and chase off the evil old woman. He managed to overtake the demonic spirit at the moment when the latter, scrambling over the garden wattle fence, caught her dirty skirt on one of the fence posts. With a heavy blow to the back of the head, the Domovoi knocked her down into the snow on the other side of the fence and with some pleasure watched the uninvited guest run away, quickly moving her bovine legs.

The Domovoi did not show any particular zeal for protecting the vegetable garden, although on occasion during the summer and autumn months he had to frighten off the village boys. On

---

1. Cow Death *(Коровья Смерть)*: an evil female spirit who takes the form of a black cow and moves among the herds, "spoiling" and bringing plague. She can also appear as a cat, usually black, or a dog, or as a skeleton of a cow.

the other hand, he paid close attention so that weasels and diseases would not kill the chicks and mother hens. Now and then he would even sweep the yard and clean up the manure. In general, he was of a submissive character, behaved soberly, and took pleasure in the little things in life.

"I have not just a *domovoi* but a real treasure!" the undemanding Ipat Saveliev would say and at times repeat to his neighbors during village celebrations when he had a bit to drink.

More than once jealous people even tried to lure away his *domovoi,* but the benefactor of Ipat's property stood firm and would not be tempted by bribery.

Once, at the very beginning of February, when the sky was just beginning to grow light and the snoring of Ipat Saveliev's family filled the hut, the Domovoi went out on his morning rounds.

Everything was quiet in the yard.

But when the faithful guard of Saveliev's property walked into the shed, the naked witch Aniska was squatting there and milking a cow of several colors. Catching the light sound of footsteps, she jumped up, turned and, upon seeing the Domovoi, burst into peals of laughter.

"Aha, so you've paid a visit! Why did you wake up so early?" she asked as if nothing was unusual.

By no means did everyone in the village see Aniska as a witch; the majority considered her an ordinary, bold young woman, with a very glib tongue, and somewhat thievish.

Her carefree laughter puzzled the Domovoi. He even took a few steps back.

"How did you get in here?" he asked, somewhat embarrassed.

The Domovoi was somewhat shy by nature, and his embarrassment on seeing Aniska naked was fully understandable.

"You're stupid, I see! Don't you know we witches can crawl through any hole? You should be a *leshy,* not a *domovoi....* You should guard rabbits, really, and watch over the forest...."

The Domovoi took offense at such words and decided, in turn, to say something unpleasant to Aniska.

"Why are you milking other people's cows? I'll give you a sound thrashing!"

"Me?" And the witch burst out laughing again and slyly looked at the Domovoi. "And how can you, you old fogey, tell me what to do?!"

"I'll show you what an old fogey I am!"

With a quick leap, which was hard to anticipate because of his venerable age, the resourceful "grandpa" landed next to Aniska. The latter was not able to jump away as strong hairy hands grabbed her under the arms, and the witch's naked back felt the touch of the Domovoi's shaggy body.

Although Aniska had even rubbed herself with a greasy magical ointment which could have turned her into a magpie, rat or frog, all her attempts to slip out of the embrace of the ardent old man proved to be futile. Their stubborn silent struggle showed the witch that the hairy "grandpa" was much stronger than she. Grabbed from behind, she was forced to fall on her knees and sensed that a bit longer and her opponent would celebrate his victory. Aniska then decided to resort to guile.

"Don't throw me down into the manure, my dear. It'll be embarrassing later to run through the village with a dirty back. . . . At least, put down some straw or hay!" she began to beg in a plaintive voice.

Trusting the conciliatory tone of his opponent, the Domovoi somewhat loosened his grip on her and panted in her ear, "And will you please me?"

"I'll please you so that . . . you'll see for yourself. I won't even try to get on my feet, just put something down!"

Without leaving his place (since he did not fully trust Aniska), the Domovoi drew himself to his full height and began to pull down straw placed on rafters above the cattle for warmth. He had not pulled down even an armful when Aniska, who was on all fours, quickly performed a few somersaults and, taking the form of a magpie after that, flew toward the window where the greyish, predawn sky was glimmering faintly.

With mouth agape and astonishment on his face, the deceived Domovoi followed her with his eyes. Throwing the straw down to the ground in a gesture of anger, the vexed old man finally sprang in pursuit of the fugitive, but the sly bird—which lingered a moment in the small narrow window—flapped her long, black tail derisively, turned her head to face him and, at the very moment when the enemy was again ready to take possession of her, took flight and disappeared from view.

It became very quiet in the shed. Only the cows chewing their cud could be heard. Scratching the back of his head, the Domovoi walked out into the yard. The dog, Zhuchka, crawled out of her doghouse and wagged her tail at him. But the old man, having suffered failure, went with resolute step into the hut and down into the cellar.

The unlucky fellow spent the whole day sitting there, huddling in a corner. He constantly remembered the resilient hot body of the resisting witch and her white back glimmering in the darkness of the cow shed. Aniska's ringing laughter would not leave his ears.

⌒

In the early hours of February 5[2] someone began to play about in the stovepipe of Ipat's hut, making squeaking noises and flapping invisible wings. The Domovoi, who had a keen sense of hearing, crawled out from behind the stove and began to investigate. He did not like to be disturbed, and for this reason was sullen.

"Who's there? What do you want?" he muttered displeased, poking his head into the stove's opening.

"It's me, dear old man. Let me in to warm up!" a squeaky voice, along with a restless scratching, was heard in reply.

"And who are you? Why are you barging into the hut uninvited? This place is already taken. . ."

"Dear old man, I myself don't really know who I am. They say I might be a *kikimora*.[3] Let me in to warm up! They've just let us out of hell. It's terribly cold when you're not used to it! Let me in! . . ."

"Oh sure, I'll let you in right away! Just keep on waiting! . . . You've been told it's taken. I know your kind. The voice is awfully submissive, but let someone like you in and you'll break all the pots, wake up the whole house, and then I'll have to answer for it. . . . You heard me, I won't let you in. Get lost!"

"My, my, look how severe you are! You probably wouldn't dare to speak to Aniska like that! . . . We know you, you strict types!"

---

2. Saint Agafiya's (the Milk Maid) Day (*Агафья Коровяница* or *Коровница*): 5 (18) February. On this day funeral repasts were eaten in memory of dead ancestors; chimneys were covered over so that evil spirits could not get in. Barns were closed and bast shoes were hung on barn doors so that Cow Death could not get in; Saint Agafiya's Day became linked with cows, hence the "Korovnitsa."

3. *kikimora* (*кикимора*): There is no one image of this demonic spirit. Some see her as the wife of the *domovoi*; others speak of her as a tiny old woman who lives behind the stove during the day and works at the spinning wheel at night. There is also the belief that she represents the restless spirit of an unbaptized child or a woman, damned in her youth by her mother, and given to playing tricks on people.

Someone began laughing in a thin voice in the stovepipe and then everything quieted down. The Domovoi felt embarrassed. He truly was not indifferent to the young witch Aniska and more than once lay in wait for her in the cow shed, hoping to catch her when she would start milking a cow.

The old man glanced out the window and thought that now was the perfect time to go and lie in wait for Aniska. Making his way out with resolute step, he pulled off, as he walked, the sheepskin with which Ipat's older son had covered himself. The "grandpa" who lived behind the stove did not do this at all out of spite, but rather so that the young boy would feel that there was a force in the house that must be respected at times.

The Domovoi walked down the corridor and out into the yard. The light snow which had fallen during the night crunched softly under his barely audible footsteps.

There was no one in the shed. The Domovoi hid in the corner and waited. All around it was quiet.

But there in another corner rats scurried about, got into a fight, and ran through the shed. They were all nipping and chasing one of their friends. The Domovoi had wanted to scare them when, all at once, the rat being mistreated did a somersault, and suddenly Aniska stood in the middle of the shed. Her long black hair cascaded down her bare shoulders and back. The witch stomped her foot at the rats running off in fright and slowly headed for the cows.

At this point someone's shaggy hands suddenly grabbed her from behind so strongly that Aniska did not have the strength to break free.

"Got you, my dear!" the Domovoi wheezed, and his soft beard tickled the neck of the captured witch.

"Oh you old dog! . . . How silently you've sneaked up on me! . . ."

And the Domovoi would not leave her alone. . . .

Aniska was in a completely gloomy mood. She liked the milk of Ipat's cows very much, but to her misfortune, Ipat's Domovoi was too enamored of her and every night lay in wait for her, either hiding in the straw left from thrashing the oats or concealing himself in a dark corner of the shed. His uninvited caresses were totally repellant to the young witch.

Aniska was proud that the Fiery Serpent[4] had already come to visit her twice and, for this reason, she looked at the Domovoi somewhat condescendingly, in any case preferring the young village men who were not at all afraid of the rumors spread about Aniska.

"What does it matter that she was seen riding a pig! You see all kinds of things! . . . And they're probably lying at that," they would say.

Although the Fiery Serpent, a recent acquaintance of the young witch, promised to teach her how to milk other people's cows without leaving the house, he had not yet kept his promise, and Aniska was forced either to deal with the Domovoi or to refrain from visiting the cows which he guarded.

She chose the latter, which drove the old man, who was doggedly lying in wait for her, into deep melancholy.

The guardian of Ipat's homestead grew thin, mangy, and unkempt; only his eyes glowed even more brightly in the dark. Once, Ipat's wife, seeing two pupils burning with a greenish light in the shed, rushed headlong out of it and, overcome with fear, could not collect herself for a long time.

The Domovoi became restless and irritable.

In the meantime the sun began to warm the snow. The flapping wings of black grouse that had been flushed could be heard in the forest from time to time; the first month of spring had arrived. This whole month the Domovoi tortured the cows out of vexation, spent whole nights sitting in the shed, and drove the horses to exhaustion, tangling up their manes.

On the 30th of March,[5] he became absolutely enraged. At night, he tried to strangle not only Ipat Saveliev's wife but even Ipat himself. He broke a pair of bowls, overturned all the milk pots, and caught and mercilessly beat the cat on the roof. The captured cat cried so furiously that it woke up everyone in the house and made Ipat's little boys go out into the yard. The Domovoi, letting the cat go, managed to roll himself under the feet of one of them. The little fellow flew off the porch and got terribly hurt. The members of Ipat's frightened family locked themselves in the

---

4. Fiery Serpent *(Огненный Змей)*: The devil is said to fly and visit women (and men) in the form of a fiery serpent. Sorcerers were also believed to be able to assume this form for love trysts.
5. 30 March (12 April): The *domovoi* was said to go into a rage on this day and not recognize the members of his household.

hut and awaited further orders. The enraged Domovoi, forgetting his age and importance, swept like a whirlwind around the yard in the dimness of early morning and gave a painful bite to a dog that happened to get in his way. From the window Ipat saw the dog yelp and then hide in the doghouse.

Then the Domovoi headed, in all probability, to the chicken coop, for suddenly such a clucking could be heard from there that Ipat's wife could no longer stand it and, grabbing a poker, ran there with a battle cry. Her spouse tried in vain to hold her back. From the window, he saw the infuriated woman, who was brandishing a poker, disappear into the chicken coop from which her furious swearing could be heard.

Then the door of the chicken coop opened wide again and Saveliev saw that something like a shaggy little ball rolled out towards the gate.

A minute later the flushed mistress of the house appeared in the doorway of the chicken coop, having obviously endured a fight that was no laughing matter. She had a rather confused look on her face, her kerchief was askew, her jacket was unbuttoned, but her hand, as before, gripped the now noticeably bent poker.

What she had seen in the chicken coop and how she had chased out the enraged Domovoi, this the woman was not able or did not want to say. It seems that she had hit the enemy not only with the poker but also with a rock hanging on a rope in the chicken coop, a rock which people called the "chicken god."[6] At any rate, the Domovoi left Ipat Saveliev's hut and homestead forever. . . .

The drunken peasant Mikita, who was returning from town towards morning, said that he apparently saw, not far from the outskirts of the village, an unclean spirit running on all fours with a red tongue hanging out a quarter of an *arshin.*[7]

Mikita even boasted that he managed to land a blow on this evil spirit with his whip, but no one believed him.

---

6. "chicken god" *(куриный бог):* a rock hung in the chicken coop, believed to contain the spirit that protected chickens from an angry *domovoi* or other spirits who liked to kill chickens or make them lose their feathers.

7. *arshin (аршин):* equivalent to 27.95 inches, hence the tongue is sticking out 7 inches.

V

To the singing of larks, Tsarevna Spring moved with inaudible steps on the still damp bosom of the earth. Lush green grass broke through under her light feet and the first flowers began to grow. Rejoicing in them, the goddess smiled, and from her happy smile different varieties of cherry trees burst forth in white blossoms, and dark and light violets gave off an even stronger fragrance. The Nightingale, the bard of Spring, who once upon a time became a gray bird for the sake of the beautiful goddess, began to sing, at first timidly, then more boldly and louder. Trees began to rustle with their first foliage, whispering among themselves. All small creatures, insects, flies, and beetles which had spent the long winter sleeping in the dark hollows of trees and under the bark awakened from their long sleep and began creeping out to bow to the goddess. Frogs, too, crawled out of their muddy ponds and came to meet her. But upon seeing a black and white stork walking before Spring on long red legs with an air of importance, they began to croak and save themselves by jumping into the water, which had not yet become covered with green duckweed. The goddess burst out in ringing laughter, and to the sound of her laughter bees began to buzz happily above the blooming hazelnut trees, and furry bumblebees began to hum, drawn by the delicate fragrance from the wreath of pink and white apple blossoms on the brow of the immortal being. The stork walked with triumphant step, paying no heed to either the beetles or the frogs. And the trees whispered to each other, "It is he who has brought out Spring from the underground kingdom for us. . . ."

Having celebrated her name day shortly before this, the talkative Magpie (a flying creature of suspicious origin), from whom nothing can ever be hidden, who knows all and sees all, had already managed on the sly to tell, here and there, that the stork was a young god who had taken the form of a bird and that he had recently vanquished the goddess of winter and awakened a young maiden, Spring, a prisoner of the tsar of the wizards, from her long sleep.

"Now he walks near her as a long-legged bird, earlier he ran on earth as a golden-horned stag and later, perhaps, we'll see him in some other image," the Magpie chattered. "All gods, just like Mother Earth, change their form from time to time. Such is their law . . ."

But the trees did not want to listen to the chatterbox any longer. They seized upon the goddess's every step, her every glance and smile. And from these smiles, stately rowan and spreading bird cherry trees burst into bloom, one after the other, and bushes of thorny blackthorn became covered with white fluff.

Spring passed over the small knolls of the cemetery already covered with bright green grass and, bending her head, sprinkled the graves of the deceased with pink, violet, yellow, and white star-like flowers.

And when people noticed such a bright, multicolored covering, they said, "Look! Radunitsa[1] has come to release imprisoned souls from their dark graves."

And the tsarevna raised her arms over the mounds of graves and ever so quietly whispered a spell known only to her; upon hearing it, the souls of the deceased left the depths of the earth. Along with the violet, yellow, and light-blue flowers, the sorrowful souls who had been imprisoned there till now joyously came to the surface and, as light butterflies and moths circling under the wind's breath, flew off to visit native fields, gardens, houses, and their nearest and dearest left behind there.

Evening was drawing near. Songbirds fell silent. The pensive stork disappeared somewhere, along with the setting sun. Tsarevna Spring was now walking alone, scattering flowers and bringing life to field and forest. Frogs in the ponds and swamps croaked from happiness in a loud, rising-and-falling chorus.

With the fog, bareheaded *rusalkas* came out of the rivers and

1. Radunitsa *(Радуница)*: An ancient spring festival which took place the day after Easter and commemorated the dead; the holiday was also closely associated with the *rusalkas*.

lakes and ran through the damp meadows, laughing and calling to each other. They rejoiced, sang, and shouted that soon their "Rusalnaya Week"[2] would be here. Clapping their hands, the water maidens frightened long-eared rabbits, roused sleepy ducks in the bushes along the shore, and ran with squeals and laughter, celebrating their liberation from wintry sleep.

In the moonlight the master of the river bottom, fat and naked and crowned with sedge, emerged waist-high from his realm. He called and shouted, imitating a bittern, and he splashed the surface of the water with the palm of his hand.

In the forest the hairy Leshy, stern and gloomy in appearance, cackled like a drunken peasant and exchanged calls with an eagle owl. He had become truly intoxicated from the smell of the blossoming bird cherry trees and tried to catch the *rusalkas,* but they only laughed at his greenish half-animal face and quickly ran away, tormented with the desire to tickle a living man to death.

The Nightingale's tender song floated on, ever louder and more ringing. He sang:

"From millennium to millennium, each year I sing the praises of your coming, O beautiful Tsarevna Spring. Rustling your silver-green garments, you walk through the land in bloom, evoking a desire for happiness everywhere and, with your smile, promise the bliss of love. . . . Accept my love as well, locked in my song, inspired by you, O Tsarevna-Goddess. Your hair smells of apple blossoms and your eternally youthful body, of sweet-scented cherry; the breath that passes your lips is the fragrance of lily-of-the-valley in full bloom! . . . Smile at me, the one who abandoned his human appearance for you, Tsarevna Spring!"

The divine maiden said nothing in response. Her attention was drawn to a silvery boat which appeared in the semi-dark heavens, in which the beautiful Tsar Moon sat clad in a glistening helmet and radiant cloak.

Flooding the earth and sky with his radiance, he turned his languid look to the goddess and, inclining his pallid face towards her, began to speak:

"In the boundless fields of the dark, blue-black heavens, there are many eternally young stars in gold and silver raiments with

---

2. Rusalnaya Week *(Русальная неделя):* the most important celebration of spring vegetation, in the seventh or eight week after Easter. Usually called "Green Yuletide" *(Зелёные святки).* Huts were decorated both inside and outside with green branches; garlands were thrown into rivers for divination.

diamond wreaths on the luxuriant waves of their long hair. They are all beautiful, but there is not one at whose appearance my boat would stop, as it has now before you. Your wreath of white, star-like, sweet-scented apple blossoms is much more beautiful than the precious crowns of the heavenly beauties, Tsarevna Spring. Climb into this boat and we will sail off together to my palace, accessible to none and surrounded by pillared towers of clouds. . . . We will be happy there together. . . ."

The pale Tsar Moon, in a silver crescent tiara, continued to speak for a long time, extending his arms to her. The eternally young daughter of goddess Earth was totally absorbed in listening, heeding his passionate pleas.

But the Nightingale, in love with Spring, interrupted the handsome Moon in a low, rolling tone full of indignation:

"Don't believe him, daughter of the sovereign of the gods! His words are full of lies and treachery. Take a look at the scars on the pale face of this knight in the silver helmet. One of them his wife inflicted on the traitor and banished him in a rage from her palace; the other, your father inflicted on him for deception, the victim of which was one of the most beautiful stars. Don't believe him, maiden! Even if he showers you with solemn promises and affection, know that before daybreak he will nevertheless leave you to meet rosy Dawn, among clouds blazing with scarlet and gold, at whose sight this god pales from passion. Don't believe him, daughter of the sovereign of the immortals!" the Nightingale finished his address.

But even before the words of the bard locked in the body of the tiny bird had ceased, the regal Moon stretched his smoky sail, and his shining boat disappeared in the haze of clouds floating across the sky.

Taking a quiet breath, Tsarevna Spring headed towards the darkening forest. The Nightingale followed her with a look of hopeless love.

It was dark in the forest. Trees rustled overhead. Somewhere nearby, a nightjar was jabbering in an incessant rumble. In the distant swamp the drawn-out screech of a crane sounded several times. In the meadows along the river shore frogs croaked in a rumbling chorus, drowning out the doleful singing of the *rusalkas*.

A gentle sadness began to make itself felt in the heart of the young goddess. "Everything around is singing from happiness and has found love, but I myself don't have time for love," she thought. "Surely not with this small gray bird which talks to it-self and claims to have been a human being?"

"Cuckoo-cuckoo! Cuckoo-cuckoo!" called a cuckoo in the branches, rousing itself in the middle of the night. "Let other birds make their nests. I'm no simple bird! My image is in the hands of the Tsaritsa of the gods herself. Let others sit on their eggs. I'm an ancient regal bird. Perun once assumed my appear-ance in order to captivate the beauty Mokosh. . . ."

"Not only people but gods as well, in the grips of passion, change their outer appearance," thought the light-footed daugh-ter of Mother Damp Earth. "Even my powerful father is subject to that law. . . . Who will be my intended one, and when? What appearance will he assume, the one to whom my lips will whis-per, 'I'm yours?'"

The air was sultry as before a storm. . . .

Together with the other *rusalkas,* Gorpina, too, went out that evening on dry land, rejoicing that she could luxuriate in the sil-very splendor of the bright moon and breathe the resinous smell of budding birches. Now blending in with the waves of late eve-ning fog, now emerging out of it, she glided through the dewy grass along the banks of the vast Yaryn. . . . So delightful is this short period of freedom after a long imprisonment on the oozy, silty river bottom in last year's slippery slime! All night long Gorpina and her friends rushed about the meadows covered by the spring flood, and when it began to get light, all of them made their way to a thick forest, which enticed them with its spring fragrances and where the recently returned birds were about to wake up and greet the sun with their happy singing.

It's so pleasant to swing on the long branches of old oaks, birch, and spreading river willows. It's so delightful to know that until St. Peter's Day[3] you do not have to return to the hateful, silty bottom of the turbid Yaryn! . . .

Oh, how sweetly the Nightingale sings! . . .

---

3. St. Peter's Day *(Петров день):* 29 June (12 July), actually in honor of two saints, Peter and Paul, Christ's disciples. On the eve of this holiday people played games, sang and danced and continued these activities deep into the night; at dawn they watched the sun rise, which was said to have special colors on that morning.

Great is the power of the goddess of gods and people, Lada: adorned with a magical gold necklace, she is eternally youthful in face and body and loves songs, passionate whispers, and kisses.

Following in the steps of Spring, she descends invisibly from the azure heavens and, with the step of eternal goddesses, walks about the flowering earth.

Immutable is her will. Inspired from on high, from the very beginning Mother Lelya[4] decided to whom the love of Tsarevna Spring, and even of the smallest butterflies, should be given.

People and animals, reptiles and fish, birds and insects, trees, grasses, and even all the unclean spirits experience the enchantments of the goddess with the enigmatic, imperious smile, the goddess who knows so well the passion and ecstasy of love as well as the bitter tears of despair which, in times of old, turned into transparent amber.

Even the sons and grandsons of Svarog[5] will accept, without a murmur of complaint, passion sent by Lada, which forces them to fight among themselves, maim each other, suffer and change their appearance, turning into animals, birds, and mortal people.

The goddesses themselves, suddenly sensing her verdict, obediently allow themselves to be carried off and give themselves not only to great gods but even to members of the human tribe, pitiful in comparison with the former. Without resistance, although at times with tears, they move from the passionate embraces of the descendants of the Sun to the wedding bed of the multi-headed gods of hell. . . .

Feeling her nearness, the hearts of the living beat faster, and the souls of those who no longer have hearts ache more painfully.

At the sight of butterflies interweaving their wings, birds pairing off in happy song, and frogs embracing and gripping each other in unrestrained loving ardor, the soul of the *rusalka* Gorpina began to moan.

And an irresistible longing arose in her to see once more the youth because of whom she was deprived of the joys of life, the one with whom she had once shared her first passion, the one who introduced her to the torment of despair.

In the semi-darkness of the spring night, the soul of the dead

---

4. Lelya *(Леля):* the goddess of passion, offspring of Lada.
5. Svarog *(Сварог):* the embodiment of the sky, the father of Dazhbog *(Дажбог),* the god of the sun, and Svarozhich *(Сварожиц),* the god of fire. Traditionally considered the father of all Slavic gods.

girl came to see Maksim, who kept seeing the sad, pale face of his once beloved in his dreams. Gorpina visited the young fellow neither to drink his blood, as vampires do, nor to give density to the transparent appearance of her soul—which was at times visible to the eye—by depriving her former lover of the life-force. The drowned girl, when she appeared to Maksim in his dreams, sought only pity and comfort from him.

But Maksim, who was fated from birth to have another's embraces, took a dislike to Gorpina visiting him even in his dreams. In order to rid himself of her, the youth made an attempt to see Praskukha, the magic healer.

"I've come to you for advice, old woman," he said to her. "I keep dreaming of that wench Gorpina who drowned last summer. She, it seems, stands at the door and keeps weeping and begging for food. . . . And since I'm sick of it, you must free me of her. Take this twenty-kopeck piece and give me whatever herbs you have so that she, the whore, won't even dare to show her face to me."

Praskukha took the twenty-kopeck piece and in return she gave him some stems and leaves to put under his pillow, but either because they worked poorly against dreams, or because Praskukha—who did not like Maksim very much—had no real desire or intention to help him, Gorpina continued, nonetheless, to appear to her former beloved in his dreams.

Then the fellow went to Aniska.

The black-browed young witch treated Maksim with great consideration. After asking him sympathetically about all the details of Gorpina's visits, the sorceress smiled, attempting to endow her smile with a hint of shyness, and said:

"Yours is a bad case. Right now she's coming to see you only in your dreams, but later on she'll begin to hang around in your waking hours, and she won't leave you until she drinks all your blood. . . . You just wasted your time going to Praskukha and bringing her money. . . . I'll even free you from your dead girl without charge because I like you so much. Only listen to what I'm going to tell you. You've got to break this Gorpinka of her habit of visiting your house. It would be good, then, if you weren't there for several nights in a row. Let her go visit other people. And during that time you spend your nights at my place. At my place she won't see or find you. I know a special spell. Only please come when it's getting dark so that people in the village don't know. . . . After all, I'm a young woman, and single . . . They'll begin to say all kinds of things about me. . . . And bring a bottle of vodka with you. I'll use it to make a sleeping potion, and you'll drink a shot of it for the night to chase away bad dreams. . . ."

Maksim took Aniska's invitation and that night truly did not see Gorpina in his dreams. Although the taste and smell of the brew prepared by the witch were not very pleasing to the youth, the effect of this sleeping potion seemed to Aniska to be highly successful.

From that time on Maksim began to be a frequent guest of the village witch, to whom he soon took a liking.

VI

Pull-by-the-Leg was glum. The Vodyanoi, who at one point got into a conversation with him, forced his worker to tell him how he went to get a little demon and what he saw in the forest and swamp while doing this. Paying no attention whatsoever to what the Leshy had told him, as if he had no dealings with him, the sovereign of the Yaryn questioned Ankudinych in great detail about the bog beauties.

"So, in your opinion, they're stronger than the *rusalka*s?"

"You bet they're stronger. One lashed another's back so hard that a boom went through the forest. They both guffawed and plopped into the mire. . . . Those girls are very fit! Not like ours— a *kissel*[1] after only one winter!"

"So here's what, Pyotra. Go and bring me one such fit girl without fail. Lure her away from the Bolotnik, say that the Water Prince of the Yaryn is asking her to become his wife. . . . And be very careful in bringing her so that your Leshy doesn't take her away from you. It's best right before morning . . ."

"And how will I get to her? The little demons will notice and start squealing and barking like small dogs. . . . And the Bolotnik is not someone to be trifled with. . . ."

"And what do I care? Have you heard my orders? Well, it means go and do it while the moon is out. Otherwise I'll feed you to the sheat-fish. . . . If you happen upon the Bolotnik, give him my regards. But watch out, don't let on why you've been sent. . . . Understand? Lively now! Otherwise! . ."

The Vodyanoi began to beckon to his faithful fish.

---

1. *kissel (кисель):* a drinkable dessert made with fruit juice and thickened with potato flour.

Like a log overgrown with moss, the huge, old sheat-fish rose from the bottom, made a sharp turn with a strong swish of its tail and, quickly swimming up to its master, stopped at the height of his head, slowly moving its fins and dark, tentacle-like whiskers.

But even before the Vodyanoi could give him an order, Pull-by-the-Leg was already crawling out of the reeds onto the shore covered with nocturnal fog and made silvery by the moon above.

"Only I mustn't run into the Leshy," he thought, "and if my business with the Bolotnitsa doesn't succeed, I'll go to the Bolotnik himself, hire on, and then we'll see."

Ankudinych began to make his way unnoticeably through the bushes to the edge of the forest looming dark in the nocturnal fog.

To go through the forest was, as last time, somewhat difficult. Accustomed to the soft silt of the river bottom and the grasses of the meadows along the shore, his puffy foot kept coming unpleasantly upon tree roots and sharp branches. The loud laugh of an eagle-owl and the squeals of various forest animals forced the *utoplennik* to stop at times and listen closely to the sounds and rustlings of the night. The road was not short. Pull-by-the-Leg was afraid to head along the path through the felling area, and consequently he was forced to make his way through the thicket not far from the forest's edge.

The pine forest, which began at the river, thinned out, with birch trees and alder bushes gradually taking over. More and more forest meadows appeared, overgrown with willows and moss and tussocks with red bilberry leaves. More and more his feet felt the pleasant cold dampness to which they were accustomed. The trees kept getting shorter, and the bushes smaller and thicker. Dry places became rarer. Here the swamp began, covered with osiers and brittle willow. . . .

"And what if my dream comes true?" Pull-by-the-Leg already began to daydream. "What if it's not the Vodyanoi but me who gets a wife who's really fit, neighs like a mare, and doesn't bring on melancholy like our *rusalkas*?!"

He had already reached the bog itself. Not having had the time yet to become covered with summer verdure, the surface of the marsh lake, a smooth black and shot through with metallic luster, was empty. Not one little demon was visible on the tussocks sticking out here and there. Neither was there any singing of the *bolotnitsas*, nor any fussing or squealing in the nearby bushes.

"What's this bad luck? No one's come to meet me. No one's calling me. I guess my dream wasn't meant to come true," the *utoplennik* thought.

~

At that particular time, all the swamp spirits were crowded together on the bottom of the wide lake, which was half-overgrown above. Moonlight penetrated to the dark lake bottom—mixing with the phosphorescent light of rotten bones and slugs covering the walls of the spacious quarters—and weakly illuminated the anxious, astounded faces of the bog inhabitants. The cause of their anxiety was very serious.

The Bolotonik's favorite wife, the fat-hipped Maryska, unexpectedly for all, gave birth not to a little demon—but to a human baby of the female sex.

"I just can't figure out how it could've happened! I never left the swamp . . . It has to be the evil eye!" Maryska said in a weak voice but with great assurance to the girlfriends who surrounded her.

"Hmm," the gloomy Bolotnik muttered in disbelief.

"Who could have put the evil eye on you, my dear?" asked in a honey-sweet, sympathetic voice one of Maryska's oldest friends, Marten-Soul, who at one time was one of the Bolotnik's "favorite wives" before Maryska.

"It must be that very same marksman I drowned last summer. While I was pulling him to the bottom, he grabbed me in his arms and looked into my eyes so piercingly that something missed a beat inside me. Well, since that time, it seems, I started to carry . . ."

"Hmm," the Bolotnik muttered again, grunting.

"I've never gone anywhere outside the swamp," Maryska drawled in a hurt, plaintive voice.

"And perhaps someone visited you here?" the bog master now asked in an almost threatening voice.

"What have you with your fat belly come up with? If I lure someone, I drown him. And to be with somebody besides you, well, never in my life! . ."

At that moment a little demon ran up to the Bolotnik and whispered in his ear:

"There's a stranger there who looks like he's not of the living, hanging around the shore and looking in the openings and, it seems, wants to get in here. . . ."

"Drag him here!" the master of the bog commanded.

"I'm going, dear master, I'm going!" was heard in answer just as Ankudinych, bowing low, appeared on the threshold of the underwater quarters.

Catching sight of the Leshy who was in the distance but drawing nearer to the lake, the *utoplennik* decided to choose what seemed to him the lesser of two evils and boldly went into the bog.

"What do you want?" the bog master's angry question thundered towards him.

"I've come to visit you and to congratulate you on your health," in his confusion answered Pull-by-the-Leg, who had grown a bit timid.

"Congratulate me?! Congratulate me on what?!" the Bolotnik bellowed in a voice not his own.

"On your well-being, your health," Ankudinych stuttered in fright.

"And just who are you?" a huge frog's mouth, with teeth sticking out like a snake's, roared menacingly close to his very face.

"We're *utoplenniki*. We've been sent to be at your disposal by the Vodyanoi of the Yaryn, your relative, to congratulate . . ," Pull-by-the Leg uttered now in a more vigorous voice—since he had managed to figure out what was what—and bit later even added, "And I've been ordered besides that to say that if you need someone to help watch over the *bolotnitsa*s, then I can stay. . . ."

The Bolotnik had not quarreled with the Vodyanoi and actually was a distant relation, as Ankudinych had mentioned. Many years ago their properties bordered on each other's, and there was a time when they used to meet now and then, but then the swamp began to be overtaken by the forest, the bogs became moss-covered—they grew smaller in size and significantly receded from the river, which also had changed its course several times. The relatives stopped seeing each other, but did not harbor any particular malice towards one another. And so the Bolotnik was astounded, it is true, but not angry when he found out that Ankudinych had been sent by the Vodyanoi.

"How did your master find out what happened here?" he asked the *utoplennik* now in a voice filled with surprise.

"They saw it in a dream. When they woke up before the moon appeared, they said to me right away, 'Go, Ankudinych, to my relative in the swamp and offer congratulations,' but how and why, they didn't explain this to me"

"Just look how smart he is," Marten-Soul uttered with some respect.

After looking over the newborn once more and becoming convinced that there was no webbing between the toes on her little feet and that the nails were entirely different from what they should be, the Bolotnik, to his own surprise, suddenly came to a decision.

"I don't need helpers. This I always say, and I say it to everyone: I can look after my girls myself. Let the Vodyanoi look after his own . . . But since he hasn't forgotten me, take him this fat little piglet as a gift from me."

He thrust the infant into the hands of the *utoplennik*.

"Now you can go. Watch out, though, make haste, because there's not much time before dawn. Go with him," the master of the bog ordered his devils in conclusion.

And Ankudinych was forced to climb out of the bog with the infant in his arms and to walk back towards the river.

But halfway there the Leshy ran into him and immediately recognized the black-bearded *utoplennik*.

"Aha, an old acquaintance! You're here again?! Well, don't be angry with me if I keep my promise, you scum!"

Pull-by-the-Leg threw the infant to the ground and tried to run away. But the Leshy quickly caught up with him and, with blows of his terrible club, literally pounded into the moss the disfigured remains of the one who in life sometimes had been called Pyotr, sometimes Ankudinych, had a pair of horses, a wife, plowed his land, and went to the tavern on Sundays and holidays.

"Just look at the smelly scum," the Leshy uttered, finishing his work. Then he spit, wiped the club on the moss and walked away.

The squealing of the child abandoned by the *utoplennik* caught his attention and forced him to return.

The master of the forest bent down, picked up the newborn female infant, sniffed her all over with his goat's nose and, after carefully examining her from head to toe, carried the baby away from the bog with broad strides.

Stopping in one of the forest meadows, the Leshy carefully

placed his burden under the branching paws of a tall, old fir tree which stood not far from the road used for summer travel.

"You had wanted to have a child at one time," he said to the fir tree. "Here you are. Take her and place her in reliable hands."

The old fir tree stirred, shivered, and nodded with her top branches and, with the low ones, covered the life entrusted to her care.

The Leshy left. It was already quite light. The disc of the sun was rising higher and higher in the sky.

For some reason Stepanida was hobbling down the forest road, returning to Zaretskoye from somewhere. The tree covered the sleeping child with its branches, as if it knew that it must not be shown to the witch. An old hunter passed by, but the spreading fir tree did not show him the child, either.

But then girls came running by, gathering lilies-of-the-valley. The fir tree looked at them and touched the baby with one of its prickly branches.

The baby began to squeal pitifully.

"Anyutka, what's that? . . . It seems somebody's crying in the bushes! Could it be some kind of evil spirit?"

"Oh sure, an evil spirit! In the light of God's day!"

And Anyutka walked up to the fir tree from where the squealing was heard.

"Lizka, it's a baby!"

"What are we going to do with it?"

"What do you mean, what? We'll take it! It's a sin to abandon a human soul to perish in the forest!"

"And perhaps not a human one . . . Take a look, the child seems to have a frog on its leg."

Indeed, there was a dark red mark on the hip of the newborn little girl, whose shape brought to mind a frog.

"What does it matter! Haven't you seen a birthmark before?" the first girl said. "Take my flowers."

And she herself, taking off her kerchief, wrapped the naked baby in it and, accompanied by her girlfriends, headed for the village.

The old fir tree nodded to them in goodwill.

VII

Every year, beginning with the morning of St. Agripinna's Day,[1] the Leshy—who was nicknamed Green-Goat because of the color and shape of his beard—tried in every way possible to win the goodwill of his Leshachikha[2] and to weaken her vigilance. The latter took a jealous view of her husband's St. John's Eve adventures and his attacks on village girls and women gathering herbs for prophesy and healing.

Already a number of times before, Green-Goat had engaged in unpleasant explanations with her about this. The Leshachikha knew herself that she was monstrous and thus was jealous not without cause.

Because of the marks which adorned her dark face, the inhabitants of the forest thickets called Green-Goat's wife "Wart-Face." Her coarse hair, which was never combed and resembled a horse's mane, was dirty with resin, dry pine needles, and moss which clung to it. Her long, grey, shriveled breasts hung and dangled like a dog's. Her dirty fur, clumped in places and smelling of mire, also made her not terribly alluring, and her nasty, quarrelsome character completely alienated all the inhabitants of the forest, including even her own husband who, if truth be told, was actually afraid of her. Only one bear enjoyed the goodwill of the Leshachikha because he happened to accompany her husband everywhere possible and reported to Wart-Face the Leshy's every misdemeanor and blunder.

---

1. St. Agrippina's Day (*Агрефена Купальница*): 23 June (6 July). The "Kupalnitsa" refers to an herb thought to possess curative powers; it was collected in the early morning of the holiday, while the dew was still on the grass. This holiday falls on the same day as Ivan Kupala's Eve. Tradition called for bathing in bathhouses and rivers and ponds.
2. Leshachikha: the Leshy's wife.

Evil tongues said, however, that this bear comforted Wart-Face when the latter was particularly sad and upset because of the long absence of her husband.

The den of the forest beings, which was made out of twigs and brushwood and set deep in the ground and smeared with clay on the outside, was covered inside with dry moss, grass, and feathers, but Wart-Face rarely changed the bedding and worried little about neatness. Making excuses about the stuffiness and bad smell in the lair, Green-Goat often did not spend his nights there in the summertime.

They did not have any little *leshi*es, which made Borodovka very happy since she could completely blame her husband for this. And the latter preferred to spend nighttime outside the home, playing a game of bones in the moonlight at the bottom of a ravine—which served as the boundary of his property— with a neighboring *leshy,* a huge, hefty fellow who was very proud of his thick, red beard. Strictly speaking, they threw not bones but stones smoothed by water and speckled with black spots. They played with zeal, losing whole herds of rabbits, foxes, squirrels, and even mice which were then driven from one part of the forest to another, from the unlucky fellow to the lucky one.

The day before St. Agrippina's Day, Green-Goat completely forgot about the game, thinking only about how to throw his spouse off guard and get away unnoticed into the pine forest where, not far from the river, lay Round Meadow, thickly overgrown with ferns. It is to this meadow that the black-bearded *utoplennik* Ankudinych had once promised the Leshy to bring the underwater beauties of the Yaryn in his care. Although this Ankudinych betrayed the Leshy's trust—he did not bring him any *rusalka*s the next summer and because of this was trampled to nothingness by Green-Goat the following spring—the hope of meeting the beauties of the deep in Round Meadow did not leave the Sovereign of the Forest, and he lay in wait for them mainly there on St. John's Eve.

It was not so easy for the shaggy master of the thickets to carry out his plan to spend the night before St. John's or Yaryla's Day[3]

---

3. Yaryla; also Yarylo *(Ярыла/Ярыло):* an ancient god of spring, fertility, and erotic love. He was associated with the renewal of life, and in a springtime rite his effigy was burned and the ashes scattered on the fields to ensure a good harvest.

as one should—chasing the *rusalka*s. Brown-Bear had probably received a strict order from the Leshachikha not to move a step from her husband and, therefore, no matter where Green-Goat went, everywhere his sharp eye noticed the bear nearby, among tree trunks or in the bushes, carefully making his way and sniffing the ground. However, the Leshy had accrued all the wisdom of the forest and thus not without reason remembered times of yore. He finally got an idea of how to fool the animal which would not leave him.

From time immemorial, in a remote part of the forest far from the river, a swarm of bees lived in an old linden tree full of hollows. It was to these bees that Green-Goat directed his course before dusk. After drawing close to the tree, he grew with his pointed head to the level of the highest hollow around which the weakly buzzing honey collectors were circling, and he began to speak quietly to them, warning them about the bear who was walking nearby.

After hearing this warning, the recklessly brave bees, instead of hiding and falling silent, raised a battle cry which Brown-Bear could not help but hear with his sensitive shaggy ears. The temptation to treat himself to honey, however, was too great for him not to stop at the tree and try to get his paw into a hollow. Digging his strong, black nails into the wrinkled bark of the old linden tree, the bear made his way to the lower hollow easily, quickly repulsing the bees fearlessly stinging him. Although this hollow allowed the bear's paw to enter with some difficulty, the paw could not reach the honeycombs stuck considerably higher. The bear began to climb higher. The next hollow was too narrow and, in order to reach the honey, he had to widen it. Stung mercilessly by the bees which kept getting entangled in his thick, long fur, and grumbling and brushing them away from him, Brown-Bear went about his business. The enraged flyers circled around him in a buzzing, warlike swarm.

In the meantime, Green-Goat was already far way.

After crossing a little stream which extended from the forest swamp towards the river, he began to walk with a hurried gait, swaying level with the treetops. His horned, pointed head with moss-like hair standing on end, appeared now here, now there. His legs, which looked like the trunks of fir trees, stepped silently through the tall saplings. A timid hare in the bushes, catching sight of the Leshy, rose up on its hind legs before him from force of habit. But Green-Goat stepped over it without paying any attention to the respectful little animal. He was rushing to Round Meadow.

VIII

On St. John's Eve, a young fellow named Senya Voloshkevich, who lived in the village of Zaretskoye, announced at home that he wanted to know his future and so would go and gather twelve types of herbs which one must put under a pillow before going to sleep.

When the sun had gone down, Senya set out not for the fields, but across a rickety wooden bridge to the other side of the river where a tall forest loomed dark beyond the meadows, somewhat familiar to him since for several years now he had gone to that area for bilberries, wild strawberries and raspberries in the summer, and mushrooms in the fall.

Senya had heard many times about the wondrous properties of the fern's flower[1] which opened that night. He decided he must see how this magical plant blossoms and, if he could manage it, even get a hold of its fiery flower. After collecting the twelve herbs in a dewy meadow and placing them under his shirt, he made his way to the forest using a road edged with bushes. It was quiet there. Only the treetops swayed slightly as if they were passing on some kind of a secret to each other in a whisper.

A sleepy bird flew out in fright from the wet bushes through which Senya was making his way. Something like a hedgehog or a mouse ran by almost right at his feet, making Senya flinch in surprise. Far, far away, probably at the Black Ravine itself, either a *leshy* or an eagle-owl was calling in a long-drawn-out threatening fashion, "Oo-oo-oo-oo!" But Senya, despite his sinking heart, used a long stick for support and walked decisively along a path

---

1. The fern is a non-flowering plant, but folk belief held that it flowered at midnight before St. John's Day.

which barely shone in the darkness and wound between trees and bushes toward Round Meadow. He was not going there alone. The village magic healers, Aniska and Praskukha, independently of one another and even without any prior arrangement, were also headed for the forest. Old Praskukha, however, was more interested in roots and herbs which had to be gathered for her healing as well as magical needs. Aniska, scorning the dogged labor of the herb collector, picked only twelve flowers and tied them to her apron with the idea of putting them under her pillow and, with their help, seeing the future. The young sorceress mainly wanted to know whether a Certain Someone would deceive her or not, the one who visited her—perhaps in her dreams, perhaps in reality—in the darkness of night and made his way through the stovepipe in the form of a fiery serpent. This Certain Someone promised the attractive sorceress happiness and a sweet existence full of all kinds of pleasures. Aniska wanted to grow rich, get far away from the village where people teased her and said she was a witch with a tail (she did not have a tail), reproached her for milking cows, and slandered her with hurtful stories. Most of all, the young practitioner of magic was angered that the birth of a little pale-green swamp demon was imputed to her—the one who was killed by the Leshy, flung out of the deep pool by the Vodyanoi, and found by village children in the reeds along the shore. It is possible that this last hurtful rumor had something to do with the influence of another witch, Stepanida, who was on bad terms with Aniska. The young, black-browed Aniska, who was not afraid of anyone or anything (with the exception of this Stepanida) and who put her trust in her intimacy with the unclean force, came to the firm decision to acquire the fern's flower for herself as soon as it grew dusk; she slipped through the backyards to the road which led to the forest.

Leaning on a walking stick, Praskukha had come out here even earlier.

The old collector of herbs was already in the fields which bordered the forest; on her way, she would stop now and then, look around, and bend down to dig up roots and pick herbs which she then put either in a large sack or a braided basket. . . . Since Praskukha turned off the road and went deep into a field gathering herbs, Aniska, who was hurrying to the forest, outdistanced her and passed by without taking conscious notice of her.

The forest was already full of all kinds of unclean spirits in a holiday mood. All of them, following a custom established thousands of years ago and which even went back to those times when bushes and trees moved about during the night before Yaryla's Day, were preparing as usual to look and see if a magical fern would bloom somewhere like a fiery bright star; to lure, if possible, a living man to this place to pick this wondrous flower and thus obtain incredible power over the secret forces of nature. No one remembers anyone accomplishing such a difficult thing in these parts. During the night before Yaryla's Day, year in and year out, it was the *rusalkas* in particular who went into the forest where the souls of trees whispered in the rustling leaves and treetops and embraced each other. At times the water maidens sensed some kinship with this whispering. Holding each other by the hand, they stopped and stared at the hazy outlines of gossamer maidens' bodies which seemed to be rooted to a fixed spot and swaying with the treetops to the wind's breathing. The older *rusalkas* told their sisters that the *drevyanitsas*[2] sometimes congregated in the spring when tree branches were in bloom in forest meadows and, transparent and silvery in the moonlight, with wreaths adorning their heads, conducted silently-solemn circle dances.

As is commonly known, any and all unclean spirits can be seen only by those simple mortals to whom they want to reveal themselves. An exception are the people who, by their nature, have the ability to see phenomena of the "other" world, or sorcerers who acquire this ability through long exercises and frightful vows.

For this reason, Aniska, who was not yet much of an expert in the dark sciences, did not see them, although she passed very close to the *rusalkas* and the *drevyanitsas* in the forest; not feeling any liking for the witch, they did not want to show themselves to her.

Reaching Round Meadow, she chose a flat place in the middle of a thicket of ferns, took a sharp knife out of the sack she had taken with her, drew a circle and sat down in the middle of it in expectation.

Praskukha was walking more slowly, carefully listening and looking all around; several times it seemed to her that the trees were whispering behind her, "Look at that old woman. If only we could bury her among the roots!"

---

2. *drevyanitsa (древяница):* a spirit that inhabits trees and is related to the *rusalka*.

"I'd first hew some boards out of you!" the magic healer snapped back and hobbled on farther. Something like a shapeshifter or a nameless forest spirit rolled under her feet in a little ball that resembled a porcupine. But Praskukha managed to strike a swinging blow at the ball with her walking stick, which she had quickly grasped in her left hand.

"Crumble to dust, amen!" she whispered angrily, and the little ball disappeared as if it had been swallowed up by the earth.

Praskukha went on—she was not far from the forest edge—shaking her head and talking to herself:

"Purple loosestrife[3] I have; I dug it up in the meadow in the evening. With it, you can pick all other kinds of plants. I've also dug up a tsar-plant . . .[4] Only it's a pity that the shoot is very small! Nonetheless, no demonic illusion is frightening when you have it. . . . I've picked enough sleep-herb.[5] Even now, my fingers are sticky from it. Now if only I could get some different kinds of burdock and thistle,[6] but you have to go to the swamp for them. . . . It won't be on my way. . . . Perhaps after midnight, when I look at the ferns, I could make my way there? . . . It's a little bit far . . . What else do I need? . . . I have bur-marigold[7] and sage.[8] I've dug up chervill[9] on the river bank. I'll have to grab some *izlyudin*[10] on my way back. I'll also

---

3. purple loosestrife *(плакун)*. In folk belief this plant had the power to frighten evil spirits and even to make them to weep. Its name literally means "a plant which causes weeping." Ryan (pp. 270-271) warns that the names of magico-medicinal plants . . . are often difficult to identify with actual plants. . . . The names . . . are frequently confused and interchanged and subject to regional variation."

4. tsar-plant *(царь трава;* also called *чертополох)*: thistle or burdock. It was believed to have the power to drive off devils and witches, to protect cattle, and cure illnesses.

5. sleep-herb *(сон трава)*: usually belladonna, but also other herbs. This plant was believed to induce prophetic dreams if placed under a pillow after midnight.

6. burdock and thistle *(одолень* and *прострел трава)*: perhaps the same as tsar plant, perhaps different varieties. It was believed that whoever had the root of одолень in his house would gain the power to overcome *(одолеть)* all kinds of obstacles. It was also used as a cure for poisons and against malefic spells. *Прострел трава* was used by sorcerers and magic healers to remove "spoiling" *(порча)*.

7. bur-marigold *(череда)*: used as protection against demonic spirits.

8. sage *(шалфей)*: used for animal bites as well as anti-magic against sorcery.

9. chervill *(купырь)*: used to treat various ailments—heart, kidney, and liver problems.

10. *izlyudin (излюдин трава)*: no English match found. It was believed that whoever ate this herb and lived would never have any grief in his life.

pick some lovage[11] when I go home. And I mustn't forget soapwort.[12] Girls very often demand it as a remedy against wrinkles
and freckles."

Thinking this way, Praskukha entered the forest inconspicu-
ously and began to walk silently on a barely discernible path toward Round Meadow.

Senya Voloshkevich had come there considerably earlier. He
entered from the side opposite the one where, in a circle drawn
with her knife, Aniska was hiding, chose a place for himself in
the branches of an old oak and began to wait.

A light, nocturnal fog hung over the meadow. The light from
the moon, piercing the fog, sometimes allowed the fellow to
make out in it someone's round hip, at times a pale, transparent
hand and even the silvery, milk-white breast of a beauty not entirely visible.

This was, of course, curious, but not what Senya dreamed of
seeing. Suddenly a rooster crowed far away in the village. It was
around midnight. A light like a glistening butterfly flew out of
the forest thicket into the meadow and began rising and falling,
fluttering above the bushes.

Aniska, too, saw this bluish fire from afar, fluttering over the
ferns. She passionately wanted this fiery butterfly to fly closer to
her, but the latter, as if on purpose, circled near the opposite edge
of the meadow; the practitioner of magic could not bring herself
to move from the circle and run there.

It seemed to Senya that voices of young maidens rang out in
silvery laughter in that same place or perhaps somewhere very
close to it. Someone's hands began to clap, now here, now there
(Aniska, who was sitting at the other end of the meadow, interpreted the hand clapping as the flapping of a roused bird's wings).
But then something more frightening began. Someone began to
call out unspeakably loudly and to scream. A strong gust of wind
suddenly passed over the forest, causing the treetops to sway rap-
idly, and quickly blew away the fog which had been moving to
and fro over the meadow. Again someone's laughter—its scale
rising and falling—was heard, then a frightened shriek, and then
everything fell silent. The sound of the wind, the clapping, and

---

11. lovage (любисток; also called зоря): This herb was used by women in love
     potions and was also said to give protection from fevers and *rusalka*s.
12. soapwort (сорочье мыло): used in cleansing.

the crackling of twigs rushed past Senya and died in the distance. This was the Leshy, who had attacked the *rusalka*s and chased after them.

Even though he did not see the Leshy, Senya's body was shaking all over from fear. Although Aniska, too, had become frightened, she noted a huge eagle owl flying by and decided that this bird was the main cause of the noise and the crackling sounds.

The small light, fluttering over the meadow, suddenly flickered and disappeared from view, as if someone had grabbed it with a dark, invisible paw. Only two or three tiny sparks, weakly twinkling with a blue flame, fell into the bush not far from Senya. He rushed towards them and managed to grab one with his left hand, but instead of a spark there turned out to be a cold wet drop on his finger, which he squeamishly wiped on the grass.

$\sim$

Getting to his feet, Senya felt his head really spinning. The stars in the sky seemed to sway, and the trees began to take on a frowning, threatening look. Because he wanted to dispel this hallucination, Senya unconsciously rubbed both eyes with his hands. At that moment the ground beneath him began to seem strangely transparent. He could make out big and small tree roots intertwined in it, fighting like snakes; nearly decayed bones of animals were visible among the roots deep in the sand. Even deeper, little streams of water were filtering through the layers of chalk and clay. . . . Senya looked all around.

The pale frightened face of a *drevyanitsa* flashed in the branches of a neighboring hornbeam, which had a sulking air of importance. The silvery, milky-white body of a *rusalka* appeared from behind a young oak. Wreathed in yellow water-lilies, the face of the *rusalka* seemed strangely familiar to the youth. He took a step in her direction.

The *rusalka* did not disappear but with a sad smile looked at Senya as if she wanted to ask him something.

Senya did not want to believe at first that he was seeing a real spirit and not the usual living, human body of some village beauty.

"Who are you?" Senya asked in a faltering, breaking voice.

"It's me," was the quiet answer, resembling the sound of leaves.

"And who is this 'me'?"

"It's me—Gorpina."

"Gorpina?! The one who drowned in the Yaryn?"

"Yes!" the phantom of the girl who had become a *rusalka* answered in an affectionate, rustling whisper.

"What do you want from me? If you want to tickle me, you'd better not come near! Do you see what a stick I have?! I'm strong, you know, and I my reaction will be such that you won't recognize your own kind. . . . So you'd better not touch me!" the youth warned.

"Why would I touch you, Senichka? I don't even dare come near you because I'm not dressed. And I don't have any evil intentions toward anyone. . . . I'm unhappy," the drowned girl said sadly.

"What are you doing here in the forest?"

"I wander about here and there because there's been no peace for my soul ever since I found myself in the water. I'm waiting to come across a good man who'd pray for me. . . ."

"Well, that's possible. I'll say a prayer myself and enter your name in Father Nikolai's Book of the Dead. He won't even know who made the entry and whom he's remembering in prayer. . . ."

"Thanks . . . And you, Senichka, better get away from here while the getting is good. There's a woman walking about not far from here who's dangerous to you and can do you in. . . . And the unclean force likes to bring harm on this night. . . . So remember, Senichka, light a candle for me or have a funeral service celebrated. Perhaps then I'll be more at peace. Oh! . ."

Senya saw a monstrous *utoplennik,* who had the look of a living man, appear suddenly from behind another tree.

With his hands spread wide, shot through with blue in the moonlight, this *utoplennik* drew closer to the youth and Gorpina as if he did not know which of the two to grab. Framed with soggy, colorless tow-colored hair, his face—with a horrid, fixed smile on full, half-open lips and bulging, tin-colored eyes— slowly moved closer to them both.

Senya froze in fear. He saw the *utoplennik* (this was another Pyotra, Pyotra the Towhead, who had replaced the black-bearded Ankudinych as overseer of the *rusalka*s) finally make his choice and grab Gorpina by the shoulders.

"Here she is, our quiet one! She clings to the living! She

doesn't want to even look at our kind! . . . Asks to be prayed for! . . . Don't push, bitch! . . ."

But Gorpina, agilely freeing herself from Towhead's gripping paws, easily and quickly disappeared into the bushes.

Not waiting for the *utoplennik* to grab him next, Senya started to run in the opposite direction.

But Towhead did not run after anyone. Scratching the back of his head, he stood in place for a little while and then slowly headed in the direction from which a doleful song of the *rusalkas* could be heard. . . .

Senya, who had darted into the bushes, again found himself in Round Meadow. Some dim silhouettes were circling in a slow dance in the middle of it. But the frightened youth did not have time to calm down and take a good look at them: loud laughter, which made the flesh creep, resounded above his head.

Senya flinched. It occurred to him that it would be much better to leave, as Gorpina had advised, while the going was good. After considering which way to go, he hurriedly made his way through a hazel-nut grove, following the path that had taken him to the meadow. But then and there someone again began to laugh loudly and non-humanly, to snap twigs very close by, and to clap his hands.

Voloshkevich cried out in fright and, forgetting everything in the world, took off running without paying any attention to the road. Some petty forest spirit, taking the form of a root, thrust itself under his feet. Senya tripped and, as he fell, hit his head on a tree stump. Not one but several fiery-red colors suddenly burst into flame in Senya's closed eyes, and he lost consciousness.

Relying on the stalks of burdock dug up by the roots, which dispel all demonic forces, old Praskukha was walking quietly to Round Meadow when a whirlwind passed overhead, swaying the tree tops; laughter and crackling sounds could be heard throughout the forest.

"They're sure making a din, those accursed spirits! They have no shame on St. John's Eve!" the old woman grumbled unhappily and moved on. However, the crackling sounds and noises in the bushes repeated and now were coming directly at her. The old woman pricked up her ears and hid behind a tree, holding her walking stick ready, just in case.

At that moment the sound of a body falling and a human cry

suddenly resounded not far off. The old woman lowered her walking stick.

"It seems a lad was screaming," she said to herself under her breath and, after waiting a bit, emerged from behind the tree.

All around everything was quiet. Not a rustle, not a human voice. Praskukha carefully took a few steps along the path . . . A bit to the side, in the bushes, moaning could be heard. After hesitating for a while, the old woman headed there and, partly feeling with her walking stick, partly looking, she spotted a human body in the semidarkness. The moon, which peeked out from behind the clouds, helped her make out a young face, covered with blood flowing from the nose and a scratched cheek.

Seeing that the boy was alive, the old woman picked up his cap, which had fallen on the ground, scooped up some swamp water from a puddle nearby, and poured it on his face.

Senya Voloshkevich started to move and slowly regain consciousness. All the visions and fears that he had experienced during the night became confused in his mind. The old woman bending over him seemed to be a continuation of them. Senya stretched out his arms at first, as if to defend himself, but after realizing that Praskukha was not about to attack him, he calmed down somewhat and tried to get to his feet.

"So you've come to life! And I thought that you had knocked yourself out for good," the magic healer began to mumble. "Don't be afraid of me. I'd never do any evil to anyone. Everyone here knows Praskukha. And you, I think I saw in the village. Is that right?"

"Yes. I'm Senya Voloshkevich."

"Aha. The nephew of the deacon's wife? . . . Right . . . Well, why did you become frightened?"

"I went to see the fern blooming . . ."

"And so? Did you see? . ."

"I did . . . It was flying in the meadow like a fiery flower or a butterfly. It was very close to me. Any minute now I'll be able to grab it, I thought. . . . But, in fact, it wasn't that close. Suddenly there was loud laughing all around; a noise began as if someone started clapping. . . . A wind came up and then disappeared, and the blue flame scattered in tiny sparks. . . . And then I even thought I saw a scary face, and all kinds of other things seemed to appear. . . . Again the noise and laughter started up. I got frightened and started running . . . I fell as I ran and broke the bridge of my nose."

"It's doesn't matter. It'll heal before you marry,"[13] the old woman said confidently. "Get up. There's nothing more for us to do here. A force not of this world carried off your flower."

The magic healer, although she had some burdock that she had dug up, did not particularly rely on it to help defend her in a clash with unclean spirits and, since a noise could be heard again in the forest, she hurried with the boy to the forest edge. She cast a spell on Senya's bleeding nose, whispering over his face something between a prayer and an incantation.

"Can you make it now to your aunt's house by yourself?" Praskukha asked when they came to the forest edge.

"I can," Senya answered.

"Well, then, go. But watch out, better not tell anyone what you saw or that you met me. . . . Besides, the fern's flower does not fly, and it burns with a red flame. . . . But if, as you say, it flew and glowed with a blue color, then before you, one has to think, was the flower of the 'flying herb'.[14] If you'd gotten hold of it, you would have been happy your whole life. . . . Still, rub your eyes with the hand you used to grab one of the blue sparks. Perhaps one day you'll even see something."

"But I've already wiped my hand."

"It doesn't matter, rub them anyway! And now, head home, God be with you! I still have to make my way to the swamp and pick some herbs, if only by morning. . . . Tonight the herbs and flowers have more power and sap," Praskukha said and hobbled along the forest edge away from Senya.

---

13. It'll heal before you marry *(до свадьбы заживёт):* said somewhat jokingly to indicate that the injury is nothing serious.

14. "flying herb" *(перелёт трава),* perhaps a type of fern. Thought to bring good luck.

IX

In the evening before Saint Agrippina's Day, Wart-Face was calm. Her husband had gone off to make his rounds in the forest, accompanied by the bear, and Brown-Bear was given strict orders to accompany the master everywhere; if he tried to chase him away, the bear was to persist, following him from afar.

It was already getting dark when the Leshachikha, who was sitting on a fallen tree near her den, lost in thought about how pleasant it would be to be surrounded by a heap of shaggy-haired and frisky children, heard someone's hesitant and timid footsteps in the distance. She perked up her animal ears. Someone was roaming in the forest thicket at a respectful distance from her lair as if he did not dare approach.

"Could my red-bearded neighbor have found out that my mate isn't at home and that's why he's turned up? How should I act with him? If you let him in, you won't be happy in the end yourself. . . . This isn't a bear who doesn't know how to speak. . . . He'll begin to boast . . . I know him . . . Any little thing, and he'll spread it through the whole neighborhood. But just the same, I must take a look . . ."

"Hey, who's there?" the Leshachikha bellowed in her booming and threatening voice. "Come on out!"

In answer, the brushwood made a quiet, crackling sound a couple of times, and the bear appeared before Wart-Face with a guilty look and with his snout drooping and swollen from bee stings.

"And where's the Leshy?" the mistress asked her favorite bear sternly.

The bear only sighed in answer and brought his guilty head even lower.

But in his sigh Leshachikha's flat, sensitive nose caught the scent of honey. Taking a closer look at the bear, Wart-Face figured out what had happened.

"Breathe on me," the shaggy-haired beauty ordered in a tone almost hissing from suppressed rage.

The bear raised his swollen nose and, looking guilty and obedient with his little sparkling dark eyes, exhaled his usual, hot, smelly breath to which, however, some fragrant honey had been clearly added.

"And what's this?! And that?!" the Leshachikha asked, pulling out bees squashed and entangled in the fur of her favorite's snout.

"Have mercy," it seemed the guiltily panting bear wanted to say.

But at that moment Leshachikha's strong, ironlike paws painfully squeezed his neck.

Brown-Bear, knowing full well that he would not be able to break free, obediently pressed close to the ground at his mistress' dirty feet, whose color brought to mind the bark of an alder tree.

After finding comfort in inflicting a beating, the Leshachikha let go of the bear's neck.

"Where is he now?" her question was heard again.

And again Brown-Bear guiltily lowered his snout, from which the mistress concluded that her cunning spouse had managed to hide from her shaggy-haired spy.

A solution suddenly formed in Leshachikha's angry head.

"We're going to the swamp!" she ordered in a sharp and angry voice.

She took off so quickly, moving nimbly between dead branches, stumps, bushes, and trees, that Brown-Bear was forced more than once to change from a light run to a gallop in order to keep up with his mistress.

As they drew closer to the swamp, the ground became damper and damper, the pine trees got smaller and smaller, and then they even became totally replaced by osier-beds and alders; tussocks appeared; dark, rust-colored water began to splash underfoot, wetting their fur.

With a jealous eye the Leshachikha scanned the section of the swamp which bordered on their territory. Her spouse could not be seen in any of the secluded places where it was possible to hide. Laughter and the singing of the *bolotnitsa*s, accompanied by the shrieks and hand-clapping of the demons, carried from the bog area which was impossible to cross without falling in, even for a bear.

"And what if that scoundrel of mine ran in from the other side and is eyeing those naked, shameless hussies from over there?" the thought flashed in jealous Leshachikha's head, and she went running to the right along the edge of the bog where the properties of several shaggy forest masters came together.

Making the tops of the bushes and the high swamp grass sway, she rushed headlong, at the same time peering attentively and ordering the bear to keep his eyes open.

However, little by little the Leshachikha understood that she would be able to find her spouse only by examining the edges of the bog more thoroughly.

She slowed her step, greedily trying to catch the forest smells with the widely dilated nostrils of her monstrous face, at times even bringing her head down to the grass like a fox; and she began to cover the thickets of bushes, tussocks, and tree stumps where, in her opinion, the hidden Leshy could be lying in wait for the *bolotnitsas*.

Wart-Face was now on the other side of the small lake, surrounded by a bog, and in a strange and unfamiliar part of the forest. The squealing and laughter from the bog carried more and more loudly and clearly. The bear was running hesitantly in front of her, serving as a scout. Then he suddenly stopped and, after turning half around, looked first at his mistress and then at the osier bushes which extended into the bog in the form of a promontory. There, without a doubt, was something which deserved attention. The bear, with his front paw raised indecisively, stood motionless. Her heart pounding, the Leshachikha began to steal up to these bushes, stopping now and then and carefully pulling the branches apart; she was all eyes and ears.

About thirty steps later, Wart-Face suddenly froze, afraid to make a move. Before her someone was taking long, drawn-out breaths, breathing just a bit heavily and noisily through his nose. Finally, the Leshachikha's sharp eyes made out a long, dark, shaggy body, with its horned head raised somewhat, sprawled among the mossy tussocks. . . . There could be no doubt. Green-Goat, having forgotten about his duty to his spouse, was spending his time reprehensibly by feasting his eyes on the swamp beauties.

Losing conscious sight of the world around her and forgetting herself out of anger and a thirst for vengeance, with one sudden huge leap the outraged wife landed on the hairy back of the prostrate man, and the first thing she did was to push him with her snout into the soggy marsh mud. The Leshy began to struggle under her; after some effort, he finally raised himself up on all fours and with some difficulty managed to pull his head out of the mud. Only at this point did Wart-Face notice that the horns on this head seemed to be different from those of Green-Goat; when her adversary, whom she had squashed, half-turned his angry, frightened face, plastered with mud and slime, she realized that she had made a mistake and jumped on the wrong being. The face did not have a goat's appearance, as did her husband's, but rather reminded her of a sheep's; the beard was not the same gray-green color but dark-brown with streaks of gray.

With a shriek of shame and vexation, the Leshachikha released the horns and neck of the stranger who was bellowing and snapping his teeth under her, and then she broke into a run. Realizing what was going on, the bear quickly joined her and galloped in front as if showing the way. The irate *leshy*, his snout filthy, frightening, chased after them with a howl of resentment and with vengeance on his mind. Needles fell off pine trees from his threatening cry, and birches and alders shook no less than the aspen.

Neither the one trying to save herself by running nor the one chasing after her yielded to the other's quickness. Notwithstanding the relatively long period of time, the distance between the two runners hardly decreased. They passed the property of Sheep-Mug (such was the name of the offended one with the dark-brown beard) and now were rushing through the forest which belonged to Red-Beard, the neighbor of the Leshachikha's husband.

At this precise moment, Red-Beard was making his usual rounds in the vicinity of Black Ravine. The Leshachikha and the bear, trying to save themselves from their pursuer, finally made their way to a thick hazel-nut grove which covered the edges of the ravine and then rushed off in different directions. Through cunning innate to women, Wart-Face hid herself nearby, but Sheep-Mug continued to run after the lumbering, trampling creature who was crushing bushes and twigs underfoot. The bear passed by quickly only a small distance away from the surprised Red-Beard, who was rooted to the spot expectantly, club in hand;

Sheep-Mug, who was carried away by the chase, smashed into Red-Beard while running and almost knocked him off his feet. Red-Beard even quacked in indignation after seeing that his neighbor, breaking all rules and traditions, was hunting on his property as if he were on his own territory.

"Stop!" he bellowed angrily, his club whistling above his head. "Why are you trying to catch my bears?! You've probably lost a wager with somebody and want to pay with an animal from someone else's forest?"

"As if I really need your animal! I was chasing your wife!" came the answer.

"My wife?! I've never been married to the she-bear. There's no point in lying. Get the hell out of my forest!"

"So you're even defending that snake!" Sheep-Mug roared and, pulling out a rather large mountain ash from the ground, shook it in rage over Red-Beard's head so that the soil flew into his eyes.

Bellowing in fury, Red-Beard threw himself at his opponent. His club pounded against the ash tree, and then both weapons pounded on the heads and shoulders of the quarreling forest spirits. At the same time, Sheep-Mug cursed the wife of Red-Beard, and the latter called his enemy a liar and robber. After breaking their weapons, the *leshies* seized each other with their paws and rolled on the ground in frenzied struggle, crying out loudly and biting each other painfully.

The Leshachikha, in the meantime, was already near her empty abode. Green-Goat apparently had not returned. Somewhat tired from his long run, the bear lay with his tongue out not far from his mistress's den, gazing at Wart-Face with an ingratiating look in his little eyes.

She, however, had no desire to reward Brown-Bear for his devotion and, after recovering a bit from the embarrassment she had endured, decided to take out her vexation on the primary culprit of all the agitation, fear, and hurried flight that she had experienced. Green-Goat alone had to pay for everything.

"Bear, we're going!" the Leshachikha exclaimed, getting up from the ground after a short rest. "If not by the swamp, then somewhere by the river we'll find the scoundrel. He'll find out what it means to leave a loyal and devoted wife!"

The bear also got to his feet, but without any particular enthusiasm, and obediently set out behind his mistress to look for the carousing master.

After moving deeper into the forest, they first went in the direction of Round Meadow where, on St. John's Eve, as was well known to the Leshachikha, the *drevyanitsas* and the *rusalkas* had been gathering from time immemorial. From there, still from afar, a noise resembling the drawn-out cry of an eagle-screech owl reached the travelers, along with what may have been the flapping of wings or the *rusalkas* clapping their hands.

Thinking of a more reliable way of tracking down her husband, Wart-Face ordered the bear to approach the meadow from one end while she herself began to sneak up from the other. Each went in a different direction.

Brown-Bear, walking out into the meadow, came upon the young village witch Aniska at the very edge of the forest, who was sitting on the ground in the middle of a magical circle, outlined with a knife, and waiting for the ferns to bloom. Not knowing whether to go around her or to crush the human being who had come into the forest at night, probably to do something evil, the bear slowed down his pace in indecision.

Aniska at that time was having some thoughts about leaving when suddenly there was a rustling sound nearby.

The young witch glanced in that direction and froze with fear.

About five or six steps from her was a large brown bear, staring at her intently with his little black eyes. He stood motionless and growled angrily.

If this had been the unclean spirit, Aniska would not have been worried. The line encircling her, the sharp edge of the knife which the unclean spirits of the night so detest, and the fifteen or so incantations that she knew should have been enough to defend her from all kinds of terrors and ghosts. But the bear . . . The bear was an entirely different matter. He simply would not notice the outlined circle, the knife would be a very poor defense against him and, as for a spell against a bear, Aniska simply could not remember one.

The bear continued to grumble and took about two steps towards her. A bit more, and he would crush the sorceress under him.

At that moment a timely thought flashed into Aniska's head—to resort to an old life-saving remedy for women who encounter a bear in the forest, a remedy counting on the bashfulness of the unsociable animal. And the witch immediately resorted to this approach. When he saw the white stomach of the woman flash in the moonlight and then saw her standing at full height before him, the bear stepped back from the unexpected nature of this gesture and sat down a few steps away from Aniska. . . . There was only the sound of grass rustling somewhere nearby and Aniska's teeth chattering.

No one knows how the whole thing would have ended if a deafening cry from the direction of the river had not reached her then, a cry which soon became a howl of despair. Almost at that precise moment, the Leshachikha's voice bellowed loudly not far from Aniska.

"So here's where he is, the good-for-nothing! Bear, get over here! Why have you sprawled out there? Let's run!"

Obeying this angry hoarse voice which did not sound human, Brown-Bear jumped on all fours and rushed to his mistress's call.

Aniska was saved.

Caught up in listening to the far-off, gentle, and mournful singing of the *rusalkas*, broken at times by the ringing, silver laughter and hand clapping of the water beauties, Green-Goat was truly happy. He was already imagining how, stealing upon the semi-visible circle of dancers, he would spot from his place in the bushes the one who seemed to him the least gossamer, run out into the meadow, put his paws on his quarry, and drag her off into the forest. The thought of this so captivated the Leshy that he could not restrain himself from laughing happily. Green-Goat could never control his laughter and, once he started laughing, he could not stop himself for a long time.

Hearing this booming laughter and then quick steps snapping dry twigs, the *rusalkas*, with their keen sense of hearing, became alarmed and, stopping their singing, started to run.

The Leshy rushed to catch them, but the water maidens were more agile. One after another they hurried to the edge of the forest, quickly ran towards the river, and hid in the bushes along the shore.

After suffering defeat, Green-Goat wandered around the dark forest for quite a while in the vain hope of hearing the alluring singing of the *rusalkas* ring out somewhere again. He lingered, paying no attention to the quiet laughter of the *drevyanitsas*, hidden in the foliage in the night and whispering to each other behind him. The Leshy was simply not in any mood for them. He roamed for a rather long time along the various meadows and paths until he came out again at the forest's edge. From there the water beauties could be seen sitting on the river bank and sorting flowers gathered in the meadows and forest glades. The orange-red moon was already disappearing. It was getting darker and the Leshy realized that, given his well-known spryness, he could even now steal up on the *rusalka*s and, grabbing one, take her to the damp moss of the impenetrable forest rustling from the whispering of the gentle night wind.

Walking away slowly from the forest's edge, Green-Goat gradually became smaller and smaller until his height was at the level of the grass growing along the banks of the Yaryn. As is commonly known, according to the laws of nature the height of a *leshy* must not exceed the tallest tree, bush, or other earthly plant near him.

Making his way through the dewy grass, Green-Goat was creeping up on the water maidens carefully and almost without making a sound.

The *rusalka*s were peacefully chatting among themselves about where they would end up after each one finished her time as a *rusalka*; would they recognize one another when they met, and would they still have to remain for long under the power of the bald and fat-bellied Vodyanoi who repelled them all.

They did not suspect that the Vodyanoi himself was sitting very close to the shore, hiding in the reeds and eavesdropping on their conversation, memorizing which of the careless beauties he would have to punish, given the chance, for her contemptible comments about his appearance.

Suddenly the *rusalka*s, jumping to their feet, cried out—some from feigned, others from real fear—and like a flock of sheep, plunged into the water. Behind them, Green-Goat, trying to grab one of the runaways, grew to the height of a brittle willow growing along the riverbank.

He even caught one by her wet, half-undone braids without noticing in his headlong chase that he was already up to his knees in water. . . . At that moment, the corpulent Vodyanoi with the fat mug appeared out of the river and forcefully pulled Green-Goat by his left leg. Green-Goat lost his footing, released the *rusalka* and then, from a prone position, with his long outstretched arms tried to grab hold of a willow bush along the river bank. Enraged by his old enemy's invasion of his tsardom, the

Vodyanoi dragged him by force to a deep place in the river, at the same time calling Towhead Pyotr to help him.

The swollen face of the *utoplennik* with the tin-colored eyes appeared out of the water; a moment later, he bravely grabbed Green-Goat by his right leg.

The Leshy, sensing that he probably would not be able to keep to the shore and that his fat enemy would more than likely drag him into his river, began to scream in fear and then to call the clumsy, lumbering creature for help. "Bear! . . Bear!" he howled in a frenzied, deafening tone, which very closely resembled the bear's own roar.

The roused ducks, quacking in alarm, flapped their wings among the reeds and took off, hissing in the darkness of the night. The snipes called to each other in the distance. . . . But the bear did not appear.

Green-Goat began to howl again. Strength was already beginning to fail him. Despite his desperate efforts to struggle free of his opponents, the Leshy was already more than halfway in the water when Wart-Face, with her hairy companion behind her, rushed to his aid unexpectedly like a stormy whirlwind. She immediately and silently seized hold of the Vodyanoi's face with her claws so that the master of the river bottom immediately released her husband's leg, but the bear did not manage even to extend his mighty paw and smash the Towhead's head when, in an instant, the latter plunged into the water where his master had disappeared earlier.

Only two or three bubbles surfaced in that spot. . . .

Green-Goat, confused and wet, crawled out on the bank and, shivering, got to his feet which were made for wading.

At the site of the recent struggle, only wide ripples in the water flowed out in various directions and small waves quietly beat against the swampy shore. . . . In the distance, the snipes along the shore called out to each other, and then everything became quiet again.

"Let's go, you good-for-nothing," Wart-Face said sternly to the Leshy and led him away from the Yaryn.

Green-Goat breathed a sad sigh and sheepishly started to walk with her.

The bear marched behind.

In the reeds somebody was laughing quietly behind them, producing a laugh that resembled the bubbling of a small brook.

Towhead did not delay in reporting to the Vodyanoi what he had seen when Gorpina, on Yarylo's Eve, went to meet a man, and also what he had heard: the young *rusalka* asking the man to pray for her.

This, according to the laws of the river bottom, was an unforgivable offense. Wanting to vent his anger on someone for the scar on his cheek that he had received from the Leshachikha, the Vodyanoi assumed a threatening, resolute look and in a commanding, angry voice summoned Gorpina. When the *rusalka* appeared and read her sentence in his goggle-frog eyes, she did not show any resistance, did not try to run, but obediently followed him from the deep pool in the river to the reeds.

The Vodyanoi conducted an interrogation and, after hearing from the girl that she had in fact asked a baptized man to pray for her, flew into a rage. He grabbed the motionless and obedient Gorpina by the hair, hit her in the chest and cheek with his slippery frog paw, and said in a whisper, "Leave the water, you miserable creature! Move between heaven and earth and find neither peace nor refuge!"

After pronouncing his curse, the Vodyanoi grabbed the doomed *rusalka* by her pale neck and strangled her with his strong, webbed fingers just like a male frog strangles the female to death in a rush of love on an April day.

Breathing hard and puffing, he then dragged the transparent, motionless body of Gorpina out onto the shore, some distance away from the water, and returned with a triumphant look of importance.

"Let it be a lesson for the others," he grumbled before plunging into the pool.

The being that he threw into the sedge was not the former heavy, earthly human being. Light and almost translucent, it was picked up by the first wind and, like the fluff of swamp flowers, flew—quivering and swaying—over the meadows along the shore in the direction of Zaretskoye. It descended near the cemetery where the physical body of Gorpina had been buried in a pine coffin a few years before.

The souls of suicides who have not found refuge for themselves usually do not part either with their place of death or with their mortal remains, nor do they move far away from them until those remains either have completely disappeared or the time on earth allotted to them at birth has expired.

X

$\backsim$

The Zaretskoye girls—the *devki* (as they were called at one end of the village) or *divchata*[1] (as they were referred to at the other end of the village)—usually congregated for their evening gatherings in a reasonably spacious hut rented from a poor lonely woman. They brought wood, groats, and fatback with them; they cooked gruel and spun linen on their spindles from home. Boys would come there with spice cookies, nuts, fruit drops, and sometimes even vodka. At times a cooked chicken would appear with the gruel, with no one questioning its origin. Somebody would bring a concertina. The girls spun and sang, but most of all they wagged their tongues about absent girlfriends, women, and boys. Maksim, who had not been seen at the gatherings for a long time, was the main topic of their gossip.

"Aniska has totally bewitched him," said the pockmarked Akulka, who remained unmarried for some time now. "At night, she turns him into a black cat and places him to sleep at her feet for warmth."

"At her feet—oh, come now," said Domna disbelievingly.

"She's given him some kind of potion," supposed the young Matrunka, who was attending the gatherings for the first time.

"Maybe she simply gave him the evil eye," Akulka retorted, "because there are lots of ways to bewitch someone: through incantation, drink, a piece of food, a footprint, or catching a person's clothing on a frog bone. . . ."

"Akulka has tried all these methods herself, but she can't get any results. No one asks for her in marriage," her neighbor and friend, Zinka, whispered to Matrunka.

---

1. *devki* is "girls"in Russian; *divchata*, in Ukrainian.

"People say there are even herbs that if a girl carries them with her, any man she desires will love her for the rest of his life," Ganna added.

"Next summer on St. John's Eve, pick some John-and-Mary[2] flowers and lovage before dawn, tie everything in a little bundle and immediately go the bath house and beat yourself with it.[3] People say that the skin becomes very white and delicate and that after that, there's no getting rid of the boys," said the unattractive, plumpish Varka.

"You think I'd go to a bathhouse[4] to sweat and beat myself at night?! Have I gotten tired of life or something?" pretty Shura exclaimed.

"Do you think he'd really strangle you?" Matrunka asked.

"Whether he strangles you or not, you can get in trouble. In Babino, someone taught two girls to tell fortunes in an empty pantry by getting undressed and looking in a mirror by candlelight exactly at midnight. Only one did the looking, and the other sat nearby more for moral support than anything. . . . And she dozed off. Suddenly she hears a scream, a noise, and a knock. . . . She looks and sees the one who was looking at herself in the mirror now lying—weeping and groaning—on the floor next to the stool, and there is a black-and-blue mark on her face. She said later, when she came to, that someone thrust his hand out of the mirror and hit her in the face. From that time on, people in Babino no longer look in a mirror to tell fortunes. . . . Who wants to parade around with a bruised mug later? . . ."

"Worse things happen," said the grave Domna. "My old aunt told me a story. She was living with some gentlefolk on an estate in the Kursk Province. There was a totally fearless young miss there, and she wanted to find out with certainty who her intended would be. People told her that the surest way was to go to the bathhouse alone on New Year's Eve, set the table for two, light two candles, and sit there and look in a mirror . . . only not in one mirror but, that is, two mirrors placed in such a way that a glass corridor is formed. . . . But you know yourselves how this is

2. John-and-Mary herb *(Иван-да-Марья):* This may be cow wheat or heart's ease.
3. A variation on the Russian tradition of beating oneself with birch twigs for health reasons, primarily for increasing circulation.
4. The bathhouse was traditionally considered to be the gathering place of various evil spirits; it was the home of the *bannik (банник)* or malicious bathhouse spirit.

done. . . . Well, she sits and looks into this same corridor and sees an officer—with epaulettes and a black moustache, young and so incredibly handsome that it's hard to imagine—coming towards her from its depths. And it seems to the young miss that he's stepped out of the corridor and is already sitting opposite her at the table. . . . Just like a living man, he eats and drinks wine that she pours into his glass for him. . . . But when the roosters began to crow, he started to say goodbye and said he had to hurry. But the miss had quietly gotten hold of the guest's sword earlier—when the latter, before sitting down at the table, took it off—and had immediately hidden it. The officer looks here and there, searching for his sword. But she says to him, 'You, it seems to me,' she says, 'were here without your sword. I don't seem to re-member you taking it off.' And so he bid her goodbye without his sword, walked out the door, and vanished. It was as if he had never been there. . . . The young miss looked all around and saw the door was latched as before, the unfinished wine gleamed red in the glasses and, when she peeked under the bench, there lay a brand new sword in a shiny scabbard, a hussar's. . . . The young miss hid the sword in her room and never told anyone what she saw, perhaps just her old nanny. And just imagine, that very year this very same officer came to their estate to buy horses for his regiment; he fell in love with the young miss, and they married in the fall. . . . The young couple moved away and settled in the town where the husband's regiment was stationed. Some time passes, and our miss sees that her young husband has lost his cheerfulness and has begun to lose himself in thought."

" 'Why are you so sad, my angel?' " the young wife asks the hussar. 'Oh, one thought keeps tormenting me: when and where have I seen you before? I just can't seem to recall. But that I did see you, I can stake my life on it. . . . ' 'You probably saw me ear-lier in some dream,' the young miss says to him. 'Of course,' he agrees, 'but still, it's strange; your face is very familiar to me. . . .' Then she stupidly couldn't resist and took out that same sword from the trunk. She shows it to him and says, 'Think carefully, did you forget it somewhere? . . .' At this point her young husband's face changed entirely, he flew into a dark rage and began to shout. 'Oh, so you got me through sorcery?' And after that, he grabbed the sword out of the young miss's hands, quickly drew it out of its scabbard . . . one, two . . . and killed his wife. Well, they tried him later. At first, people say he admitted how everything was, but then he began to deny his guilt and placed all the blame on his murdered wife—that she showed an awful lot of interest in other officers. . . . Only the judges found out this wasn't true, and on the Tsar's orders, they reduced him to the ranks for the rest of his life."

The spindles which had grown quiet began to hum once again.

"But you know, Aniska will probably marry Maksim," Matrunka said, returning to their earlier conversation.

"Marry him! . . . She can't go to church except before the Great Holiday (Easter). The unclean spirit won't forgive her for such a step and it'll strangle her. And he's not that enviable a bridegroom," Akulka said, expressing her opinion.

"I daresay she was unable to take her eyes off that same Maksim all spring long," Zinka, who had a malicious tongue, whispered again to Matrunka.

XI

The one about whom the girls were so zealously wagging their tongues really did spend his nights at Aniska's. At first the youth went there only so that he could stop seeing Gorpina in his dreams, and then his visits became a matter of habit for him. Aniska's bad reputation, that she was a witch, did not frighten Maksim for some reason, and he even asked his new girlfriend several times not to hide her art from him.

"Show me," he kept pestering her, "how you milk other people's cows."

"I turn into a magpie at night, fly out through the stovepipe, run into someone's shed as a rat, do my milking, and bring the milk home. . . . Why do you ask such stupid questions?! You saw yourself that I have my Burenka."[1]

"No, Anisushka, my dear friend, don't play with me and don't evade my questions. At night you don't go flying anywhere, but instead you lie in the same place all the time. And as for Burenka, I myself brought a feed bag with fodder into the shed for her and have at times seen you milking her. Your Burenka doesn't give very much milk, yet you sell it even to the teacher, and you store away cheese and sour cream. And just look how many earthenware pots you have in the storeroom. They aren't from Burenka. . . ."

"If you know a lot, you'll soon grow old," the witch tried to laugh it off.

However, it was not so easy to shake off Maksim. When the youth wanted to, he knew how to make himself surprisingly affectionate.

---

1. Burenka (from *бурый*, meaning "brown"): a popular name for cows that are brown in color.

"Anisushka, you know how much I love you," he said. "I'd probably do anything for you. And I'd like so much to help you at times. If you really have anything to do with 'them,' then teach me as well. So that we can live together and both be responsible . . . I could be something of a right-hand man for you," more than once he buttered up his girlfriend in the night hours.

"I don't need your help. But so you know I'm not deceiving you and know a few things, and have power over some people, I'll show you something right now if you like. . . . Lie quietly and listen," she said.

Maksim pricked up his ears. Everything was quiet. Only every now and then, water dripped into a basin from a copper washstand that hung in a corner, and cockroaches made barely audible sounds on the table near the breadcrumbs left from supper. The youth was about to say that he didn't hear anything when the witch, lying next to him, nudged him in the side with her fist to keep quiet; in that very instant Maksim heard something like a heavy cat jumping from a bench to the floor, making a clear pouncing sound, then running to the corner where the stove was, jumping up on the raised part of the stove, and scratching the stove's iron door with its claws. . . . Aniska did not keep a cat in her hut.

"A rat," the young man thought and wanted to express his assumption aloud when suddenly something first made a knocking sound on the ceiling in the middle of the hut and then fell with a plop to the floor, like a pillow. Something again ran this time toward the bed and at first even began to scratch, as if wanting to climb up, and then to scratch itself and rub against the wooden legs of the bed.

"Anisuchka, enough, light a lamp! Otherwise they'll climb on the bed," Maksim begged in a whisper.

Aniska struck a match and lit a kerosene lamp which stood nearby on a stool. In the light the fellow satisfied himself that there were neither cats nor rats in the hut.

"See, they don't dare in the light," Maksim noted.

"Do you think I won't be able to summon them even in the light? . . . Look at the ceiling!"the witch ordered.

Maksim obeyed. Again some time passed. Aniska's more rapid breathing could be heard.

Then a shadow flashed on the white-washed ceiling. The fellow looked intently and in the shadow made out the outline of a rat as big as a large dog. This shadow not only shifted from place to place on the ceiling but also moved its paws, back, tail, and head; it turned, contracted into a ball, crouched down, and then rushed towards the opposite corner.

Maksim looked at the lamp, the floor, and finally at Aniska herself, who was lying motionless with knitted black brows, eyes closed, and a look of concentration. There could be no doubt. The shadow moved independently of his girlfriend who was lying absolutely still under the blanket. Now the ghost of the rat rushed about not only on the ceiling but also on the walls.

"I'm afraid it'll pounce on me," the young man thought.

"Anisushka, enough! Stop them, those things of yours, " he begged.

The witch did not seem to hear his words right away. Then she mouthed something soundlessly, and the rat's shadow faded and collapsed somewhere in the corner. Aniska opened her eyes and smugly looked at her lover.

"Well, did you see?" she asked him sternly.

"I did, Anisushka! No more! And I won't ever ask you again," Maksim answered.

"Well, what did I tell you? Only watch out! If you betray me, 'they' will find you wherever you are and won't give you any peace until you're in your grave," the witch threatened.

Maksim hastened as best he knew, with words and caresses, to win over his girlfriend whose body, he noticed, had became totally cold after the test she had conducted.

A few days later, Maksim managed to prevail upon Aniska to show him how she milked the neighbors' cows. After receiving a frightful oath from the youth not to reveal her secret to anyone, the witch woke Maksim before dawn, forced him to get dressed and follow her into the shed with several empty, cleanly-washed earthenware pots. When they got there, Aniska ordered him to roll over to her a wooden log which was in the cattle shed, sat down on it half an *arshin* from the wall, and told him to put an empty pot in front of her; she took a long rag out of her pocket which had been washed clean in water over which a spell had been cast, threw the rag on a wooden nail which stuck out of the wall at the height of the cow's udder, took both ends of this rag in her hands and, just as when she had been showing the rat's shadows, froze again in position with fixed expression.

"Quiet, Mashka," she unexpectedly said after some time, as if she were addressing a cow which Maksim could not see. "Quiet . . . give me your leg!" Aniska continued and, with eyes closed, began to pull on one end of the rag and then on the other. Milk began to stream from the witch's fingers into the milking bucket standing there.

"Leave that one alone and give me another,"Aniska ordered curtly.

Although the wooden bucket was only half-full, Maksim took it obediently and carefully replaced it with another.

Next, after an interval of time, the witch spoke to a Ryabaya[2] as she milked her; and thirdly, she spoke to a black cow, asking her to stand still. As she did this, the entire time Aniska kept pulling on the rag from which the milk was streaming. Finally, in the usual way, she milked her own Burenka, who gave her only half a pot of milk. All of this milk Maksim helped Aniska to take in two buckets to the storeroom.

From that time on, the witch began to wake up the youth—who was spending practically every night with her—before daybreak and to take him to the cattle shed so that he could carry the pots and position and change them during milking.

Aniska had somehow quarreled with another village witch named Stepanida. This was a widow of venerable age with a rosy face like a child's, who seemed much younger than her years. They quarreled over nothing—who should milk the neighbors' cows that had just calved—and after quarreling, they had a falling out.

Aniska also had had the impudence to add a few unnecessary words:

"And why do you need milk if it doesn't satisfy you and you use something else for food?"

"What something else?" Stepanida hissed in answer, turning dark with anger.

"You know yourself what," followed the evasive answer.

"I'll remind you of this later."

And the witches parted. . . .

---

2. Ryabaya (from *рябой*, meaning "mottled"): a popular name for spotted cows.

"She'll be the ruin of me, that damn blood sucker," Aniska, who had become frightened of her rival's threats, said later. In some respects she felt weaker than Stepanida and began to take a whole series of precautionary measures, from turning her bottom skirt and blouse inside out to carrying on her herbs which guard against "spoiling" and the evil eye.

"Why do you call Stepanida a blood sucker?" Maksim asked.

"Because I never do evil to anyone for no reason, with the exception of using other people's milk, but she's not like that. She—that miserable creature—destroys innocent infants . . . . You can always recognize us, witches, at the morning services during the week after Easter, if you come with a piece of blessed cheese in your mouth. Each of us stands with a milk pail on her head, our backs to the altar. People don't see this and don't suspect it, but we know everything about each other. . . . So, if you come to the morning services with blessed cheese in your mouth and say to yourself, 'I have cheese,' then you'll see not only a milk pail on Styopka's head but a towel around her neck, all covered in the blood she pumps out of the infants."

"How's that done?"

"The same way we get milk from cows. First she spots a suitable little child during the day, and at night, as she's thinking of it, she lets the blood out of that child through a knot in the wood in her cattle shed. And the father and mother don't know why their child is getting thinner and turning pale."

"Oh, that damned woman!" Maksim got all emotional. "If I saw her, never in my life would I forgive her."

"You can see her if you sneak up on her carefully. Only if she's not doing her business by the light of a candle made out of human fat . . . Then you won't be able to spy on her . . . But you can try."

And Aniska and Maksim began to keep track of Stepanida.

A whole number of nights passed without any success. Sometimes the young witch and youth managed to spy on Styopka through slits in the cattle shed as she used a towel to milk cows in the light of an almost burnt-out candle. Maksim had already begun to doubt what Aniska had said, when one day she sneaked up to the old witch's shed and signaled to him to step more gingerly.

"Look," the young witch whispered in the fellow's ear, giving up her place to him by the chink in the shed's wall.

Illuminated weakly by the melting, yellow candle, Styopka—with a greedy face and licking her lips in impatience—was milking quickly not into the usual milking pail but into a small earthenware pot, using a red belt. Filling the pot half-full, she drank the contents greedily, once more licked her lips, and wiped her mouth with her hand; Maksim also managed to make out that it was not milk in the pot but something dark.

"Need to leave some for another time as well," the witch said to herself, her face happy, almost intoxicated, and her eyes sparkling.

No matter how hard Maksim tried to keep quiet, he could not restrain himself from exclaiming lightly, "Ah!"

Because she probably heard this, Stepanida instantly blew out the flame.

"Let's run as fast as we can," his girlfriend whispered, tugging the youth's sleeve, and both rushed to Aniska's cottage.

Spurring Maksim along, his girlfriend ran down the street with him past her own cottage so as to confuse the old woman about the road she took, then quickly ran through the neighbor's orchard and, turning at the wattle fence, came tearing along to her own place from the side of the vegetable gardens.

Closing the door behind them, Maksim and Aniska heard Stepanida's door banging shut in the distance.

They both froze and stood in the hallway, listening closely to whether anyone was chasing them.

Their ears caught neither Styopka's voice nor the sounds of footsteps shuffling through the street mud. Everything all around was quiet.

"That damned woman went looking for us as a cat. Lie down quickly on the bed and keep still, or even better, snore, because she'll be listening by the windows and the stovepipe," Aniska whispered.

Collapsing on the bed, Maksim and his girlfriend could not fall asleep all night until daybreak, listening to every rustle, light noise, and crackling sound around the cottage.

Trying to seem carefree, the next day Maksim walked bravely past Stepanida's windows, heading for the estate where he worked by day. Had he thought of looking back, he would have seen the old witch running out of her cottage almost immediately and, bending down, examining his footprint.

"You have trouble, my dear fellow," his girlfriend greeted Maksim when he returned to her place that same evening.

"What is it?"

"It's just that Styopka cut out your footprint, and now you don't have long in this world to drink vodka, eat white bread and sausage, and visit young women," Aniska continued, putting her treats on the table.

"What'll she do to me with my footprint?" Maksim wondered, already half-frightened.

"After she cut your footprint out, she wrapped it in a rag and now will be drying it in the stove, as it is done, with a spell on it. . . . The footprint will dry and you'll begin to dry and waste away, and finally die from wasting away. . . . Only don't grieve, my dear fellow . . ." Aniska suddenly stopped, slapping Maksim—whose face had become transformed with fear—on the shoulder. "In her malice she doesn't understand what she's doing. She took it into her head, the fool, to remove your footprint in the middle of the day, a footprint made in watery mud, where there are so many footprints that you can't tell whether there's one or four. . . . I've already asked my neighbor: 'What have you done to Stepanida to make her remove your husband's footprint after he passed by?' The neighbor turned pale as she listened to me. . . . But, that really has nothing to do with it. When you were walking in the mud in the morning, did you, you know, try to use the path?"

"Yes, I used the path, where there were a lot of footprints even before mine."

"Well, then, nothing will come of her sorcery. No matter how strong a spell she might have, if the footprint isn't clean, not a damn thing will come of it. . . . So you, when you go in the woods, take care that she doesn't track you down. If she takes out your footprint there, the whole thing will be an entirely different matter. . . . Best of all, take an advance from the contractor for work floating timber. He was looking for some extra men yesterday. And for this spring get a good distance away from here while you're still alive and well. As for what's next, we'll see."

Saying these words, Aniska only partly had in mind saving Maksim from Styopka. He was hampering the witch somewhat just as the Fiery Serpent had taken to visiting her recently. Their meeting each other, which she had averted up to this point, would have been unpleasant, first of all for the witch herself.

Maksim listened to his girlfriend, took an advance, and in about two days left with an *artel*[3] of young villagers for lumber work in the neighboring district.

In essence, he need not have worried and left his native village since the neighbor, warned by Aniska, had climbed through a poorly closed window into Styopka's hut in the old witch's absence and stolen the footprint drying in the stove in a piece of rag.

But Maksim did not know this.

~

After catching the sound of noise and crackling in the stovepipe, Aniska jumped up from the bed and held her breath. There could not be any doubt: someone was clearly scratching the stove door with his nails. Aniska blew on the coals in the hearth, lit a candle with a bit of straw, and, drawing her face near the stove, asked quietly, "Who's there?"

"Receive a guest from earthly heights," a hoarse, somewhat whistling male voice was heard in reply.

Aniska moved the stove door aside and in that instant something blew on her from the stovepipe. The candle went out. Sounding like a pile of wet laundry, something heavy plopped to the floor and began to move about in the dark hut.

The witch immediately blew on the coals again and lit the candle which had gone out. In its light Aniska saw a corpulent man with the look of a gypsy, about thirty-five or forty years old, dressed in a red caftan, wide black velvet trousers, and strangely shaped shoes, with sharp forked toes turned upward.

"Recognize me?" he asked, smiling at the half-dressed woman peering at him with affected embarrassment.

"That's exactly why I've lit the fire, so that I could tell whether it's you or someone else pretending to be you," answered the witch. "Although I recognized your voice, I still thought it's better to see with your own eyes."

"Test even with your teeth or some other way, there's no deception on my part. Or does someone else fly here to see you?"

---

3. *artel (артель)*: cooperative association of workmen or peasants.

"There's a lot of your kind hanging around my stovepipe, asking to come in and warm up. Let them in, and they won't want to go back . . ."

"Perhaps someone even stayed with you? There seems to be a light smell of man and tobacco."

"That's true, there's a light smell of that. All kinds of people come here during the day, but I don't let anyone stay the night. . . . Search, if you want to. You won't find anyone here except the unclean spirits who like to live behind the stove."

"Well, you don't have just the stove unclean spirits; there are all kinds of petty spirits here."

"The petty spirits don't count. The petty ones exist almost everywhere," Aniska answered. Just look at the forked toes you have," she added, trying to change the topic.

"Everything of mine is forked," the red caftan guffawed in answer. "Don't you remember? . . You've really filled out since I last visited you," he continued with a contented smile, admiring the witch's bare shoulders and full arms and even stroking her magnificent breasts approvingly.

In answer to such attention, Aniska, casting down her eyes and turning red, shyly gave her honored guest "the fig,"[4] the usual greeting used by the unclean force.

Touched by such a sign of attention, the visitor in the red caftan began to give even more free rein to his hands, leading the mistress of the house to hurry and blow out the candle.

"What if someone spies us through the window! Then I won't be able to get rid of the shame," she uttered displeased.

It became dark in the witch's cottage. In the darkness some rustling, bustling, and whispering could be heard, then the bed, on which the night guest probably sat down, squeaked loudly. Then some panting was heard, again whispering and, finally, some words loudly spoken by Aniska, "Will you bring me a satin blouse?"

Again everything grew silent.

Right before daybreak Aniska would not allow her visitor to leave until he taught her a quick way (without doing three somersaults) of changing into a magpie, frog, dog, and rat. As for how to change into a pig, the Serpent did not know or did not want to teach her.

---

4. to give someone "the fig" (*показать кому-нибудь кукиш*): a gesture consisting of an extended, clenched fist with thumb between index and middle fingers.

In turn, he made the witch promise that, when summoned, she would appear at the night meeting of the unclean spirits, which Aniska had stopped attending after taking up with Maksim.

She tried to excuse herself on the grounds that she had quarreled with Styopka and did not want to meet up with her, but the Fiery Serpent objected:

"Styopka is not your senior now and can't harm you. People have started to say that you want to separate yourself from us . . . That you've come to an understanding with some young fellow . . . You plan to marry him, the rumor has it."

"Me? Get married?! It's Styopka who's spread those lies about me out of jealousy, that I've grabbed a fellow right out from under her nose. She started that rumor out of spite."

"And what do I care? You can have even ten fellows, but you must come to the sabbath."

"All right, I'll come."

"Not by and by, but as soon as the call goes out, and without any excuses like the other times," the guest said in a didactic tone, rolling into a ball of reddish smoke with whirling blue sparks, and then entered the stove's smoke opening. . . .

When dawn came, Aniska saw a wide skirt of pink silk left by the guest on one of the benches. The skirt was dampish and had two or three spots, probably from mold. But you could dry it out, re-sew it, and wear it happily. . . . The moldy smell should vanish as it dried. Without asking pointless questions about where the Fiery Serpent had obtained the gift he had brought her, Aniska got busy with stoking the stove so that she could dry the skirt as quickly as possible.

XII

When Maksim, after a long absence, came the next winter to the get-togethers, no one asked him why he had not come for so long, and instead everyone pretended that they had parted with him only the evening before. Only Akulka could not restrain herself and, instead of giving Maksim a friendly slap on the back with her powerful hand, as she usually greeted the boys, she suddenly remembered someone's words about Aniska turning her beloved into a black cat and began to beckon to the returnee with the words, "here, kitty-kitty."

The easily amused Zinka could not restrain herself and burst out laughing uncontrollably. Without leaving their spindles, the girls exchanged meaningful looks. But Maksim, who knew about the jokes making the rounds at his expense, did not lose his head and, looking over Akulina's magnificent body, in turn addressed her with the following words:

"I suppose you want to offer me some milk? I thought it had already disappeared. . ."

After such a snide remark, even Akulka got embarrassed. Domna tried to stand up for her girlfriend. "Look, my dear friends! Someone has really given Maksim the evil eye: he mistakes girls for cows. . . . I suppose he was making his way to someone's shed and wound up here by mistake!"

"And you, my dear, don't play up to me and don't try so hard around me. I won't milk you. You're far from pretty," the youth snapped back at Domna, annoyed.

His friend Antip, wanting to deflect attention from Maksim, who had become the victim of derisive looks, tried to change the conversation to a topic that was still about sorcery but less dangerous.

"We were saying here without you, Maksim, that if you catch a male black cat without any marks on it and boil it in a covered cauldron at midnight, at a crossroads, then without fail there should be a small bone in it with which you can become invisible and steal everything you want."

Maksim, wanting perhaps to show his innocence in things that had to do with magic, hastened to ask how you find this bone.

"Here's how. As soon as the meat is boiled soft, you have to separate it from the bones and take one bone after another in your hand. You have to cook the meat and pull it apart with another person. One takes a bone, the other looks. And as soon as he stops seeing the one holding a bone in his hand, it means that the 'bone of invisibility' has been found."

"How did you learn this?" Domna asked.

"Your mother taught me," snapped back Antip.

"That she taught you when you were a little boy and stole chicken eggs from us, that's for sure. Only she taught you with stinging nettles,[1] not magic. . . ."

"Enough of your quarreling," good-hearted Fyokla stepped in. "The man has come just in time for gruel and fried eggs and brought a small bottle with him and, for all we know, a whole one, and pockets full of sunflower seeds, but you won't leave him alone! Sit yourself here, Maksim, and show me your sunflower seeds. Are they roasted?"

And Fyokla put her five fingers into the bulging pocket of Maskim, who was sitting next to her.

"How's your mother?" she asked, spitting out the shell sticking to her lips.

"And what does she have to worry about? She got a three-rouble note from a rich uncle the other day. And so she's happy. . . . A benefactor, so to say!"

"Ah, so that's why you've brought vodka," Fyokla realized.

"No, I bought it with my own money," Maksim explained in embarrassment and pretended that he was paying close attention to the talk about how to cook a black cat.

"You can't imagine how much easier it is to steal with a magic bone than with a dead man's hand. The hand you even have to carry around the hut, and if someone's sleeping, you have to pass

---

1. stinging nettles *(крапива):* in village life, a type of weed often used in place of a strap or whip to punish a child.

it in a circular motion over his head, but the bone . . . it's the simplest way. Put it in your pocket and go where you like," Antip related matter-of-factly in the meantime.

"What do you want to say? That you've tried both ways?" the gloomy Anton asked the speaker maliciously.

"I haven't tried, but people have told me about it. I myself probably couldn't even cook a cat . . . I wouldn't have the courage."

"Oh? Or are you afraid of the sin?" Matrunka asked.

"It's not the sin, but people say that while you're cooking this cat, you get attacks of fear. Someone told me that he tried to cook one. The water had just barely begun to boil and the lid of the cauldron to clatter, when there was a noise out of nowhere, as if a whole cavalry was galloping. You could even hear the horses snorting. Such a frightful clatter of hooves and people's voices really near . . . At this point, my buddy got scared and took off! . . . He ran and ran and all the time seemed to sense that he was being chased. In the darkness he fell into a ditch and stayed there until dawn. The good thing was that there was no water in it. He was afraid to go out into the fields. And when dawn came, he looked all around and went to the place where he had been cooking the cat. . . . He comes and sees the ashes, coal, and blackened twigs, but there's no cauldron, no lid, no cat. There's nothing . . . as if someone had carried them off."

"Of course someone carried them off," Anton and Fyokla and Akulina and even Red-Haired Fedka, who was usually silent at the get-togethers, said in unison.

"A black cat's bone will certainly be better by far," Anton expressed thoughtfully after a minute's silence. "It's not hard to cut off the hand of a corpse, but you can get in serious trouble. . . . But boiling a cat, it's a simple matter. They're not going to try you for that."

Akulina, at this time, began singing a melancholy, plaintive tune—either an outlaw or convict song. Her girlfriends joined her, and for some time laughter and gossip in the soot-covered hut were replaced by drawn-out singing in which the thin, lightly ringing voice of the young Zinka stood out clearly.

⁓

"You know, Maksim, I might have guests coming tonight, and it's better for you not to be seen by their kind," Aniska said one wonderful winter morning to her boyfriend, who had come back to her.

"Why?"

"I'd feel bad about what would happen to you. You'd die for no reason at all."

"I don't like leaving you alone, Anisushka. Who knows what might happen, people could hurt you," clever Maksim answered in a sweet voice. "Perhaps I'd even be of some use to you . . ."

The youth had a terrible desire to take a look at the unclean force. He once had happened to hear a story at the mill about a landlord whose worker associated with devils. This landlord treated his farm laborer to some alcohol and persuaded the laborer to let him see his acquaintances when they next came to visit him. The worker reluctantly agreed. He demanded half a bucket of beer, diluted it with a great deal of water "so that they wouldn't get out of hand," and told the landlord to stay in the house so that he would not be seen by his acquaintances. This farm laborer permitted him only to sit by the window and look from behind the curtains at the guests passing by.

When those guests were passing by, the man missed his chance to see them. He only heard drunken noises in the barn, where the worker lived in the summer, and only saw the guests staggering and walking through the yard to the gate.

The guests were dressed in shabby clothes. They all had human faces, only each face had some kind of flaw: one had a crude face twisted to the side; another, a mouth extending to his ears, revealing animal teeth; a third had a bad nose; and a fourth did not even have a face, just a bearded blob covered with a cap full of holes. They all had such a vile and frightening look that the landlord gave strict orders to his farm laborer not to admit them in the future and, later, when the year's hiring came to an end, he did not keep him on either.

Maksim wanted very much to test whether the unclean spirits were like the ones he had heard about in the story.

"Give me, Anisushka, some 'invisible herb'[2] and put it, along with me, in the wardrobe where your clothing is hanging or in a chest, and I'll watch from there through the keyhole," he began to entreat his girlfriend.

---

2. "invisible herb" (*неведим трава*): a reference to the fern, whose flower had the power to make the person holding it invisible. The fern is a non-flowering plant, but it was believed to flower at midnight on St. John's Eve.

"Do you probably want to lose an eye? A guest is supposed to visit me who, for all we know, can carry you off with him into the stovepipe, and I'll get it as well because of you. . . . I have no desire whatsoever to have you watch my pain! Spend tonight at your own place!"

And thus Aniska did not allow Maksim to stay the night.

The youth, however, tortured on the one hand by jealousy—he was afraid that instead of the unclean force, the steward from the neighboring estate would be visiting his girlfriend—and, on the other hand, curious to see just what this hostile force[3] looked like, walked out of his hut before midnight and began to wander about not far from Aniska's cottage.

There was no light in the windows there, and everything all around was quiet. It was a frosty, moonless night, and only the stars were burning brightly in the blue-black sky. Maksim got good and cold as he waited, and even wanted to go home when suddenly a red star flashed in the dark heights and, falling in a fiery streak, showered Aniska's roof with small sparks. Maksim saw that these sparks, before disappearing into the stovepipe, came together and assumed the form of a golden-red, coiled winged serpent.

"Uh huh," the fellow said through his teeth and, without lingering any longer, headed home. He lost all desire to visit Aniska that night. He had no wish whatsoever to compete with the Fiery Serpent.

Right then and there, on the way home, he decided that tomorrow he would take the advance offered to him by the steward and, in the approaching period of fasting, leave again for work floating timber.

---

3. "hostile force" *(вражья сила)*: another way of referring to the unclean force or the world of the demonic.

XIII

Fat Maryska was very unhappy with what had happened. The child, to which she unexpectedly gave birth as a result of the hurried caresses of a hunter she had dragged, in the end, into the depths of the forest lake, began to appear in her dreams and to frighten her at night. The Bolotnitsa began to lose weight and even lost her title of "favorite wife" which, as it happened, did not revert back to Marten-Soul but passed on to the latter's younger sister, Malinka.

Taking advantage of her master's weakening attention, Maryska made the firm decision that as soon as an occasion presented itself, she would run to the river to find out the fate of her infant from the *rusalka*s there and, if possible, even to see it in person. She worried, incidentally, how river water would affect her child who was not web-footed.

Maryska managed to fulfill her intentions, however, only after a year had passed, due to various obstacles.

One day, seizing a convenient time toward evening, she made her way to a neighboring lake, quickly swam across it and, finding the place where a small forest stream began, quickly followed its flow to the mouth.

The forest in this place was pine. It was only along the banks of the stream—particularly in those places where the violet-yellow trunks of the pine trees retreated from the banks—that hazel-nut, alder and osier bushes were visible here and there; small long-legged sandpipers, water rats, and wild ducks, which had made nests for themselves in the bushes, peered out of them from time to time.

Maryska waddled from side to side—the usual gait of a swamp she-demon—without sinking into the swampish mud and almost without leaving any traces of her webbed feet. She looked at neither the red squirrel which had just leapt over the stream and was swaying in the fir branches, nor at the two rabbits who were cautiously sniffing each other in the clearing. The *bolotnitsa* had only one thought on her mind: to reach the river as quickly as possible and to find out from the *rusalka*s there about the child who had been taken away from her.

Not paying any attention, therefore, even to the bear who appeared for an instant among the trees and then hurriedly ran off, Maryska stepped businesslike along the winding stream, not foreseeing the suddenness with which her trip would end.

The fact is that the bear, who had encountered the swamp she-demon, did not fail to report to his mistress, the local Leshachikha called Wart-Face, that some kind of being—perhaps a *rusalka*, or a woman getting ready to bathe, but with strange feet—had appeared on their property.

Not tolerating any being of the female gender whom her spouse (Green-Goat, to be precise) might take a liking to, the Leshachikha immediately decided to remove the uninvited guest from her property and, if the latter had any business or relationship with the Leshy, to remove her with particular haste.

Following the stream's flow, Maryska came out upon a small oblong-shaped, open meadow and noticed up ahead, to the right of her, the tall, shaggy-haired, and scraggly Leshachikha also walking there, accompanied by Brown-Bear. Noticing that they had stopped and seemed to be waiting for her, Maryska slowed her pace but continued to walk.

"Why are you roaming about here, you fat-ass toad?" she heard unexpectedly after she had taken about four steps toward Wart-Face.

Maryska glanced at the speaker and saw that she was in a state of furious rage, about to burst forth any second now.

"I have things to attend to, up the river . . . Is there no road here?" the Bolotnitsa asked, trying to seem calm although in her heart she was dying of fear, since she sensed a storm brewing.

"Here's your road!" And a terrible blow from an almost wooden right hand knocked Maryska off her feet, throwing her a couple of steps to the side of the path. "Don't roam around where there's no trail. Don't run around with other women's husbands!" Wart-Face burst out in rasping laughter, seeing the swamp she-demon fall.

"Like I really need your bear! Embrace him yourself!" snapped Maryska—who had seen a thing or two in her life—as she got to her feet. "I'll tell everyone! I'll give you a bad name throughout the whole swamp and forest! Sheep-Mug didn't chase you and that clumsy, fancy bear of yours off his land for nothing!"

The Leshachikha could not bear such obvious slander. With a cry of rage and vengeance she pushed her rival–who was not standing firmly on her gooselike legs–down on the grass again and began to drag the Bolotnitsa by her wet, black braids. Maryska, defending herself, put her sharp demon's nails into action, leaving marks on Wart-Face's hands and rough cheek. Then the Leshachikha enveloped her fat rival tightly in her long, hard paws and, squeezing hard, tried to crush or strangle her. The swamp she-demon, who was short in comparison with Wart-Face, managed somehow, nonetheless, to bite her on the chest with her sharp, pike-like teeth.

Letting out a scream from the pain, the Leshachikha pushed her opponent away forcefully, and Maryska—all red and disheveled—rushed to find salvation in the stream. But she had not yet reached the river bank when a strong blow from Wart-Face's fist—which resembled a bony, angular, gnarly bunch of roots—forced her to do a somersault and plop in the water.

Although not fully in her own element, but at least now in a related one, Maryska managed nevertheless to turn into a frog—granted, with little paws the size of a bird's and reminiscent of a duck's, which she painstakingly drew inward—and, concealing herself among the plants growing in the water, sat all the while on the bottom of the stream while the Leshachikha looked for her unsuccessfully.

Only after it had grown dark did Wart-Face—straddling the stream—spit into the muddy water and, after promising to strangle Maryska if she dared again to wander onto her property, did she go into the forest.

Only then did the Bolotnitsa dare to stick her head out of water. Looking around fearfully, she immediately headed home, first in her frog form, but then, after becoming convinced of the difficulty of swimming against the current, in her previous form of the Fat Maryska.

She managed to return to the deep pool in the lake only before dawn.

"Again you've started going who knows where?! Trying to get

someone to put the evil eye on you again, is that it?" the old swamp she-demon, who was either her mother or aunt (it was difficult to figure out these things in the pool), asked Maryska. "Look out, Marten-Soul or Malinka will find out and have lots of gossip for him. It won't be good for you!"

"It's already been bad for me. I barely got away," Maryska said, groaning and showing her bruises.

"Who did this to you, sweet girl?" the old woman now asked in an entirely different tone, sympathizing with her.

"The Leshachikha . . . may she burn! . . . I ran into her when I was going along the stream to the river to find out about my child, and she jumped me. . . ."

"Oh, the bitch! If only we could get our hands on her!" the she-demon threatened. "And you, don't go chasing around after your infant. Say to yourself: what's gone is gone. And if you're bored, then get a new child. You know how . . . the evil eye!" the gray-haired she-demon joked.

"It isn't that easy, auntie, to find an object for this evil eye. You yourself, I daresay, know that," Maryska tried to joke back.

"I used to know at one time . . . But now let's go as quickly as we can to the bog. I'll massage your sides and back with frog roe. It won't be noticeable at all . . ."

Predawn fog lay suspended in the air; the cranes, sensing the sun, were calling; it was time to plunge into the black water of an opening in the swamp.

XIV

From early morning on, there was the din and noise of a tambourine in Aniska's ears, one minute quieter, another minute louder. With the exception of women who knew the unclean force, no one in the village heard these sounds, and the young witch was well aware that the tambourine was a call for all local sorceresses to come to a demonic gathering the next night. Such gatherings, in Aniska's memory, happened rather rarely. She had even avoided them for various reasons, but now, after the talk with the Fiery Serpent, it was impossible not to show up.

Anisia was not herself the whole day. Her heart kept constricting and stopping from the waiting. She found the people who came to have their fortunes told, or to get some advice from her, annoying. Her face contorted with rage, Aniska shouted so loudly at one fellow she knew—who gave free rein to his hands from force of habit—that he became totally confused, apologized for a long time and, after receiving the powder he needed, hurried to depart, leaving the magic healer a bottle of vodka. As he was leaving, the fellow did not even dare ask her, as he usually had before, to treat him then and there to a bit of the bottle.

Aniska was so anxious about her upcoming journey that even if Maksim had returned to her then from his seasonal work far away, she would have chased him off without any regret.

Disconnected thoughts and fears rushed swiftly through the sorceress's head.

"And what if that envious Stepanida has managed to complain that I saw her and showed Maksim how she milks blood through a red belt? Then I'll get a dressing down! . . . Or what if He Himself comes and chooses me to be his bride?! Rarely, they say, can one endure such passion and torture without screaming. . . . And then, what should I fly on? They can steal my poker. I have a new one, made of iron. . . . Invariably some low-life will be tempted. They can take the broomstick accidentally at any time. You mount it in a hurry when everyone is leaving, and it—not being your own—takes you to someone else's cottage about a hundred versts from your own home. Run then, try to find your way home from there! . . . And you're lucky if they don't strike you dead in that cottage when you appear. . . . I'll put the broom on an old stove fork! Perhaps that way they won't take mine and leave theirs instead while I'm dancing. . . . And oh, will I dance! . ."

Well in advance, the witch took a large, white clay pot with a strong-smelling ointment out of her trunk, prepared a pot for boiling a magical potion, and let the coals die down in the cast-iron stove. She had wanted to outline her eyes with soot—which were black even without it—but remembered in time that she would sweat and then the soot would run down her face. She was forced to give up making herself beautiful. "I'll probably be the best of all just the way I am," the witch thought, trying to re-member who could rival her beauty at the witches' sabbath. "Perhaps the fair-haired one with the manorial hair style and creases on her hips from the corset? . . . Except that she's too skinny . . . It's doubtful anyone would be tempted by her except the Master Himself. And if he hankers after her, it serves her right! . . . Should I take something edible to the sabbath for sup-per? I have fatback, but it's salted. If you bring it, they'll even beat you up. Devils don't like salt. You also can't bring our sim-ple bread. There you need a special one . . . I'll grab a ring of sau-sage and today's bottle . . . But how do I take them? After all, there aren't any pockets on the body. The sausage can be threaded through the stove fork. But then, I'll still have to hold the bottle in my hands or under my arms. . . . No, it could very well break. I'll stick it into the broom and tie it . . . Just mustn't forget to grease them both," the witch thought.

In the meantime, dusk set in. In the corner of the stove a coal fire had been laid long ago and a pot full of herbs, covered with water, had been prepared. The witch covered the windows, walked up to the exit doors, opened them and listened for a long time as she stood in the hallway.

Somewhere, on the edge of the village, girls' singing fell silent. In the vegetable gardens someone screamed once in a voice feign-ing fright, a few voices guffawed in return, and again everything grew silent. Bright stars were already flickering on the smooth surface of the summer night sky.

"It's a bit light," Aniska mumbled, shaking her head pensively. But then she grew calm. "I'll fly out of the stovepipe with the smoke. They say it's not noticeable in the smoke. . . ."

The witch returned to her hut. She latched both doors behind her. Then she placed a large, strong broom on the handle of the stove fork. Inside the broom she placed the bottle with the vodka and tied it tightly. She threw the ring of sausage on one of the prongs, also tying it for safety's sake. Then she moved the coals from the corner to the front of the stove, added new coals and fanned them, and again placed the pot with the concoction she was cooking on them.

When the water began to get warm, Aniska checked once more to see if the windows were well covered and began to undress. Rustling sounds could be heard as she took off her skirts, jacket and blouse; her shoes made a knocking sound as they fell near a bench. As she bent over the coals, her lightly red face and glowing pink neck and shoulders flashed for a second in the rosy light of the coals on which she was blowing. . . .

The water was already beginning to boil. A lightly intoxicating steam rose from the pot; its smell was not very strong yet, more pleasant than not, with just a hint of resin.

"I'll have a splitting headache tomorrow," Aniska said to herself as she inhaled the steam and reached for the jar of ointment.

The ointment smelled even stronger, although somewhat differently, than the concoction she had cooked. The witch massaged her temples, the area behind her ears, her neck and chest, under her arms, the palms of her hands, the soles of her feet, and other places. The greasy potion burned and cooled at the same time.

Then the wooden stick and the metal of the stove fork were painstakingly greased. The witch's hands also touched the broom top and the sausage and the vodka bottle. Both palms were then wiped on her hair.

"It's time!" Aniska threw one leg across the stove fork-broom which was resting against the stove. With her left hand holding the metal end of the fork and her right hand on the front ledge of the stove, she began to inhale the steam which was now billowing thickly from the pot.

The witch's head soon began to spin; she could feel an unusual, almost weightless lightness and weakness throughout her body, combined with an uncontrollable urge pulling her into space. Aniska's legs—she had been standing on tiptoe all this time—bent under her, her heart grew still, her eyes grew dark and, feeling that she was falling into an abyss, the sorceress lost consciousness.

This state lasted only an instant. In the next moment the witch had a clear sense that she was not falling but swiftly ascending, that she was flying on her fork-and-broomstick to sacred Mount Osiyan.[1]

The coolness of the night enveloped Aniska's body; there was whistling in her ears, perhaps from the speed of the flight, perhaps from the headwind tousling her unbraided hair. Frequent, intensely bright stars flashed like sparks before her eyes. Somewhere far off, the sound of a tambourine could be heard, its din and noise gaining in strength the nearer she drew. . . .

Just now in the distance a bright-red dot which did not look like a star flashed below and then grew into a body of interlaced fires. After flying closer to them, Aniska made out that these bonfires formed a fantastical union of circle and square. You could already see the scarlet tongues of these inviting fires, varying in length, shooting upwards towards the sky and licking the gloom of the night.

Gripping the stove fork with her hands and grasping the broom with her heels, in the midst of the howling and screeching of sorceresses and spirits flying from everywhere to the gathering as she was, Aniska rushed to the nocturnal, demonic celebration with a sinking heart. "Live it up, dear woman!" an exclamation she had heard somewhere flashed through her head. At that point in time, the barren plateau of Mount Osiyan was growing closer and closer to her, its bonfires glittering, where beings of all kinds, limping and running with awful wails, were already visible.

Aniska's legs touched the ground smoothly and painlessly. After placing her stove fork with the attached broom against a large rock around which several pestles and brooms, two-three

---

1. Bald Mountain *(Лысая гора)*, near Kiev, was said to be the site of witches' sabbaths. The choice of Mt. Osiyan *(Осиянская гора)* may be Kondratiev's oblique reference to the "ancient epic poems" that James Macpherson (1736-1796) claimed to have collected in the highlands of Scotland and attributed to the legendary Gaelic warrior Ossian. Macpherson's books of Ossian "translations" aroused great controversy but helped to draw attention to ancient Scottish poetry. Perhaps Kondratiev saw his own utilization of Slavic folklore beliefs as something akin to James MacPherson's creativity.

pokers, about a dozen pointed objects, a small trough, benches, and other contraptions for night flight had already been placed, the witch turned to her stove fork and broom, bent over, and whispered, "Stand here and wait for me, but don't let anyone take you."

Not far from her, a middle-aged dark-skinned woman, as she was repeating an incantation, used one of her long hairs to tie the bread shovel on which she had just arrived to the lone blackthorn bush growing there.

Fixing her tousled hair and then untying the sausage and bottle of vodka, the young witch headed with a light step to the brightly burning bonfires, smiling happily.

She was outdistanced by a disheveled old woman, gray-haired, with a slight limp, seemingly drunk, who was dancing and slapping her sagging behind and stomach. A young devil—with the legs of a dog but dressed in manor-house clothing and even wearing a straw hat cocked over his half-animal face—jumped out of the bend in the path which wound between large rocks and pinched her bottom amiably but painfully. The old woman cried out as if she were frightened, but then she burst out in artificial, jingling laughter and began to talk with the unclean spirit as if with an old acquaintance. He embraced the old witch and, wagging his dog-like tail, led her toward the bonfires.

A familiar voice behind her forced Aniska, who was walking up the mountain, to turn around. A woman from a neighboring village, also a witch, was walking unsteadily with two young daughters and singing loudly:

> It's not me who's walking,
> The devils are carrying me,
> And tiny little devils are shaking me . . .

Incidentally, there was no one around her except her daughters. Aniska quickened her step.

The night was likely cold since the young woman was feeling a chill the whole time. She wanted to draw closer to the bonfires as quickly as possible and to warm her chilled, naked body near them. The witch pushed away someone's ice-cold, slippery hand which was trying to embrace her torso, and let a remark fall to the hand's owner—a frog mug with eyes bulging from surprise or perhaps passion, and with whiskers like a cat's:

"Get away! You miserable! . . It's cold even without your paws, you foul scum!"

The frog mug, however, would not leave her alone and, probably wanting to show his agility and flexibility, began to turn somersaults and do cartwheels across the road before the annoyed Aniska. Another man—short, with a little belly and a half-goat face, wearing torn men's boots—ran up to Aniska from the side and grabbed the witch firmly by her left hand.

"You're going to the Master Himself, my beauty? Then I'll accompany you so that others won't hurt you. . . ."

The smell coming from him was unbearable, but Aniska didn't feel like picking a fight, particularly since her suitor with the flat goat nose and beard was happily calling out in a vile tone to his comrades who showed up here and there and clearly shared his feelings. Although considerably more witches than devils appeared for the holiday, you could not rely on their help since no special friendship could be observed among the witches.

When she saw the Fiery Serpent's familiar red *kuntush*[2] in the glow of a nearby bonfire that now was burning without making any crackling sounds or smoke, Aniska even rejoiced and called him to help her in a voice that was not her own:

"My dear little Serpent! Come here! I'm looking and looking for you, but this loafer . . . this miserable . . . won't let me through!"

Aniska knew that the more you used foul language in this place, the better.

The Serpent heard the despairing call of his acquaintance, the sorceress, and rushed to her aid.

"Leave me alone, you insolent thing! Don't you see, my *kum*[3] is coming!" Aniska said to the goat in boots, who continued to press her left hand.

"After you and I become acquainted, then I'll be your *kum*," he replied, unruffled. "And if your red one gets in my way, I'll spear him on my horns!"

After removing the torn cap from his head, Aniska's companion revealed small but rather sharp horns. These horns were pointed unequivocally towards the approaching Serpent.

---

2. *kuntush (кунтуш):* a kind of overcoat, worn by Ukrainians and Poles, which resembled a caftan with wide sleeves.

3. *kum (кум):* literally, godfather of one's child; often used to indicate a close friend.

The Serpent noticed the gesture of the goat-like unclean spirit but, pretending that he was paying no attention whatsoever to him, cheerfully shouted to the young witch:

"Ah, Aniska, so you've dragged yourself here after all, you fat ass! . . . It looks like you're carrying sausage and vodka. Now you're talking! . . . And you've even brought a goat with you. Now that's really good! Because our cooks are complaining that there isn't enough goat meat for supper. They can roast one leg and part of the back . . . Don't be afraid, my friend! We'll give you a new leg, if only a frog's or a dog's . . . Hey you, cooks, come here quickly!"

The Serpent whistled so loudly in his fist that Aniska even closed her eyes. When she opened them again, the Serpent stood before her, rolling in laughter. There was no trace of the smelly half-goat.

Only a stocky swamp devil slipped past Aniska, trying a boot on his head that had been lost by the goat during his hurried disappearance.

"Let's go!" said the Serpent. "There'll be a good supper tonight. You're probably hungry?" he continued, amiably pinching his companion's stomach as he walked. "Don't forget to place the sausage and vodka at the hooves of the Master Himself when you're bowing to him or give them to the old woman in black who stands beside him. . . . He'll be so happy with the vodka that he won't even bother asking you about your actions. . . . Don't forget, also, to kiss the idol's tail," he added. "You haven't been here for so long that no doubt you've forgotten all the rules."

Sometimes passing others, sometimes being outdistanced by the witches and unclean spirits streaming in from everywhere for the holiday, Aniska and her companion passed through the second chain of brightly burning fires. It was noticeably warmer here. The Serpent led his girlfriend to a high chair made out of either brightly polished copper or red gold. It was again cold near this throne-like chair. With his feet on a small red bench, the Someone was sitting there—large, displeased, breathing heavily and noisily through his nose—winged and black. The bluish flame between his large bent horns illuminated his arrogant, half-animal face with its sparkling, keen, and penetrating dark eyes.

Getting on her knees, Aniska made "the fig" with her left hand for the Sitting One, and with her right hand she laid the

bottle of vodka and the sausage at the feet of the Master overgrown with thick, black fur.

"Not salted," she either whispered or thought, bowing to the
ground and kissing the cloven hoof, cold as ice, which was oblig-
ingly raised to her lips. The old woman with the dark-brown face
and dressed in a long black shift, who sat by the throne, put away
the offering in a wicker basket.

Aniska got up from her knees and, led by the same Fiery Serpent who had been respectfully bending before the Master, circled the ruler's throne and again bent down in order to kiss him
through an opening in the seat. The reflection of the brightly
burning fires shimmered on the reddish metal of the throne
chair. After she placed her head under it, Aniska suddenly recoiled in horror but got hold of herself and, with an incredible act
of will, forced herself to kiss. . . . Her own pale face accepted the
kiss on cold, motionless lips with an apathetic and lifeless
look. . . . [4] There was the barest smell of raw vodka from the
mouth of this stone-like face, familiar and, at the same time,
alien.

The Serpent helped Aniska to get off her knees and dragged her
to the side.

"Quickly!" he either whispered or hissed in the witch's ear.
"Or he'll start asking you how many animal and human souls
you've ruined, how many illnesses you've called down on people,
how many cows you've robbed of milk. Then he'll even punish
you for your laziness. Let's go quickly, while he's guzzling your
vodka."

Mixing into a crowd of naked witches and pale devils with
grayish blue-green faces, who were covered with fur or dressed in
clothing full of holes, Aniska and her companion saw from afar
how the goat-legged Master gave an order to beat a witch who
had appeared before him without any special deeds to her credit
as well as empty-handed.

Not sparing their long tails, two devils began to whip and in-
flict terrible pain on the woman who was either slow-witted or
too greedy. She howled and asked to be released, promising to try
hard in the future and the next time to bring a whole quart of the
best homebrew as well as a silver ruble.

---

4. She observes herself kissing the Master's tail in the reflection in the metal
of the chair.

One by one, the witches approached the throne, boasting of the illnesses they had called down on their neighbors, cattle they had milked until they were bleeding, weddings they had spoiled, and other such deeds. A young dark-skinned gypsy with wiry hair even brought a two-week old infant, whimpering quietly, which she had stolen somewhere. At the unspoken signal of Black Goat, dozens of hands with hook-like fingers reached for the gift, and the little white body, squealing pitifully, disappeared among the multi-furred retinue of the Sovereign of the nocturnal celebration. The one who brought the gift was noted and favored with the Master's claw, who scratched some kind of sign on the forehead of the happy sorceress.

"Let's get a bit closer to the tables so we can get a better place," the Fiery Serpent invited Aniska.

"Only can't we get farther away from the Black One, from the Master? I'm afraid of him. I'm afraid he'll hurt me."

"All right. I myself am not about to give you up to him. . . . Just fall into his hands, and he'll spoil you for the rest of your life," the Serpent answered, making his way through the witches pushing one another and shamelessly flirting with the devils and through the unclean spirits brazenly boasting of their members, which resembled a horse's, donkey's, wolf's, or other animal's. Some of them were clearly proud of the long claws on their hands and feet. Some wore hats, hiding their sharp-pointed heads and horns; others, on the other hand, not without some vanity, displayed them. Two or three had horn growths in the form of claws not only on their fingers but even on their elbows and knees. A significant majority of the unclean spirits were disfigured with some kind of a defect: noses twisted to the side or flat like that of cattle, mouths extending to ears, crossed eyes, or hairy ears which stuck out—revealing the non-human origin of their owners.

Aniska involuntarily glanced at her companion and made out that when he laughed, you could see thin, sharp teeth shaped like those of a serpent.

The witch became frightened and began to shiver.

"Too late! You should've taken a good look earlier," the Serpent said roughly and, turning his face away, led Aniska to the tables. . . .

On wooden and clay plates, serving dishes and flat platters the following were spread out in abundance: fatback cut in thick slices, cooked and roasted meat shredded into fine pieces, sausage, goose, cheese, sour milk, piles of sliced, gray, crumbly bread—clearly with something added to it—mountains of cooked potatoes, and a large quantity of bottles and jugs with different drinks. No eggs, fish, or salt cellars were visible.

Several old witches, lustfully licking their lips and wiping their wrinkled, vein-covered hands, and one very young witch, still a girl, with a fat stomach, thin neck, and an unusually long slit that was her dumbly smiling mouth, were already moving about near the tables. The young witch's whisker-like hair stuck up in uncombed, hard strands. She was shoveling piece after piece of food into her mouth from the dishes near the edge of the table. A large white borzoi dog sat near her, salivating.

"That's a changeling.[5] She must soon die," the Serpent explained when he noticed the surprised look of his companion.

A thin, strikingly sharp sound of a small silver bell came from where the throne of the Black Goat stood. The witches immediately grew quiet and, placing their hands on their stomachs, stood rooted to the spot with a prayerful look. A toad, sitting on the shoulder of one of them, did the same. A fat, grey-haired, and gloomy fellow of some rank, either a sorcerer or a warlock in a black cassock, passed near the tables, quickly approached the idiot girl-changeling, and hit her with a stick. With a stupid grin, the girl said a foul word to the old man and quickly hid under the table. The dog, who also got hit, yelped and, with his tail between his legs, followed the idiot girl. . . .

In the midst of the ensuing stillness, the loudest words of Black Goat's sermon came through clearly, drowning out the excited whispering of the sorceresses which resembled the croaking of frogs in spring.

"Bring harm! . . Let them go hungry and grumble . . . Don't spare your efforts . . . Look after each other . . . Hide from other people . . . I'll reward you secretly . . . Wreak vengeance, wreak vengeance, wreak vengeance!" the Master of the celebration said, finally ending his short but powerful speech.

When she noticed the familiar, rosy face and ungainly figure of Styopka in the distance, Aniska started to worry, and it was only

---

5. changeling (подмёныш, from the verb подменять, meaning "to exchange or substitute something secretly"): an ugly, stupid, or strange child believed to have been left by the devils in place of a pretty, normal child.

when Styopka sat down that the young witch took a place at another table, as far away from her rival as possible.

"I don't like either carrion or human flesh," she quietly turned to the Serpent. "When I eat them, my stomach aches every time. What could I eat here so that I don't feel bad later?"

"If you have a weak stomach, which I didn't notice earlier," he answered, "eat and drink dairy stuff. Best of all, cheese or milk fresh from the cow. You can also try potatoes, and when it comes to drinking, drink only vodka."

"And where did such beautiful pink meat come from?" Aniska asked.

"From different places. There's even some from the cemetery," the Serpent whispered quietly in her ear.

He himself was fearlessly devouring fatback, and sausage, and shredded meat with cabbage, and bread, all of which disappeared in large chunks into his wide maw with numerous sharp teeth.

"From the cemetery?! That means that my silk skirt, which you brought me, is from there too," thought Aniska. "Should I drink out of grief?" And she reached for a large decanter made of thick, cloudy-green glass.

Although the homebrew was poorly filtered and not even that strong, it tasted as if something intoxicating had been added to it.

The Serpent was attentively pouring her cup after cup.

Thanks to the bright light of the bonfires, Aniska could examine this small cup of fine porcelain with a broken handle and a barely noticeable crack inside. Outside, on the smooth greenish surface, there was a winding, intricate, dark design.

"Where's this cup from? Probably from the manor house?" Aniska asked.

"A little girl brought it to the Master not long ago when she was paying her respects," answered the Fiery Serpent, apparently rather well-informed about household matters.

The witch looked down the long rows of standing tables. Among the witch-like faces of the village women, who predominated in number, donkey, wolf, dog, and bear snouts could be seen here and there, chomping and eating quickly—at times without the help of hands—from the plates and dishes they had drawn closer to themselves. Very few of those present used forks. Forks could not be seen anywhere, partly so that the guests, when they quarreled, would not cut each other up, and partly so that a knife would not accidentally form a cross with a fork.

Little by little the plates and dishes on the long tables covered with coarse, home-woven tablecloths were emptied. The pitcher and almost all the bottles were drained dry as well. The good and drunk unclean spirits and the drunken women were shouting loudly, arguing, screeching, and bawling out songs. Some were settling old scores with each other. Two witches even got into a fight because of someone's long-dead cow. One of these women, whose head was crowned with a wooden milk pail, let the other have it with a ringing slap.

The insulted one grabbed the milk pail—which had almost fallen to the ground—by the handle and hit her enemy on her half-bald, gray head. The one who received the blow managed to grab a fork and attempted to stab her opponent in the neck, but she missed and hit her on the shoulder on which a large, gray-brown toad was sitting. The stabbed reptile began to croak strangely. The witch who had been hit with the milk pail let forth a stream of blasphemous profanities in a loud voice, and the possessor of the toad, apparently also grazed by the fork, quickly donned the milk pail and ran off somewhere, squealing like a pig. After breaking up the gathered crowd, a being with a mug that half-resembled a horse got up on the table and, making stomping sounds with hoof-shaped boots and laughing in a way that resembled neighing, began to dance among the empty glasses and dishes.

Aniska finished her cup and felt completely drunk. It seemed to her that she was either rising upwards or that the table with the remains of the banquet was moving underground. In an instant the bench also disappeared somewhere, and Aniska would surely have fallen if the idiot girl-changeling, who chanced to run out on all fours from under the descending table, had not turned up beneath her. The girl, trying to scramble out and free herself, bit Aniska in the leg. The witch let the girl crawl out from underneath her and then, staggering along the uneven, seemingly rippling ground, walked away.

The place of the recent banquet was now an empty and level area where sorceresses, young and old, were getting ready with the same degree of fervor to throw themselves into dance.

At a signal given by Black Goat, the tambourine, made out of the skin of someone who had hung himself, began to thunder again; little swamp demons blew on pipes crafted from the bones of the dead and made vile sounds; and musicians, who had taken to drink in the old days and had not found peace beyond the grave, loudly imitated trumpet sounds.

Black Goat opened the ball with the thin, fair-haired witch with the manor-house hairdo, just as Aniska had assumed he would. The witch's shining, wide-open eyes were completely motionless, as if she did not see anyone or anything around her. Following them with incredible lightness, a raggedy old woman began to circle alone, shaking a broom on a long bent stick which she had grabbed. A young red-haired witch, slapping the back of her heels, began to jump and squeal alone as well. The unclean spirits, shouting and howling, began to circle around them in dance, mixing in with the witches. Some of the witches, including Aniska, broke through the demonic circle and danced in pairs. It seemed to the young witch that she was flying in the air in the strong embrace of the Serpent. . . . Someone she had knocked down grabbed her by both legs and tried to take her and run away, and someone else scratched her painfully on her behind. Aniska kicked someone, laughed from being tickled, and screamed with all her might.

Finally, the suitor dressed in the red *kuntush* pulled his girlfriend out of the crowd and sat her on his shoulders. From above, Aniska was able to see for a moment that a sizeable part of those who had been dancing were now intertwined in the most diverse and surprising combinations, some on the ground, and some as they continued to move and even dance. At that moment, the Serpent, performing an intricate dance which forced others to marvel at his nimbleness, tripped over something or someone, and Aniska and he fell down again into the pile of the unclean spirits, who were howling and panting as they wallowed in the witches' embraces. She felt again that she was being bitten, massaged, licked, and pinched; that they were breathing raw vodka and awful, stinking smells on her. This continued until the Fiery Serpent, who tore himself free of the clinging sorceresses, got to his feet and again extricated his girlfriend from the crowd. Grabbing her in his arms, the Serpent ran to a pile of rocks where the witches' brooms stood. Furious that the unclean spirit in the red *kuntush* was avoiding them, the crowd of witches chased after him and Aniska with howls and threats. Such a solid and strong male—by the looks of him—as the Fiery Serpent represented an enviable enticement for the women grown mad with lust, who were already tired of the half-sleepy affections of the living dead and all the petty spirits of the forest and the swamp.

"Get on your broomstick and fly with all your might! Otherwise they'll either torture us or tear us both to pieces," the Serpent more hissed than said hoarsely in a faltering, alarmed voice; he ran, wrapping himself in his *kuntush,* which had been ripped to shreds and now exposed his dark, scaly body.

Spotting her stove fork and broom, knocked down to the ground by someone, with pieces of string still on them, Aniska mounted and whispered the secret word. In an instant she soared up into the upper regions and again felt the air sounding in her ears as she cut through it.

After she caught the sound of the wild cries following her in pursuit, Aniska turned around and looked down at the earth below. There, down by the bonfires, a pile of triumphant witches who had managed to catch the Serpent in the red *kuntush* was swarming. . . . You could see that this time Aniska's friend would not be able to free himself from their grasp. His pitiful pleas, hisses, and cries mixed with the swearing and threats of the voluptuous and vengeful sorceresses, young and old.

The way back seemed much shorter to Aniska. The stove fork and broom, which had been generously greased with the magic ointment, knew the road well and moved swiftly in the direction of Zaretskoye.

With her head down and holding onto the rusty stove fork with her weakening hands, the sorceress dove into the stovepipe and more fell than crawled off the stove's raised portion onto the floor. As she did this, Aniska hit the back of her head rather badly and, partly from pain, partly from weakness, she again lost consciousness.

The naked witch came to on the wooden floor of her hut with a head heavy as lead, shivering from the cold. The stove fork with the attached broom and pieces of string lay under her. Her body was covered with soot and marks from the pinches she had received; a large scratch smarted on her behind. Her stomach, back, and chest ached as if she had been beaten. Aniska's whole being was enveloped in incredible weariness.

All day long she worked either on getting rid of her hangover or moistening the scratch on her behind with a concoction of healing herbs. A woman came to have her fortune told, and the witch promised her so many blows from her husband, sicknesses in the home, and other unpleasant things that the woman stopped visiting her from that time on.

XV

Having established that he had a rival—and a rival with whom it was not only shameful (that was the least of it) but also dangerous for a baptized man to meet and, what is even more, have something in common—Maksim decided to break up with Aniska. An opportune moment arrived unexpectedly. The youth inherited from his childless uncle, who had died suddenly, five plots of land which, with his own two-and-a-half, gave him the possibility of becoming a well-to-do man. In order to start his own independent household, the young and single man lacked only a strong and healthy wife.

Maksim sorted through all the village girls in his mind, one after another.

"The most strapping, of course, is Parakha. Her fists—now they're something! Don't get caught by her when she's angry and ready to fight, and particularly if you've been drinking. But, on the other hand, she works like a sturdy mare. Akulina is strong, too. Once she landed such a blow on Antipka's mug that he walked around with a black eye for two weeks. . . . And her personality would probably be a bit more lively than Parakha's. . . . Only there are many poor relatives. And who needs to have brothers and sisters come a-begging? We suffer losses because of the wife's family, but we have to welcome them, that is, pay the honor that is their due. . . . Parashka, therefore, would probably be the more reasonable choice. Her father (a rich *katsap*[1]) has more than ten plots. While he's also cheap, if you haggle with him well, then you can certainly wrest a plot or two from him in dowry."

---

1. *katsap (кацап)*: a jocular as well as pejorative term for a Russian.

Maksim decided to ask for Parakha in marriage.

There was no refusal on the part of Parakha's parents to the owner of seven-and-a-half plots of land—a red-haired fellow dressed like a dandy, his hair even greased—when he came to talk about marriage and brought a cottage loaf of rye bread and several bottles of vodka with him. Parakha, who had been of marriageable age for some time now, agreed as well after some thought, demanding only that the groom break off his connection with Aniska.

Maksim gave this promise and the following day went to see the black-haired witch for the last time and have a talk with her.

With some anxiety he crossed the threshold of the cottage which was as familiar to him as his own and, with feelings of both sadness and worry, he glanced at Aniska, who now seemed totally alien to him.

Aniska, standing by a table covered with healing and magical herbs she was sorting when Maksim entered, began to listen to him with outward indifference.

Maksim, after saying that he had witnessed the Fiery Serpent visiting Aniska, announced that he no longer wanted to meet with her and compete with him and, for this reason, would no longer come to her cottage.

"I don't want to be the brother-in-law of all kinds of demonic reptiles," he proudly finished his emotional speech.

"And who told you why the one you've mentioned visited me?" asked the witch, severely knitting her thick, black brows which almost came together. "If you spied on us and eavesdropped, then of course you don't have long to live," Aniska said through her teeth calmly and ominously.

"When it comes to how you entertained and comforted him, that I didn't see. But then, there's no need to see. Everyone knows why fiery serpents and all kinds of unclean spirits visit witches," Maksim answered without losing his composure.

"Well, and if you didn't see who came to visit me and why, then be quiet while you're still alive! . . . But no, you go on, 'I don't want to be the brother-in-law! . .' Do you think I really need you, you scoundrel with the greased hair?! And because you spied and roamed outside my cottage when I forbade you to do it, I'm kicking you out myself! And I'd also like to add: You won't be able to marry any Parashka. And if you do marry, nothing will come of your wedding! Do you hear me? Now get out of here before I turn you into a mangy dog," Aniska shouted angrily, waving her wooden walking-stick at her former beloved.

The youth did not wait long and dashed out of the hut.

He understood that with his loose tongue he had earned himself a dangerous enemy in the person of his former girlfriend.

"I should've said to her I'm afraid of this Serpent. But I started to get a swelled head and called him a reptile. Of course she's become embittered . . . Now watch out, Maksimushka," the youth thought and worried as he walked at dusk to his little shack from which, any day now, he was getting ready to move to the spacious house he had inherited from his uncle.

Aniska did indeed take her vengeance.

When after the wedding ceremony, surrounded by friends and relatives, Maksim walked out onto the church porch with Parakha—who was smiling with her wide, full-lipped mouth—a familiar, shrill, and loud voice was heard in the crowd of fellow villagers behind a fence.

"Maksimushka!"

"What?" he responded unwillingly.

Instead of answering, Aniska hastily began to tie knots in a rope which she had brought with her; it was not very long, about a quarter of an *arshin*.

"While it's knotted, it won't straighten out," she whispered with malicious glee and, hiding the rope, disappeared into the crowd.

Maksim turned pale. Although he did not see what his former lover was doing, he understood that she had not come to his wedding to do anything good.

Confused, forgetting about his bride and muttering something under his breath, he climbed into the cart and was followed by the wide-hipped Parakha—all dressed-up—who was trying to hide her displeasure and glancing suspiciously, first at Aniska running off and then, at the faces of the girls and women standing around.

The young woman lived up to Maksim's opinion about her power. On the day after the wedding, the newlywed, who had not fully recovered from his hangover, appeared with bruises from the blows which the young bride—deceived in her expectations—bestowed on him in a surge of unsatisfied passion.

The relatives of the newlyweds found out about the unpleasant matter which befell Parasha and Maksim. After long counsel and gossip, it was decided to invite a "knowing man"[2] from a distant village. When they brought the man, he examined Maksim, tried unsuccessfully to examine Parasha at the same time, then asked for a glass of water and gazed in it for a long time, shaking his head in sympathy and distress.

"It's tied," he finally said with a far from happy look. "If you had gotten advice from me before the wedding, I would've told you: pour flax seeds into both shoes. But now this won't help . . . I'll do what I can . . . Only take care that no one tells that woman what I'm going to do . . . And that she doesn't know I was here."

Then, whispering incantations, the black-bearded "knowing man" from the distant village demanded oat and wheat straw, picked several straws that were of similar length and, after pouring a drop of mercury into each of them, sealed the ends with wax and ordered the straws to be put under the young couple's bed. In addition, the sorcerer gave Maksim a vial of a greenish liquid, several drops of which he was to take mixed in a shot of vodka every evening at supper.

"It would be best if the rope with the knots could be stolen or bought from that Aniska," he said as he was leaving. "If you manage to get it, immediately untie the knots. Then the curse will be removed even more quickly. . . . Only I'll say again: God forbid she find out I was trying to cure Maksim."

The black-bearded man was handed a ruble and a half in silver and a cottage loaf of wheat bread and, with them in hand, he departed for home.

It is not clear whether it was the liquid taken internally or the mercury-filled straws over which incantations had been uttered and then placed under the bed, but for a while the remedies prescribed by the sorcerer worked, albeit weakly.

Unfortunately, Aniska, who found out about this in some

---

2. "knowing man" *(знающий человек)*: another term for a sorcerer. See "practitioners of magic" in the appendix.

amazing way, added several new knots to her enchanted rope, and Maksim and Parasha became utterly gloomy.

They argued with each other, and the newlywed endured many unpleasantries from Parakha, who had become irritable and almost turned into a witch.

The annoyed young wife wanted to break the windows in Aniska's cottage and beat up the witch, but her relatives talked her out of it.

"What if that bitch does something even worse?" the women warned in a whisper.

~

His former friends kept laughing at Maksim, jokingly offering to take his place in his marital duties. Parakha openly despised her husband, upon whom this unpleasantness had been visited. The unhappy youth turned to her namesake,[3] the old sorceress Praskukha. She gave him herbs and a powder, but those remedies worked poorly. Maksim grew sad and began to chase away his grief with vodka. Sometimes Gorpina, sometimes Aniska appeared in his drunken, delirium-filled dreams. One beckoned to the lover who had abandoned her, and the other chased him, threatening to suck out all his blood because he had dared to look in the window when the Fiery Serpent came to visit her through the stovepipe.

Maksim's feverish deliriums, in which he mentioned blood being drunk, cows being milked, and the unclean force appearing, so frightened his young wife that she did not want to be alone with him. The sleepy chatter of her husband about his former relations with Aniska and Gorpina also affected her for the worse.

The image of Gorpina often beckoned to him, promising forgiveness and new affection. The phantom of the drowned girl tried to persuade Maksim to abandon his earthly human life and be with her where there was no need to work by the sweat of one's brow or worry about paying taxes and harvesting crops. In comparison with the gloomily scowling and unhappy face of Parakha, the features of his former lover appearing to him in

---

3. Parakha and Praskukha are derived from Paraskoviya (Параско́вья), which has the variant Praskoviya (Праско́вья)).

dreams were so pleasant and comforting that Maksim got used to her and was even unhappy after nights when he did not dream of Gorpina.

This did not interfere, however, with the young peasant slowly getting used to the many tasks and hard work involved in being an independent homeowner. He would come home toward evening tired and, after exchanging a few matter-of-fact remarks with his wife, collapse into sleep immediately after supper.

One night Maksim woke up, thinking he heard someone drumming quietly on the window. At first he thought it was rain, but the sound had a somewhat different quality, and the man of the house got out of bed alarmed. It was quiet in the hut. The even breathing of Parakha, who slept separately, could be heard from an adjoining bench, and the snoring of Maksim's aunt, Akulina—who had been taken on to help with the household—reached him from the stove.[4] A stream of moonlight was pouring through the bare window and stretching in a long streak along the floor. Someone was standing outside, behind the window. Strictly speaking, Maksim already knew who, but seemingly wanting to check, he got up from his hay mattress and walked up to the window. Yes, indeed, one and a half steps away from him, Gorpina was standing frozen—motionless like a statue—and looking into the hut. When the strange look of her glassy eyes met the glance of her former beloved, the chalk-white face of the girl's phantom seemed to come alive and her lips began to move silently. Although no words could be heard, Maksim felt the meaning of this soundless, and yet compellingly appealing speech with his whole being. Throwing the heavy cloth coat—which he used to cover himself at night—on his shoulders, the young master of the house quietly opened the door, walked out into the hallway, and from there out into the yard.

"Why have you come?" he asked in a quiet, suppressed whisper.

"For you," was the dour answer.

"Where am I to go?"

"Wherever you want . . . even into that shed. Leave your cloak and your body for your fat wife there, and then, light and

---

4. The Russian stove, a great mass of clay or brick, had a place on top for sleeping.

unburdened, go off with me. I have no one to play with, and the others laugh that I'm constantly alone. I've forgiven you and don't want to part with you again. Come fly away with me!"

And Gorpina, stepping toward the half-open gate of the hay shed, beckoned for Maksim to follow her.

"My dear one," the phantom whispered to him affectionately. "There's a rope here with a noose on the end, a strong rope. . . . You carry hay to the horses with it. Tie it to the beam and let the long noose hang down. Hang your body and leave in this noose. Then I'll kiss you, caress you, and we'll fly away from here forever. And Parashka won't have anyone to push around anymore."

Maksim silently and obediently did all that the lover who had come after him asked. Throwing off his heavy cotton coat, he made a loop at one end of the rope, the other end he tied securely to the "legera"[5]—a rafter that stretched between the opposite walls of the shed under the roof. Then standing on a rung of the ladder that he had put in place, he—the lost soul—put his neck in the noose and glanced at Gorpina. She walked up very close to him and with her wide-open eyes looked at Maksim tenderly and waited, a smile on her face.

The youth smiled in turn with a perplexed look and, after a short period of hesitation, pushed the ladder away with his feet and jumped. The hands and feet of the suicide victim began to move and jerk. . . .

The noose was squeezing Maksim's neck painfully, like a piece of iron, and breaking it; there was a red fog in his eyes, and his hands and feet jerked convulsively as if he were swimming in that fog. Gorpina's face disappeared, and only her once familiar, now almost forgotten laughter rang in the ears of the man swinging in the noose. The red fog kept getting darker and Maksim, trying in vain to find Gorpina in it, was hanging by the rope and making circles that seemed large to him. . . . In fact, these circles were becoming smaller and smaller. The rope, little by little, stopped swinging, and the man hanging from it no longer moved.

In the morning Parakha and Akulina noticed Maksim's absence in the cottage. Sensing something ill, they both headed out to search immediately. They did not have to search for long.

---

5. Kondratiev inserts this dialectal term in quotation marks and then uses the more common бревно, or "rafter" in English, to explain its meaning.

Walking into the half-open shed, the women stopped, rooted to the ground.

Maksim was hanging without moving, dressed only in his underwear, from the rope which was used for carrying hay to the cattle. On the face of the man who had hanged himself was a frozen expression of surprise and fear.

Wailing loudly, both women ran out of the shed into the yard.

XVI

"Where could that Ankudinych have disappeared to?" the Vodyanoi asked his wise oak friend at times, unhappy with
Ankudinych's replacement, Towhead.

"You, it seems, were getting ready to feed him to the sheat-
fish," the idol answered dispassionately. "Your servant probably
preferred to arrange his fate somewhat differently. . . . You gave
him, I seem to remember, an assignment?"

"That's true, I did . . . to bring me a she-demon from the
swamp."

"Well, then look for him there . . . if, of course, you can make it
there," the idol added with some doubt in his voice.

"And do you really think I'm afraid to go there or that I won't
make it?" the Vodyanoi retorted, his anger aroused by the lack of
faith in his strength. "I'll go tonight! At least I'll see someone and
hear intelligent conversation."

Evening had barely come when the master of the river bottom,
turning into a grey drake, swam upstream, following a brook which
flowed into the Yaryn. The lord of the Yaryn knew very well that
this brook flowed from a forest lake overgrown with moss, where
his second cousin on his mother's side, the horned Bolotnik,
lived.

He made the firm decision that after he reminded the Bolotnik
of their kinship, he would ask in marriage one of the beauties
subject to the master of the bog.

Quacking from the anticipated pleasure, the Vodyanoi—who
had transformed himself into a drake—swam on, paddling with
his black feet, swimming past motionless pine and fir trees
whose tops had disappeared in the pale-dark gloom.

The evening stars were reflected in the brook babbling through the exposed roots of the trees. A slightly late woodcock, preparing to alight in the foggy meadow, flew low over the Vodyanoi's drake head. Some animals were making noise, squeaking in the bushes along the banks. A timid hare, hearing something rustling in last year's reeds, pricked up his ears and, smelling the spring air, rose up on his hind legs. After noticing that it was only a drake and there was no reason to worry, the hare settled back again on all four legs and, ignoring the bird, began to drink the cold water that rushed past.

"It's good it's not a fox. It would probably bite through my neck in an instant before I could explain its mistake or assume my former appearance. I'm afraid some big animal will grab me . . . The brook is narrow . . . I'd better shuffle on with my own legs."

Diving into the water and turning three somersaults, the cautious lord of the Yaryn instantly assumed his usual appearance of a bald, fat old man on frog legs.

"Of course, to walk around like this is also not without danger. An ancient *vodyanitsa*[1] lived here once, in the brook. And the local *leshi*es so annoyed the old woman with their pestering, mockery, and insults that she got tired of living here and went who knows where. . . . Well, it isn't that easy to offend the tsar of the Yaryn," the Vodyanoi decided.

Up to his knees and, at times, up to his waist and even deeper in the brook, he ambled with a sure step until he reached the swamp where the brook originated.

Since the brook's bed was packed in places with moss-covered snags and had become overgrown with osier bushes, the Vodyanoi finally chose to walk along the bank, which was becoming more and more boggy.

The moss rug bent under his steps and swayed in rolling waves. The round holes of the openings, in which the stars of the night were reflected, loomed dark in places among the tussocks.

But these openings, judging by the untouched, untrampled look of their edges, did not serve as entrances into the Bolotnik's dwelling. There were no more trees visible anywhere, and it was empty and quiet in the middle of the bog, covered with last year's dry sedge, creeping bushes, and moss.

The Vodyanoi tried to recall in what part of the swamp he had

---

1. *vodyanitsa (водяница):* feminine form of *vodyanoi.*

last visited his relative many years ago, but the area had changed so much that it was difficult to figure anything out.

A squeal that resounded not far off forced old man Vodyanoi to turn around and take a good look at a dark thicket of low, dark bushes. Two beings ran out of there, the somewhat bigger one chasing the smaller one, whose piercing squeals were either from pain or fear.

The Vodyanoi's experienced eye immediately recognized these two beings, still without horns or claws, as typical young members of the swamp-demon tribe. The smaller of the two demons rushed by and hid among the tussocks in last year's grass, but the pursuing demon, the one of larger proportions, ran into the stranger standing motionless. The young *lozovik* got so frightened at the sight of the stranger that he became rooted to the spot for a moment, and the lord of the Yaryn took advantage of this and grabbed him.

Squeaking hoarsely and kicking, the little demon first threatened with the wrath of Grandad Bolotnik, then begged pitifully to be released, and was very surprised when the Vodyanoi promised to let him go as soon as he showed him his master's dwelling.

"It's not far. There, beyond those whortle-berry bushes, which I jumped out of, are low-lying pine trees . . . not very dense. Don't be afraid, dear uncle, you can get through. And behind them is again a bog with a small lake in the middle. . . . The entrance is not from the lake but more towards the edge, not far from the forest." The little demon, who had become somewhat calmer, showed the way, and the Vodyanoi, who kept holding him in his arms, moved quickly but not without dignity, along the mossy swamp.

A swamp she-demon who appeared near one of the openings began to motion with her finger to the guest from the Yaryn, but when he came nearer and the bog charmer verified that beside her stood the same kind of unclean spirit as she, the swamp maiden spat from vexation and quickly dove into the thick, black water.

"What did she get so angry about?" the Vodyanoi asked.

"She, dear uncle, wanted to have a little fun with a living man in secret from our master. Not so as to drown him, but to let him go, so that in the future he could visit her. . . . Oh, how you have to watch our girls!" the little demon began to explain to the guest from the Yaryn.

"And why aren't you watching?"

"We do watch. But can you really keep an eye on them?! They can cover their tracks more cunningly than any fox."

Talking this way, the Vodyanoi and his escort made their way almost to the Bolotnik's dwelling. The little demons who met them, a bit older with little horns already showing through, squatted respectfully, gave their guest "the fig," and politely made way for him.

"Here, grandpa," they showed him the entrance into which the lord of the Yaryn wasted no time in sinking, after first letting the escorting little demon go.

In the pale shimmering produced by pieces of rotten wood that had been worked into the walls and the refraction of the moonbeams in the swamp water, the Bolotnik—warned about the arrival of his guest—sat in state on a snag that had been gnawed evenly by his small demons. When he saw that it was not just anybody, but his relative who had come and, what's more, one of the honored and distinguished ones with whom he had never had to settle any scores or unpleasant business, the Bolotnik joyfully opened his frog mouth, got up from the snag, and moved toward the guest from the Yaryn. The relatives greeted each other with "the fig," which was not a very easy thing for the Vodyanoi's fingers, since they were webbed; then they slapped each other's large stomachs and found out who ate what that day. Then the horned Bolotnik with the yellow mug seated his guest next to him and asked about the infant that he had once sent through the *utoplennik* Ankudinych as a gift to his cousin.

"What infant? . . I did send, at some point, this Ankudinych to you, but he didn't come back. I even thought, brother, that you kept my servant for yourself. . . ."

"What do I need your *utoplennik* for? I have about twenty of my own in a neighboring lake. He did ask me to take him on, but I didn't let him stay and instead sent him to you with a gift. Let my brother's wives, I said, amuse themselves."

"He didn't come back to me. He probably fell into the Leshy's clutches on the way back. Now they've become so angry, and those bearded things have multiplied so! They say that a number of them live near your lake."

"It's not that they've multiplied so much; the forests around here bring them together. And so they crowd together more tightly in one place," the Bolotnik explained.

"I don't know the reason, but where there were one or two of them earlier, now there are five or six. Day and night they roam along the banks, searching for *rusalkas*. They'd love to grab one and drag her off into the forest! . . ."

"And I have almost the same situation. A little demon wanders off just a little farther than usual and the *leshies* invariably choke it. Oh, and what enthusiasts they are for the *bolotnitsas*. Their females are so awful, all covered in fur, and that's why they have taken a fancy to my wives, daughters, and nieces (the Bolotnik did not want to admit that he had many generations of descendants). They lie for hours on end in the willow bushes, those accursed things. They breathe heavily and noisily, with their tongues hanging out, like dogs. Or they neigh like horses and cackle and whistle. And they whistle so much that the leaves fall off trees."

"You, my dear brother, should drag one or two into the lake."

"How can I do that?! I'm afraid he'll butt me with his horns and rip my stomach apart. It doesn't take long to get in trouble! . . ."

"I almost dragged one into the river last summer. He tried to catch my *rusalkas* and ran a little too close to the water. And so I grabbed him by his leg. The bearded fellow fell down, started to grab the bushes, and I, of course, kept pulling him. He would've been totally mine, but his accursed Leshachikha came running with her bear and started to pull him away. I saw that things were not turning out well, so I let the rascal go. Now he doesn't even dare come close to the river."

"I've come to you on business, dear brother," the Vodyanoi added unexpectedly, surprising even himself.

"What business?" inquired the master of the swamp and reeds, worried.

"I want to have some memory of you, and so I've decided to ask you to give me one of your daughters in marriage or, let's say, one of your nieces, as you yourself call them. I would keep her as my chief mistress. . . ."

"But don't you have your *rusalkas* for that, dear brother?"

"Oh, those *rusalkas*! You know yourself our drowned maidens. At first she sulks and howls, walks around frowning and grumbling about something, and the longer she stays, the less substance her body she has. You've just gotten used to her, and then you look and there's almost nothing left of her. Only vapor,

you might say . . . There's no sweetness to them, those *rusalka*s
. . . Let me at least marry a niece of yours, brother!"

The Bolotnik frowned and lowered his eyes as if examining
whether the reed matting was lying evenly on the floor. He did
not like the request of his importunate relative. But suddenly he
remembered Maryska, with whom he was again unhappy.

Marten-Soul, in due course, had found out somewhere about
her rival's absence from the swamp and, fearing the possibility of
new favoritism for the latter, informed the master that his former beloved had once returned from somewhere toward morning, all beaten up, and that the old she-demon had massaged the
blue marks on her sides and back with frog roe. At the time, the
swamp tsar had let this denunciation go without any consequences (the swamp females level all kinds of charges against
each other as they compete among themselves) but, nonetheless,
he took note of the information.

The thought of satisfying the demands of his fellow brother
from the Yaryn and at the same time getting rid of his disloyal
wife suddenly flashed into the head the sovereign of the bog.

Assuming, therefore, a solemn look, he stood up on his
webbed feet and said:

"For you, dear brother, there's nothing so sacred to me that
you can't have it. I'll marry you off to my favorite niece. Now
you'll see for yourself, how well-filled-out . . ."

And turning to the little demons sitting along the wall,
scratching and tickling each other on the sly, he shouted, "Hey,
you! Bring Fat Maryska here immediately!"

The hairless beings, who looked somewhat like a cross
between a frog and a cat, ran to fulfill his command.

Soon the one they were talking about appeared, decorated with
a wreath of yellow water-lilies and wearing a belt of long stalks
and dark, round, glossy leaves from swamp plants.

Maryska first looked at the Vodyanoi, then at the Bolotnik.
Both fat-bellied old men seemed equally repulsive to her and
even somewhat similar to each other. The master of the bog had
a more yellow face and a darker and dirtier body, while the Vodyanoi had a lighter face and was fatter and hornless, with webbing between the fingers not only on his hind but also on his
front paws. The Bolotnik's fingers, just like Maryska's, were
human—with short, sharp fingernails.

Catching a water insect in his short, thin beard, he squashed it loudly with one of his nails, then puffed himself up as if he were trying to impart even more importance to himself. His frog goggle-eyes were filled with solemn majesty.

"Maryska," he began, "being tied by old friendship and blood kinship to the river-bottom sovereign of the Yaryn, I give you to him to be his wife in order to strengthen this kinship even more and to seal our friendship. Be loyal and obey him. Caress and entertain your new master just as you would caress and entertain me if you had stayed here."

Maryska bowed low, both to her old lord as well as to her new.

Then the Bolotnik started to praise the merits of the *bolotnitsa* he was giving in marriage, and the Vodyanoi listened happily to him, squinting his round fish-like eyes at his future spouse.

"Do you like her?" the sovereign of the bog finally asked his guest.

"She looks good. She's also resilient to the touch . . . Well-filled-out . . . And as for the rest, I'll find out later," the lord of the Yaryn answered.

"If you want to celebrate your marriage here, take care to send a few baskets of large and small fish here and . . . what do you call them? They say they pinch painfully with their hard paws and whiskers. . . ."

"You mean crayfish? Fine! There'll be crayfish. . . . Only I'm thinking of celebrating the wedding in the river where I invite you to come, too, dear brother, with all your wives, nieces, and daughters. Let my bride go with me now so that she can help with the preparations for the wedding feast. There'll be no moon at all in four nights. The road will be safe, therefore, for you."

The Bolotnik agreed to let Maryska go immediately (with this he particularly wanted to please Marten-Soul), and the fat she-demon departed for the Yaryn that same night with her betrothed, accompanied by several of the older little swamp demons.

Following the same brook without stumbling upon anyone and without even changing into birds or frogs, they safely reached the river into which they descended exactly at the moment when the predawn fog, which had enveloped the river banks, was beginning to thin.

The five little demons who had been accompanying them to the Yaryn started to run back to the swamp. In the forest, they came across Green-Goat, who ran after them, but he could not catch any of them. Two were forced to return to the Yaryn, to Maryska, however, and three reached the bog safely.

XVII

When at the appointed time the Bolotnik, accompanied by his seven or eight nieces and wives—young and old—and a dozen older little demons, appeared at the designated place by the river, no one met the honored guest; no one even glanced out of the water or the bushes along the riverbank. For some reason the Bolotnik was afraid to go into the river without an escort and, after unsuccessfully quacking and making calls to the Vodyanoi, he finally decided to try to summon at least Maryska.

However, she did not appear for a long time in reply to his call, and only in response to the familiar sound of a strong hand slapping the water's surface did she finally show her sleepy, unhappy face on the surface.

"What d'you want?" she asked angrily, as if she did not recognize her former master and head of the household.

"What do you mean what do I want?! We've come for your wedding."

"We've celebrated it already! I gave that fat-bellied bald-head so many injuries that ever since he ran away yesterday, he hasn't come back. . . . Was there a lot to laugh about! He jumped out onto the riverbank but was afraid to run into the forest. Well, so he took off down the river. He kept running along the river bank until he disappeared from view. . . . Have no fear, he won't be back! . . ."

"If that's the case, then let's go back to the bog together," the Bolotnik proposed.

"Beat it! Go into the bog yourselves! I'm fine in the river. I'm now fully in charge. If you want to, come here. I give you my word, I won't touch you. I only scratched my old man here and there, but you . . . all right . . . I won't hurt you. . . . Don't want to?

Well, as you wish. . . . Leave me a pair of your little demons so that I won't be so bored," Maryska concluded, seeing that her frowning, former master and his retinue were getting ready to go home.

The master of the bog did not give her any little demons, and grumbling unhappily, shuffled off through the wet-meadow along the river. The she-demons, whispering among themselves and glancing back at the river with envy, followed their lord. They still had to face the difficult and dangerous passage to their native bog. The Bolotnik, who was walking in front, glanced back now and then, not permitting his little demons to fall behind. He was not sure that, after finding out about Maryska's free and easy life in the pool of the river freed from its master, they wouldn't run there themselves of their own free will.

In the always tranquil, silty river pool and in the adjoining river-bottom areas of the full-flowing Yaryn, the change in power occurred under the following circumstances. Disappointed in the old Vodyanoi as her spouse, Maryska wanted to console herself with the joys of motherhood and, through two little demons who had returned and stayed with her in the Yaryn, she began to make detailed inquiries about the black-bearded *utoplennik*, An-kudinych, and about the infant he was supposed to bring on the night he disappeared. Time and again, she whispered with these little demons and sent them on errands in various directions.

The new servants of the new wife took their example from their mistress and were inclined to recognize only her. The lord of the Yaryn, used to the slavish submission of his *utoplen-niks* and *rusalkas*, did not like such independence, which could be a bad example for the other inhabitants of the river bottom. Unhappy with the fact that one of the little demons had not bowed low enough before him, the Vodyanoi gave the unfortunate one such a slap in the face that the small, little *lozovik* fell and could not get up on his little hind legs for a long time.

Maryska took advantage of the small demon's punishment and used it as a pretext to pour out all the bile that had accumulated in her heart.

"Don't you dare touch my servants, you fat-bellied frog of a man!" she shrieked. "They're not your *utoplenniks*! Why those goggle-eyes, you old freak? . . . You frog mouth! No need to make scary faces! I'm not afraid!" the she-demon continued, pouncing on the Vodyanoi.

The Vodyanoi, panting in a threatening way, bared his pike teeth and wanted to grab Maryska's splendid, black braids with his strong, webbed fingers.

But she warned her spouse and, shrieking again and clearly reaching for his goggle-eyes, dug her sharp claws into his swollen mug, which immediately lost its threatening look. The Vodyanoi managed to wrest one of her hands from his torn nostrils, but that was not the end of it: her demon claws slipped down his stomach so that his entrails almost spilled out. The second hand followed the first, scratching and seizing everything that could be seized.

The sharp claws of the swamp beauty made such strong and cruel welts in various places on the fat body of the river-bottom master that he, forgetting himself from the pain, jumped out of the river and ran along the river bank for a long time, not daring to go down into the waters which earlier had belonged to him completely. Only when it had become almost totally light did he plop into the fresh water which pleasantly cooled his body, hot from the run. There, the exile rested on the silty bottom under a high, steep bank. The yellow-green murk, in which particles of sunlit dust quavered and glimmered along the river bottom, soothed and refreshed his bulging eyes.

At this point he understood that to return meant to doom himself to the constant torment of anxiety and humiliation. The Vodyanoi decided, therefore, not to return but move as far away as possible downstream on the Yaryn, settle somewhere near a deserted mill, and hide there until his wound—an offense to his dignity—had healed. *Utoplenniks* and *rusalkas* can be found everywhere, and the old man counted on his being able to acquire a new household and wives. The Vodyanoi was sad only at the thought that he was now deprived of such a loyal friend and conversation companion as the wooden idol of Perun, who shared winter boredom with him and patiently endured the bad moods of the lord of the Yaryn.

The old Vodyanoi did not know that the treacherous she-demon who had disfigured him not only had declared herself mistress and made all the local *utoplenniks* and *rusalkas* subject to her power, but had even encroached upon the tranquility of his oak friend. Discovering that he once had been a god, Maryska ordered the wooden idol, half-covered by silt, to be dug up. Then rendering the homage due the idol, the she-demon proclaimed the idol of Perun to be her husband and the new lord of the Yaryn.

And he, who in the past drove about and rumbled among the dark storm clouds in his chariot flashing blue flames and hurled scorching arrows at frightened demons, he who used to embrace heavenly goddesses with his powerful arms, now became an unwilling plaything of the swamp she-demon, who forced him to be her spouse.

Maryska adapted rather quickly to her new position as the sovereign of the Yaryn. As for the *rusalka*s, none had any pretensions to such high office, and thus there were no rivals in this respect. The new mistress established fear and respect in the *utoplennik*s with her animal claws. They all saw that the Vodyanoi himself had run away from the angry she-demon. Maryska gave her orders mostly through her loyal, little swamp demons in the name of the wooden god whose wife she had proclaimed herself to be. In full view of all the inhabitants of the river bottom, she would embrace the wooden body of the idol, press close to the old man, and whisper in his ear (so that all could hear) words filled with the most demonic passion. And sometimes she would bring her ear close to the idol's lips—which had been decorated once with gold whiskers—as if she were listening to his soundless speech, and then immediately she would pass on the instructions of the new lord of the Yaryn to her frightened subjects.

But this was only for the benefit of the dependent folk, the *utoplennik*s and the *rusalka*s who were subject to her.

In her real and unfeigned dealings with her new husband, Maryska had entirely different discussions with him.

The she-demon was unhappy that the idol, who had been deprived of his gold mustache and the precious stones around his waist and uncomplainingly accepted the affections of his wife, not only did not return his wife's affections but had no desire—or was not able—to give (if only for the benefit of the river-bottom population) however small a sign that he was not simply an indecent and motionless dolt, skillfully crafted from large and small pieces of petrified wood, but that he had something resembling a life and could at times even demonstrate its existence. That the idol had thoughts, moods, feelings, and a double or shadow, Maryska knew from her first hour of married life with him. For this reason she kept pestering her silent husband day and night:

"Come out of your wooden stump and show yourself as tsar and god to the goggle-eyed crowd at least for an instant," she begged, pressing close to her spouse.

"I don't have the power to do that," he usually answered. "I have grown much too weak over the last centuries during which no one prayed to me, loved me, or brought me sacrifices."

"Don't I love you enough?" Maryska asked.

"Your love only inflames my desires, but it cannot sate them. It can't give me back the strength to move and be touchable and visible outside my wooden home. You yourself, from time to time, need the passion of living beings—people or animals. I know very well why you run out of the river at night and return only toward morning. In my mind's eye I accompany you and, knowing who you are, I can't blame you. . . . Understand that I too need, if not fully alive, then at least those bodies that have a bit of their own or someone else's life force. . . . In ancient times I used to inhale this life force in the smell of the blood of the youths sacrificed to me. Content with these sacrifices, I thundered among dark clouds, cleaved them with blue-white lightning, and my abundant seed, spilling with the spring rain, made the insatiable Earth fruitful. Acquire some life force for me so that I can again become bold and mighty."

"Even now your oak limbs are inexhaustibly strong, but since you need it, from now on I will share with you the life force that I accumulate on the river banks," Maryska promised. "Henceforth, I'll try to accumulate this force from people and animals for us both."

And now in the form of a cat, or a dog, or a bathing woman, Maryska started to disappear more and more frequently during the night. . . .

～

Thanks to the efforts of his spouse and she-demon, so much life force gradually accumulated in the idol that on one stormy night he was able to separate his double, which glowed with a steel-blue luster, from himself. That double, to the consternation of the *utoplenniks*, *rusalka*s and even the tsaritsa of the river bottom, moved slowly along the river bottom and emerged on the bank where, because of the flashes of lightning and frequent peals of thunder, Maryska did not dare follow. In his lightly glowing semi-transparent attire, decorated with closely-set feathers, the double of the wooden god stood on the dam and, with his once powerful arms crossed on his chest, attentively watched purplish flashes cleaving the black, stormy sky. The face of the divine ghost changed strangely. At each new flash of lightning his light, gold mustache, which had not existed on the idol for a long time, burned ever more brightly. His thick, dark, shaggy eyebrows, as if made from tarnished silver, frowned more and more menacingly. He wanted to shout in the rumbling, threatening voice that used to make the offspring of Night all a-tremble: "Who dares ride in my chariot?! Give it back to me! Give me back my palace in the clouds! Return my wives and children! Return my power over the earth, nature, and the sky! . . ."

But the weak phantom of the god who had come to life did not have a voice; he had neither power nor strength. Instead, someone else, who paid no attention whatsoever to the phantom of the forgotten deity, was thundering in the heavens and enjoying his power.

After standing for a short while in the rain and surveying the area illuminated by flashes of lightning, Perun's shadow sighed sadly and slowly descended back into the waters of the Yaryn in order to unite with the motionless body of semi-petrified oak on the silty bottom, where the unbridled, ardent caresses of his mistress, the swamp she-demon, now awaited the former lord of the heavenly expanse and the former, stately spouse of cloud-wives.

XVIII

The child found under the fir tree, about whom the sovereign of the Yaryn worried so much, eventually was taken in, first by the childless Gordeichuks and then, when about five years later both died in the same week from cholera, Maryska's little girl—who had been given the name Ksenka or Ksanka—passed into the care of her distant relative, Praskukha. Living in the Russian end of the village and more Russian than Ukrainian herself, the old woman renamed her adopted child Aksyutka and became very attached to her. While she was still very young, Aksyutka learned not only the names and properties of herbs (which the girl helped gather) from this grey-haired but still vigorous magic healer, but she also picked up so many other bits of knowledge that she was able to cast spells on burns, blood, and even toothache.

The village girls did not like the sullen "little witch child," as they called Aksyutka among themselves, and almost never invited her to play with them.

The birthmark on her hip, in the shape of a frog, which they somehow noticed during swimming, led to all kinds of mocking comments about the poor adopted girl.

"And even her feet are big, just like a frog's or duck's," the girls would say. "Her mother is a large swamp frog and her father is an *utoplennik,* or even the Swamp Grandpa himself."

The derisive questions about her parents, directed at Aksyutka by her peers, became the reason that the little girl, who was not sociable to begin with, stopped taking part in their games entirely and amused herself alone as best she knew how.

Sometimes she was seen talking with Praskukha's cat, almost as old as the magic healer herself.

The cat, we'll assume, did not say anything and only purred from time to time in answer to Aksyutka's words. The fellow villagers who saw this did not fail to explain such intimacy as the foundling's innate sorcery.

Aksyutka never questioned Grandmother Praskukha about her origins, since she was mainly interested in Praskuhka's craft as a magic healer, a craft in which Aksyutka truly showed quick progress, given her age.

Sometimes the old sorceress herself marveled at her progress.

"Who taught you that?" Praskukha asked sternly, seeing the girl beating a puddle of a questionable color with a twig during a drought so that bubbles appeared in the liquid. "Why are you doing that?"

"No one taught me. I simply want a pouring rain to come and for bubbles just like this to bounce in real water puddles in the middle of the street."

"So no one really taught you?" Praskukha persisted.

"No one," was the short answer.

"Oh, my girl, then you are truly born for this . . ."

"A born witch, you said so yourself, grandma, keeps doing only evil. But think back, who ever saw any evil coming from me? In my whole life I think I thrashed only Vanka the Lame, and even that was because he was torturing a cat! . . ."

"That's true. But nonetheless, it's strange to see all this," the old woman said, shaking her head.

"Have no doubts, grandma, there'll be no evil from me. The unclean one does torture me almost every night when I'm going to sleep and tempts me to do bad things, but I don't give in to him. He tries this and that so that I'll start to do harm. 'Put your hand,' he says, 'on the back of Tanka's red-brown cow and make a wish that the milk disappear.' But I don't give in . . . Well, and then he begins to torture me. . . ."

"And how does he torture you?"

"He says over and over inside me, 'Give me, give me your soul. All the same,' he says, 'it will be mine.' And so, my dear grandma, he pesters me as if he's unraveling my very soul like a thread into his foul clutches. . . . At such times I can't find any peace anywhere. Might as well lay hands on myself!"

Praskukha again shook her head and uttered only one thing, "That's not good!"

The girl spoke the truth when she asserted that no one had

ever seen any evil from her. She did not show any inclination to take vengeance on her peers who teased her, and she was not interested in milking cows dry, or "spoiling" cattle, or other ways of bringing harm. But on the other hand, she loved to question Praskukha about various forms of divination, the interpretation of dreams and, at times, pressured her to teach her incantations and how to summon the unclean and mysterious force.

The old woman, however, who knew something about such things, did not want to share her knowledge with the girl, either because she considered it too early for her, or simply because she herself was not terribly fond of entering into dealings with the unclean force. In her own hut, she did not allow anyone to say any charms or incantations in any form that mentioned questionable names.

"You unintentionally say some undesirable name and he, the unholy one, appears right then and there.[1] The dark force, people say, responds to its names without fail, but to get rid of it later . . . oh, that's difficult!" the old magic healer would say.

Once, when the girl, somewhat more persistently than usual, began to pester Praskukha to teach her how to deal with the unclean force, the old magic healer led Aksyutka to a small forest brook which flowed out of the swamp and, after throwing a piece of cheese over which she had whispered something in advance, ordered her ward to look carefully into the water.

"What do you see?" she asked curtly, holding the right hand of the girl over the dark surface of the water.

"Beetles, or perhaps spiders with tails, small and almost transparent, have appeared from the bottom of the brook and are tearing the cheese to pieces."

"In the same way the demons will tear your soul apart in the other world if you're going to have dealings with them in this world."

"They won't tear mine!" Aksyutka said stubbornly and with conviction.

"You all think that: they'll tear apart others, but they won't touch me. Watch out, Aksyutka, don't lead yourself into misfortune. And why do you want to meet them?"

---

1. Folk belief holds that if you invoke the name of the devil, he can materialize before you.

"I have to find out about my father and mother," the girl said matter-of-factly.

"That you have to find out in the cemetery."

"I was there already. I tried to find out. They aren't there," was the quiet answer.

"Well then, perhaps they're buried in another cemetery, or in the woods, or in the river, or by a road . . . and perhaps they're even alive," Praskukha argued.

"No, granny. My heart knows that I won't find them among the living and that I have to go to the swamp. It comes to me in dreams," Aksyutka admitted.

"Oh, so you're that fearless," the old woman could only say in reply.

"I'm not at all fearless. I just can't find the courage to go to that swamp at night. If you go there with a prayer, not a single demon will come out, but if you go without a prayer and without an incantation, then you might even not return," Aksyutka continued pensively. "Dear granny, humor me, teach me the spells so they won't be able to touch me. You probably know them and can help me. I really don't want to go to Styopka."

"Oh, my dear, where would I have learned them?! I do repeat something like a prayer in order to close them off from me when I collect herbs at night near the swamp. Those *lozoviks*, we can assume, don't dare to come close. They shout from afar, swear, and make me, an old woman, the object of their laughter, but nonetheless they don't dare come close. Even the shapeshifters don't come close. They probably know I have gentian[2] and monkshood with me, which are used to fend off the unclean spirit. . . ."

"So they can't touch you when you have gentian and monkshood?" asked Aksyutka.

"Of course they can't. If you have some gentian sown in your clothing, particularly if the gentian has been blessed in church, and a wreath of monksbood on your head, plus a handful of blessed poppy seeds in your pocket, neither devils nor vampires dare to touch you. Just don't take them off! Sometimes it happens that the unclean spirit appears as such an incredibly handsome

---

2. gentian *(тирличь)*: This plant was believed to calm the anger of those in power; it was also associated with witches' sabbaths and flying ointment (rubbed into the armpits and backs of knees, allowing the witch to fly up the chimney).

youth that you really have to get a hold of yourself! He utters words of affection and promises to marry you and only asks that you take off your wreath. And you've barely gotten the wreath off when he grabs you like a cat grabs a mouse. . . . They really have a strong liking for the girls, those beings with tails . . . . The boys, they have it easier. Some, who know what to do, walk out of the water and swamp completely dry. In my time there were even men who went into the bog to get acquainted with the swamp she-demons and got gifts from them for doing this, to boot. Now, of course, it's not like that. People have become ignorant. There aren't many of us left who have the knowledge," the old woman finished saying.

The girl took into consideration everything she had heard from Praskukha and decided to put her admonitions into practice the first good chance she got.

‿

Among the things which troubled Aksyutka's soul there was one disturbing dream which she had from time to time. In this dream, the girl saw herself sitting on a tussock in the middle of an unfamiliar swamp, with her feet lowered into the water and her hair flowing free on her bare shoulders and back. At times she combed her wet braids with a comb made out of horn, totally unlike the ones which she had in real life. But in her dream, this comb, with half of its teeth broken off, seemed strangely familiar to her. The full moon, with all its spots, seemed familiar, too, which she, in waking reality, not only was not interested in but did not even like. At times in this dream, the girl was singing and waiting for someone, looking at the flat swamp, overgrown with low, sparse pine trees. And when in the distance, among those small pines appeared the figure of a man in the moonlight, approaching with hurried step, Aksyutka's heart began to contract and beat faster. She knew that the man who was approaching, although he stopped from time to time, was nonetheless supposed to come and attempt to carry her away from the swamp. And she was not sure whether this made her happy or afraid. At the same time a desire seized the girl's sleepy soul: she wanted not only to be carried off by this man, but to enfold him tightly in her arms and drag him down to the oozy bottom of the pool in the swamp. This craving for a struggle, a craving to measure her strength against a man's, troubled Aksyutka's soul in the disturbing dream which she had from time to time.

Sometimes her dream would break off, particularly if the approaching man stopped at the edge of the swamp and Aksyutka woke up from the sound of her own singing. At times her girlish dream ended with both of them—both Aksyutka and the man who made his way to her—tightly embracing each other in a silent but sweetly horrific struggle and descending together into the dark water.

"What strange songs you sing in your troubled sleep," the old Praskukha sometimes would say to her foster daughter in the morning, "Where did you learn them?"

"What songs, grandma? I just don't remember," Aksyutka usually answered, not wanting to reveal her secret for anything. "I didn't even have any dreams."

"Oh, so you didn't have any! Tell me, you secretive one!"

"Really grandma, I didn't have any," the girl usually refused to say anything more.

Nonetheless, she made the firm decision to somehow make her way to the swamp in order to find the places that she had seen in her dreams.

"Perhaps I'll even see the person who can tell me about my mother or father," the young day-dreamer said to herself, justifying her desire.

XIX

Spring was beginning. Senya Voloshkevich, who had gotten himself a hunting rifle the year before, was thirsting for an opportunity to hunt wood grouse.

Easter had come early. The snow had already disappeared from the fields, and only here and there was it visible in white patches in the gloom of the forest. The bleating of a "lamb" snipe could be heard in the sky, and ducks quacked from pleasure in puddles which had collected in the meadows. The calls of the long-legged storks, who had returned from distant places, could be heard in the swamp. Timid rabbits, who had not yet changed the color of their winter fur, felt uncomfortable on the yellow-grey-green coloring of the moss and last year's grass. They timidly hugged the forest, staying close to the patches of snow which remained in its shadow.

Old Fedot, who "amused himself" with his rifle and knew the breeding ground of the wood grouse, agreed to take Senya with him for a bottle of vodka in payment, and both hunters walked out of the village before sunset, since it was a good ways off to the breeding ground.

Fedot wanted to make it to the birds' evening roost and walked hastily along the path, paying no attention whatsoever to whether Senya—with bag, rifle and other hunter's supplies hanging on him—was managing to keep up with him.

The old bridge across the Yaryn and the meadows along the river bank were already long behind them. Following the edge of the forest, they made their way to the swamp. There, where it was very boggy, Fedot—who had a good memory—rather quickly found long poles tied together with willow branches, spread out in the moss one after another in twos and threes.

No matter how much Senya and Fedot hurried, they did not make it in time for the birds' evening roost. By the time the hunters were approaching a low sand hill which rose from the swamp, the sun had already set. Once or twice along the way they heard the flapping of wood grouse's wings above them.

After they climbed the knoll, the travelers stopped. At first Fedot, and then Senya, who imitated the old hunter, removed their rifles from their shoulders, hung their bags on a tree at the height of a grown man, and breathing heavily from the quick pace of their walk, squatted in the sand. Their hearts were beating hard.

Somewhere far away, a woodcock was flying, making a "feeing" sound plus another sound that was like someone spitting. A sleepless bird warbled its song several times. A big dung beetle circled and buzzed very close by; it would descend and then begin to circle again. Not far away a wood grouse, flying up a tree, flapped its wings and broke off thin, dry twigs.

All around it was getting dark quickly. Sitting under an old pine tree, in a thicket of heather, the hunters listened attentively to the voices of the forest.

Fedot was pondering whether the wood grouse would begin making their mating calls in the evening, and Senya, forgetting everything in the world, became absorbed in the contemplation of nature which was falling asleep.

"Will we spend the night here?" he asked Fedot some time later.

But the old man only waved his hand in reply and began to listen even more attentively.

In the distance something like the quiet trilling of birds could be heard, alternating with a sound like the buzzing of flies in a spider web or the intermittent sound of a grindstone against a knife.

Senya saw Fedot, who had been listening hard to the sound, get to his feet and, taking his rifle, gesture to him to stay there and wait while he himself began to move quietly and carefully in the direction from which the sounds came.

Soon Fedot's sheepskin coat blended in with the darkening forest. Dead branches snapped a few times where he walked, and then even those sounds could not be heard. Only the occasional trilling of the wood grouse carried from afar.

It became completely dark. Senya, who had been waiting rather long already, had begun to worry when he heard again the crackling of dry twigs. Instinctively, he reached for his rifle. The snapping of branches repeated, but closer this time, considerably to the right of the place from where, in his opinion, Fedot should appear.

"Can it be a bear?" he thought. At that point a familiar cough showed the youth that he was wrong.

"Senya!" Fedot's voice was heard in the darkness.

"Well?" the young hunter asked, now calm, when the old man was already near.

"The wood grouse started to trick me as soon as I stole up on him, and then he grew completely quiet. I waited and waited and saw he wouldn't sing until morning. And so I headed back . . . Did you get dry twigs for the campfire?"

"No. It didn't occur to me."

"No matter. We'll gather them now. We can't sit all night in the dark."

And both of them, after putting aside their rifles, began to collect dead branches and to break off the dry lower branches of some pine trees. They stripped off birch bark for starting the fire, and soon a flame was leaping up, small at first, then growing bigger and brighter. The hunters put dry twigs on it and more birch bark until the flame—crackling and devouring the offered food—turned into a happy campfire illuminating the surrounding heather, stumps, rose colored-trunks, twigs, and needles of the adjoining trees with its flickering light.

After lugging in an extra supply of dead branches, the hunters sat down by the campfire, instinctively peering into the bright-red gold of the limbs and branches which had turned to coal. "It's always more reassuring to spend a night in the forest by a fire. No wild animal dares come close, and you feel happier in your heart," said Fedot.

"Have you ever had to spend a night without a fire?"

"I have. I've even spent a night around here. A pouring rain caught me in the forest in the evening, and my matches got all wet. Well, I chose an old pine tree with wide, full branches and decided to take shelter under its lower branches until dawn. I have the old folks to thank for teaching me that before you crawl under a tree, you must first ask it to let you spend the night: 'Mother Pine Tree, protect me from dark night!' As soon as I said this, it creaked in answer as if to say, 'Come!' Well, I crawled under . . . It was just like in a tent under the lower branches:

there's no wind, and it's dry, and the fallen needles are soft to lie on. I pulled my wet coat over my head, got warm and dozed off. . . . And then I hear, as if in a dream, someone calling nearby, 'O mistress of the branches! Come towards us, we'll sway together!' And someone very close by answers, 'I can't, I have a guest.' And so then I slept peacefully until morning."

"Who said that?" asked Senya.

"Who knows! The tree was talking. The tree, it also understands, you know. It's not just you and I who have a soul. A tree can even defend you sometimes. Here's a story Uncle Levon told me. He, in his time, spent a lot of nights in forests. Once he also asked permission of a pine tree, as one is supposed to, and lay down. At night he hears somebody come and say, 'You have a stranger. Give him here. I'll crush him!' But another voice replies from the tree, 'I won't give him up. He came to visit me and asked honorably.' The one who wanted to crush him doesn't walk away but swears and wants to crawl under the branches where my uncle is. My uncle is paralyzed with fear. He hears someone large and heavy as a dog, or perhaps a bear, suddenly jump off the pine tree and fall right on the newcomer who was about to do mischief. And they begin, at this point, to fight and roll on the ground. They snort like cats, pant and breathe heavily. . . . Then things probably took a turn for the worse for the stranger. He tore himself away and took off, and the other one approached his tree and then like a cat jumped up the trunk about one-and-a-half *sazhens*[1] off the ground and then started climbing up—you could hear him. But my uncle didn't dare crawl out from under the pine tree until dawn in order not to have the misfortune of running into the one who'd been ready to crush him. And when he crawled out in the morning, he saw the moss not only had been trampled but was lying in clumps around the pine tree. . . . They must have really fought," Fedot finished his story, throwing a dry branch on the campfire.

Smoothing out his red moustache and graying beard, the hunter reached for the knapsack hanging nearby, got a thick slice of bread from there, some salt tied in a little piece of rag, and several boiled eggs. Food, as everybody knows, helps to while away the boring night hours.

---

1. *sazhen (сажень):* a Russian measure, 2.13 meters or 7 feet, so here about 10.5 feet.

Looking at him, Senya quickly got his bag and pulled out a full bottle of vodka, sealed with red sealing wax.

"As promised," he said, extending the bottle to Fedot, "for taking me with you to the breeding ground," he added.

"Now that's a nice thing," the old hunter approved. "We could do without that, of course. I would've taken you anyway. . . . But still, vodka, is a good thing," he continued, breaking away pieces of the sealing wax around the neck and cork with his knife.

"Here, take a swallow," Fedot extended the bottle to his young friend after finishing his work.

"You know, Uncle Fedot, I don't drink."

"You don't? That's just as well . . . there's less expense," the old hunter agreed and, with the taste still in his mouth, again brought his lips to the glass neck; the cool liquid, which he poured into his mouth, warmed his insides. Nevertheless, he decided to save half for morning.

"Are *leshi*es afraid of fire, Uncle Fedot?" Senya asked, swallowing a small piece of pie and boiled salted pork which he had taken from his bag.

Chewing the food slowly with his strong teeth, Fedot thought for a while and then began to speak.

"Sure they are. A *leshy* doesn't like fire and won't go near it willingly, but there've been cases when the pointy-headed one approached a campfire. Andrei Savostiyanov—there lived such an old man in Zapoliye, I saw him when I was still a child—told my father this story. There was a hunter, and he had seen and heard a lot in his life. And this Andrei had a brother, Savva. And so once in the spring, Savva lay down by a campfire in the forest and fell asleep. Suddenly he hears someone's footsteps not far away. Savva raises his head and looks. Something that looks like a man is approaching him. He's dressed in a black kaftan, seemingly of cloth, and has gray pants and shoes and a cap on his head, but there's no face at all! And before Savva could grab his rifle, he ran up to him and began to strangle him. Savva broke free and ran away from the unclean force and started to run around the campfire. And when he had run around it three times, the unclean force disappeared. Andrei later told my father that he himself saw blue marks on his brother's throat. . . . After that, Savva would not set foot in the forest. He began to get ill and died in three years."

"Who's that?" Senya suddenly asked, when he heard an inter-

mittent cry, drawn-out and shrill—partly sounding like clucking—which made him shudder because it came so suddenly.

"It's a white partridge . . . You should catch a few winks.
There's still time."

Senya, however, could not sleep. He kept throwing dry
branches on the campfire, delighting in the dancing tongues of
flame shooting upwards and unconsciously rejoicing in the
warmth emanating from them. It seemed to the youth that he
had been living in this forest for a long, long time, sitting by the
fire, listening to the crackling and hissing of burning twigs,
sometimes chewing white bread, and looking at the bright sparks
circling and flying up into the dark sky.

The crunching of someone's footsteps on dead branches roused
Senya from his daydreaming and forced him to prick up his ears.
Fedot, who had dozed off after the vodka, also roused himself and
reached for his rifle, listening tensely to the rustling of the forest.
The dead branches snapped again in another place, about twenty
or thirty steps away from the campfire, and then in yet another
place. It was clear that someone was circling the hunters, afraid
to show himself in the illuminated area.

"Who could that be?" Senya asked, not without some alarm in
his voice, holding onto his rifle.

"Who knows?" Fedot answered. He cocked his single-barreled
gun, rose to his feet and, turning his back to the fire so it would
not blind him, began to peer into the dark night.

The crackling of the dead branches continued. The hunters listened with strained attention.

Some time later, a loud yet muffled cough which did not
sound human reached them. After a few moments, the cough
was heard again.

"An elk," Fedot said, breathing easier. After carefully relaxing
his trigger finger, he leaned the rifle against a tree and sat down
where he had been sitting before. Senya followed his example.

"I wondered for a moment if it was the Grandpa himself," the
old hunter revealed his earlier unease to the youth.

The elk walked a while around the campfire and left without
showing himself to the people. The only thing that could be
heard was the brushwood snapping under his feet, growing ever
weaker and more distant.

The storks in the swamp called to one another. The snipes by
the brook followed suit, although not for the first time.

"Soon, even the black grouse will start hissing, and the wood grouse will follow them, making their mating calls. The night is already drawing to a close. Nowadays it gets light early," said Fedot.

Senya looked at the sky. It was still completely blue-black, with constellations of stars burning brightly in it. The youth was thinking about what his companion meant by the word "Grandpa" (a *leshy* or a bear?), but for some reason did not ask.

Time passed.

Finally, somewhere far away in a forest meadow, a black grouse broke the silence of the night with a drawn-out hissing sound; a little later, his second "chu-fy-y-y-sh" was heard.

"Now it's time," said Fedot. "All right, you go to the first wood grouse that makes its mating-call. . . . Remember: approach at first lightly and, when you have stolen up on it so that you can clearly hear it humming, start taking leaping steps toward it. Try to steal up on it sideways, so that it's to the east of you, where the sky is lighter, and you'll have an easier time taking your aim. . . . Now let's listen. When it begins to trill, it'll be too late to talk."

The hunters moved away from the campfire and began to listen carefully. Soon a distant sound carried from the swamp which was like a bird's trilling or perhaps a sound like the one made if someone had put a stick between the stakes of a fence and was rapping it from side to side.

"Go quietly," Fedot whispered to Senya, "but watch out, aim carefully."

After realizing that the knapsacks were lying on the ground by the fire, the old hunter went back to hang them up again on the tree. Fedot remembered that one of them contained the open bottle, took it out, sat down (he did not like to drink standing) and, uncorking it, upended the neck in his mouth.

A pleasant languor overcame the old hunter. He decided that he would be able to hear the second wood grouse perfectly even sitting by the fire, which poured a pleasant warmth over him and which he was so reluctant to part with.

"It should make a mating-call somewhere nearby . . . Surely I'll hear it, I won't fall asleep," he thought, hiding the bottle under his shirt and closing his eyes, which had grown weary of looking at the fire.

Fedot tried to remember for a while how much he owed the

store for his shoe-making materials, but his thoughts somehow became strangely muddled; they became displaced by a picture of a red-hot stove and loaves of bread which his wife was putting there.

The hunter's head, which nodded involuntarily, dropped to his chest. Fedot gave a start and, opening his eyes, took a look around. Suddenly he became afraid. In the place that Senya had left now sat a shaggy stranger. The reddish coals of the dying campfire illuminated the half-animal mug—either like that of a bear or a goat—which suddenly began to speak.

"Why do you smell so good, human? I've been sitting nearby for a long time now and smelling the vapors from your mouth. What was the stuff you poured into your throat a short while back? Treat me to some, too!"

And the shaggy newcomer extended his long, gnarled paw towards the hunter.

With a sad sigh, Fedot drew the half-empty bottle out from under his shirt and, trembling, passed it to his strange guest. . . . The latter tried to drink it without taking out the cork; he inserted the neck of the bottle into his mouth and apparently got angry when nothing came out.

"Why don't you take out the cork?" said Fedot, who even became amused at the Leshy's absurd attempt.

And he showed, by gestures, how to uncork the bottle.

An instant later, the vodka poured into forest master's throat and his shaggy face lit up.

Fedot, despite his fright, sadly watched the precious liquid disappearing in the bottle.

Leaving a little bit, the Leshy magnanimously returned the bottle to the hunter.

"You drink, too," he said.

Fedot, however, afraid of defiling himself with the bottle's neck which the lips—those of an unclean spirit, after all—had touched, decided to show his magnanimity as well and declined.

The Leshy did not spend much time trying to persuade the hunter to take a drink and quickly tipped the remaining contents of the bottle into his mouth. Then, trying without success to slip his long tongue into the bottle's neck, the shaggy guest sighed and gave the empty bottle back to Fedot.

"You people have it good," he said a bit later, again sighing. "You have everything: huts and women, and cows with calves, and vodka. . . . Why haven't you brought bread?!" the shaggy newcomer suddenly added loudly and angrily.

Fedot hastily gave him the rest of the food from both bags: the unfinished pie, what was left of the thick slice of bread, and the salt in the little piece of rag.

The Leshy began to chomp and eat noisily like an animal, devouring the bread and the pie but not touching the salt. When he finished, he brushed off the crumbs which had fallen on his long, greenish beard and now, in a less unhappy but commanding voice, said:

"Always bring me a treat when you go into the forest and don't put it on a stump but hang it in a piece of rag on a dry pine, and high at that, because your village fools always put the bread so low that either a fox or a bear invariably runs off with it."

Unhappy that he had been forced to give his vodka to the unclean spirit, Fedot kept silent, thinking, "And what is it that you've done for me that I should start bringing you bread?"

"I drive birds or animals in your direction. I always drive them closer to those who show me respect," as if in answer to the hunter's thoughts Green-Goat said in a querulous voice, creaking like a dry tree. "You people have it good! You have well-filled-out, chubby women almost without any fur. And they bake pies for you . . . Once, a woman said to me, 'Let me go! I have to bake a pie for my husband at home. . . . ' She promised to bring me some, but she didn't. . . ."

"Perhaps she brought it," Fedot tried to defend the woman he did not know, "but she couldn't find you. Did you show her your dwelling?"

"How can I do that when my Leshachikha is in it? If she found out, no one would fare well. . . . No, I told that woman I would wait for her the next day in the ravine, that she should come there around noon and bring me a pie. . . . And how she kept promising me! With tears in her eyes she kept vowing, 'Only let me go, my dear Leshy, and I'll bring you both vodka and pie!' That wasn't your wife, by any chance, was it?"

"My wife's an old woman already."

"Oh, it's all right that she's an old woman! Some of those old women are so . . . Ahhh!" Green-Goat wheezed, finishing his speech.

"And don't your *leshachikhas* bake pies for you? What kind of food then, let's say, do you have?"

"We eat you!" suddenly getting angry, the Leshy bellowed, and his animal head, with its wide-open maw, reached for Fedot.

Forgetting himself from fright, Fedot quickly got to his feet, grabbed the rifle and, jumping back about three steps, fired at the shaggy lord of the forests.

A shot rang out. The hunter, with eyes closed from fear, opened them again and looked around. The Leshy was nowhere to be seen. There was no crackling in the forest. Only in the distance, in the direction in which Senya had gone, a second shot went off from a gun as if in answer.

The sky in the east was growing gray.

Disturbed by what had happened, Fedot did not know whether he should go while the going was good and get away from the enraged forest spirit who could return at any moment, or whether the latter had been just a hallucination when he was not fully awake.

Suddenly catching the crunching of approaching steps, the old hunter began to load his single-barreled shotgun with trembling hands but calmed down when a hail in Senya's familiar voice reached him.

The youth came back, happily excited and proud of his first wood grouse, which he had already managed to tie to his waist and was stroking with his hand. He fully believed what his old friend Fedot had told him: that he had fired hastily at a wood grouse that had become frightened by something and flew by not far from the fire, and that the wood grouse had descended into a thicket and was hiding somewhere in it.

"He's probably run off with a wounded wing. As for the others, you almost can't hear them," Fedot finished his story.

The hunters listened attentively. The wood grouse, probably frightened by the shots, fell silent. Only the sound "chu-fy-y-y" and the muttering of the mating black grouse carried from the swamp and fields along the river, and even from the village.

"It's time to go home," Fedot said, picking up the empty bottle lying near the dead campfire.

He still didn't know, by the way, whether you can drink from the washed neck of a bottle which may not have been touched by a devil's lips, but nevertheless, by those of an unclean spirit. . . .

The old hunter did not return empty-handed, however. When it was already light, the hunters, passing through a forest meadow, ran into two field grouse, absorbed in fighting. Quickly taking aim at one of them, Fedot killed it with a well-placed shot from about thirty steps away. The second black grouse, seeing its opponent lying motionless, sat still nearby for a few moments, then took off and flew away before Senya could manage to take aim and shoot.

～

Green-Goat, hit with a charge of shot from Fedot's single-barreled gun, quickly ran away from the fire. After he had covered about half a verst, he stopped, recovered a bit from his fright and, feeling incomprehensibly weak, leaned against an old pine tree. In those places where the small shot had pierced him, the Leshy experienced a sensation of unusual weariness and chill as if a cold wind were piercing his whole being.

Green-Goat dropped down on the thick roots of an old tree which were sticking out of the ground. His shot-through body shook and ached. The master of the forest understood that something bad had happened, and that he had to run as quickly as possible to his Leshachikha so that she would pick some healing herbs and, after chewing them, plug the small, nastily aching holes in his stomach and chest with the chewed-up mixture. Only first he had to take revenge on the man who had burned him with fire from a black stick. Most likely the man had fallen asleep again and was not waiting for an attack. . . .

Mustering his strength, the Leshy rose to his feet and wandered back quietly to the campfire, trying to step noiselessly and carefully in order to catch the enemy unawares.

"I'll grab him and sit him on top of the highest fir tree. But first, I'll break off all of the upper branches so that he won't be able to climb down. Then, that good-for-nothing will really sing," Green-Goat daydreamed, sighing at each step and stopping to catch his breath.

But when the wounded Leshy finally approached the red coals of the campfire that was dying out in the predawn gloom, there was no longer anyone there. Only a fox, sniffing the ground, was running nearby on a barely noticeable forest path in the direction of the low grumbling of a black grouse.

"He's gone," Green-Goat whispered, his feelings hurt.

A strong chill racked him. An icy cold like the winter wind through the crevices of a den penetrated his body, draining him of the warmth of life, making his limbs lose strength, and inducing the dying half-god to sleep.

The Leshy lost his unconscious fear of fire, which is usually present in his tribe.

"If only I could get warm," he creaked hoarsely and fell into the pile of dying embers. Giving himself an unpleasant burn, the Leshy did not have the strength, however, to get up; he turned a bit and stretched out, sighing, across the campfire.

His wet fur began to hiss on the hot coals. Then it dried out, began to smolder, and finally burst into crackling, bright flame, from which the rest of Green-Goat's body caught fire.

He burned rather quickly, producing a thick, white smoke (which, for a moment, took the form of the Leshy) which smelled pleasantly like pine needles mixed with wild strawberries and emitting a whistling noise that sounded like a complaint. In a short time, all that remained of the lord of the forest, once full of strength, were some ashes and something that resembled the charred and blackened roots of a burned stump.

Returning on the same path, the fox—sated after a successful hunt—stopped for a moment, sniffed the strange smell in the air and, with one leap, disappeared into the bushes.

XX

Having donned a wreath of monkshood and madder, with gentian tucked around her waist and about two handfuls of blessed poppy seed in her pocket, just in case, Aksyutka headed on a moonlit night for the forest swamp.

It was a damp summer, and the pleasant coolness of wet patches here and there in the forest, as she made her way, enveloped her feet. Thanks to the moonlight, it was possible to bypass piles of prickly brushwood and not stumble over roots and rocks. With a walking stick in her hand (using this stick she had once separated a frog from a grass snake that had gotten hold of it, and for this reason such a walking stick had to possess some magical properties), the young girl made her way down a barely noticeable path trodden by cattle, which wound through alder bushes, young aspen trees, and birches. In a small meadow, a brown bear—the friend of the Leshachikha who was called Wart-Face—happened to come towards her. The animal stopped, bristled, and started to snarl.

Aksyutka, who did not become frightened at all, waved her stick at him and walked towards the animal after raising the hem of her skirt, just to be on the safe side; the latter gesture was supposed to act upon her opponent's alleged shyness.

Whether the animal was truly shy, or because Aksyutka's fearlessness had an effect on him, the bear—without even listening to her incantations—did not wait for the touch of her magical club; he turned around and unhurriedly ran in the opposite direction, snarling loudly and making a great effort to spit in disgust.

The young girl triumphantly continued her journey.

After passing a thicket of shrubs that grew in the area where the trees had been cut down earlier, she entered a grove of tall pine and fir trees whose prickly branches intertwined high above her. It was totally dark here, and only the little path beneath her feet was dimly visible. This path brought the traveler to a large meadow, in the middle of which, on a stump, sat the stern Wart-Face, almost imperceptible against the dark foliage of a nearby bush and seemingly blending in with its shadow in the moonlight.

Burying her somewhat hairy chin in her calloused knees and with gnarled fingers clasping her thin legs overgrown with brown fur, the Leshachikha was pensively recalling her lost husband. She particularly liked to imagine him sitting on just such a stump and picking at his bast shoes full of holes in the moonlight. . . . "Where is he?" she thought.

Wart-Face had no knowledge whatsoever of the fate which had befallen Green-Goat, and she thought only that her spouse, convinced of her infidelity, had moved to a different forest. And the Leshachika dreamt how she would find her run-away husband again and prove to him that his suspicions were unfounded and that it was useless to run away from her. . . .

The sound of someone's barely audible steps put Wart-Face on her guard. She pricked up her shaggy ears. The steps were coming nearer. A young, female human being (as Wart-Face quickly identified her instinctively), dressed in a white shirt and a dark, short skirt, with a wreath of some unpleasantly-smelling herbs on her head, came out in the meadow flooded with moonlight.

When the girl was side by side with the stump, the Leshachikha, without changing her position (she only turned her head slightly, which had been resting on her knees), asked imperiously in a hoarse and creaky voice, "Where are you going?"

Startled by this unexpected question, Aksyutka stopped, rooted to the ground. Then, after taking a good look at the one inquiring, the young girl, although she had become frightened, quickly recovered and, trying not to show her confusion, took on a casual air and in turn asked her own impertinent question, "And what are you doing here, you old hag?"

"Oh, I'm just sitting here and guarding my forest so that all kinds of trash like you don't roam about here at night," Wart-Face creaked ominously, seemingly growing out of the stump and extending her long, dark paws with uneven, hooked fingers. One almost reached Aksyutka who, frozen in place and numb with fear, unconsciously thrust a half-dry gentian flower into the Leshachikha's gnarled hand closest to her.

The Leshachikha's hand, which grabbed this flower, flinched as if burned and jerked backwards, and Wart-Face herself, snorting like a wild cat, suddenly began to change shape and grow smaller in size.

"You've been taught," she hissed maliciously, rolling to the ground and seemingly dissolving into the black shadow cast by the bush in the moonlight.

Aksyutka saw the grass weave and snake as if from a streaming wind, and again everything grew quiet, as if no Leshachikha had been sitting just now on a damp stump in the shadow of an alder bush, illuminated by the moon.

The girl sighed, looked all around, and continued her journey. In half an hour, after following the bends of the stream that meandered through meadows and then through a willow thicket, she approached the Great Swamp.

It was no easier to walk there than in the forest. At times Aksyutka's bare feet sank in the rust-colored bog so that the water came up to her knees and even higher. The moon, as if intentionally, kept hiding in the broken clouds floating in the sky. A pre-dawn wind whooshed in the high swamp grass and in the osier-beds. A large owl hooted in a small pine tree and then flew off after catching sight of Aksyutka. In the distance, little swamp demons whistled to each other from the deep openings that looked like puddles.

Raising the hem of her skirt almost to her waist, the fearless girl made her way between these puddles across the unsteady surface of the bog to the main lake in the middle. She wanted to go up to the very edge of this lake and summon the demons and shapeshifters found there and, when they appeared, to ask them if her parents, whom no one seemed to know, could not be found among the human souls who had perished and were imprisoned in the boggy swamp.

Recalling the place, the bushes, the location of the deep pools glistening like black steel, and the bends in the path through the sedge that someone had made—all of which she had seen in her dream—Aksyutka stood almost knee-deep in the rust-colored bog. She felt gurgling bubbles slipping down her knees; she looked first all around and then at the dark sky with the quickly moving clouds.

"In my dream, there was a full moon then, and there were many more trees," Aksyutka pondered. "Where are they?"

The nocturnal heavenly body, which peeked out for a little while from behind the clouds, poured silver on the dark, round openings and the sedge rustling in the wind, the stumps of pines cut down a few years earlier on the nearby knoll, and on the young girl standing motionless, with the wet hem of her skirt raised high. The head of Maryska's daughter slowly turned from side to side and incomprehensible melancholy stirred in her bosom.

"Who are you, my girl? And where did you get such a mark on your hip?" a non-human voice, rustling and hoarse like that of an over-strained toad, was suddenly heard from somewhere below.

Knowing that you must not reveal your name to any unclean spirit if there is no special need, Aksyutka looked silently in the direction from where these words resounded.

The head of an old, swamp she-demon was visible in the dark mirror of the opening glistening now in the moonlight, under the branches of a willow bending over this opening. Rust-colored water was pouring down her thin grey hair—covered with slime and mud—to her swollen face with old, bulging eyes and criss-crossed with wrinkles.

"Who are you, my little beauty? And why have you come here to our place?" the fat wrinkled mug, poking out of the water, continued to question.

"I've come to see your kind and have a talk," the girl answered, trying to be bold.

"Why not, we'll talk. Who were your father and mother, my dear?"

"I don't know. They found me under a fir tree in the forest," was the answer uttered in a gloomy voice.

"Raise your skirt just a little bit on your left side . . . So! You say you don't have parents? They found you in the forest? . . . Hmmm . . . I just knew you couldn't have real parents. But I remember the birthmark on your leg . . . When you were born in our swamp, I, my dear, swaddled you myself and even then marveled at your birthmark."

"Did you know my mother, too?! Tell me, who is she? How did she come to be in your swamp?" Aksyutka asked anxiously.

"Just like me and just like you. Your mother was called Fat Maryska and she was, like all of us, a swamp demon."

"Then I'm a demon, too?" followed the dismayed question.

"Who knows? I never saw your father. I think he was then a man. Who he is now, I don't know. But your mother was a real demon, and if she hadn't married the Vodyanoi from the Yaryn twelve, perhaps more, years ago, I would've called her here to admire her daughter. . . . Don't be hurt that your mother's a demon. Maryska was always a fine and well-filled-out girl. I was friends with her, although she was much younger than me. There were times when she'd run off into the forest for the night and return only toward morning after some fight. I always massaged her bruises and scratches with frog roe. . . . As for with whom she got together and begot you, she didn't tell me anything that made sense, or perhaps she did, but I've forgotten. In my old age I've begun to confuse what happened to someone and when. He was either a hunter or a tramp . . . It seems he drowned later somewhere. Quite a few of them drown!" the old woman muttered pensively. "But I remember you, my little beauty . . . I held you in my arms. . . . So, if you've come to visit us and don't intend to stay forever, then better go back where you've come from. Our life isn't terribly sweet. Your mother would often shed many a tear because of our Fat-Belly. You know, if you don't show him respect, he beats us sisters—when we're young and pretty—so much that life is no longer dear. . . . Better go off while you're in one piece," the she-demon advised.

"I'm not afraid of your Fat-Belly! You see yourself what I have on my head and around my waist."

"Your herbs, my dear, are only good on the ground, but in the water, even if it's swamp water, they have no power. If somebody knows some of the right words, they can be useful at times, but the herbs, no. For this reason, my big-eyed little frog, if you don't know these words, turn around and go where you've come from so that you won't have to shed tears later!"

"To which Vodyanoi did you marry off my mother?" Aksyutka continued to inquire.

"You've been told that it was from your Yaryn! He lives there, they say, at the river bottom near a mill. Something like our master. Also very fat, a red mug, and grey hair on his chest. He's the one who took her away. . . . About half-a-dozen small demons were also enticed away at different times . . . . So don't persist in looking for her, that is, your mother, without a spell. Her Vodyanoi is no better, they say, than our Bolotnik."

Aksyutka sighed and, after bowing and giving the old she-demon "the fig" out of respect, she began to slosh back sadly through the boggy swamp.

The painful awareness that, even if she was not a full-blooded demon, she was in any case a half-demon, gave her no peace.

XXI

It was getting dark. The village witch Styopka had just finished cleaning her cottage. She was pensive. A question was troubling the sorceress: just how healthy was the infant she had taken a fancy to at the far end of their village? The witch adhered to the rule of sucking the blood of only completely healthy children.

"I'll have to go and see if the little baby has a cough," she decided and walked out of the cottage in order to make sure that there were no curious women or mischievous boys around.

Standing near the porch, Styopka began to look around and listen carefully. In the distance she could hear girls' voices, the sounds of a harmonica, and bits and pieces of a song sung by some youth and broken intermittently by laughter, but there was no one nearby.

The witch returned to her cottage, closed the door on a hook behind her, walked up to the window, and opened the tiny ventilation pane a little. After a boy had hit her with a rock, Styopka did not like to fly out through the stovepipe in the form of a magpie before nightfall.

Today, she decided to try her luck after changing into a black cat.

The little kids, who had gotten their fill of running around all day, were now having supper. Then some would go to bed, and others would ride out to the meadow where the horses were pastured at night "I'll run unnoticed through the vegetable gardens as a cat, and the way back will be completely safe," Styopka thought, taking off her blouse, skirt, and slip.

Then, from behind the stove, she got a small, wooden board with small iron nails hammered in it from end to end, put this board with its sharp edge facing up in the middle of the floor, and began to quietly mumble incantations.

Because of the closed red-calico curtains on the windows, it became almost completely dark in the hut. Only hoarse, fitful whispering and stamping were audible, followed by the thuds of a naked woman's body against the wooden floorboards.

Three times, carefully, in order not to hurt her back against the nails, Styopka executed somersaults across the board.

A small, dark shadow flashed on the window's curtain; the ventilation pane squeaked ever so slightly, and then it became quiet in the cottage.

That same evening, Red-Haired Fedka ("Shameless Thief,"[1] as the village boys teasingly called him), was walking with his friend Makar the back way, that is, not following the main street but taking the path along the vegetable gardens, and Makar was telling Fedka how dogs attacked him once near the priest's barn.

"I barely got away. One tried to get his teeth into my sheepskin coat, but I fended him off with my sack. But he, the stinker, caught my sack in his teeth. I barely wrested it free. I had to patch it later. Look what a piece he tore off!"

Makar took out from under his shirt a carefully folded sack with a fresh patch and showed it to him.

"I always have it with me," he ended, folding and hiding his sack again.

Fedka suddenly stood still and grabbed his friend by the hand. Makar looked in the direction in which his friend was pointing with his finger. An animal, clearly of the feline species, completely black, was making its way among the vegetable garden beds.

"That's just what we need," Fedka whispered to Makar. "If only we could catch it!"

Having heard the story about the magic bone earlier from his friend, Makar immediately realized what was up.

"You go first," Fedka said to him, "and stand behind the corner of Ipat's shed. As soon as that black cat slips through there, you grab it . . . Run!"

---

1. In the Russian, Red-Haired Fedka *(Федька Рыжий)* and Shameless Thief *(Вор Бестыжий)* complement each other in rhyme and rhythm.

Makar ran quick as a flash to Ipat's shed; Fedka stood still, for he noticed that the cat would have to run past him. . . .

Styopka, who had assumed the form of a cat, was running and thinking about illnesses which spoil the blood of infants. "Our fellow sister-witches put the evil eye on many of them, and then they suck that very same blood. Before you adjust the red belt to the child, you have to look it over and listen hard by the stove-pipe to hear if it's coughing; Then slip through to it in the form of a rat and make sure it doesn't have a rash or scabs. . . . Our sisters need only clean infants. Oh! What's that?" she suddenly wondered, when Red-Haired Fedka suddenly reached and almost grabbed her arched back.

Jumping lightly and agilely across the vegetable beds, Styopka rushed from Fedka to Ipat's shed. Here, a very natural thought occurred to her: to turn the corner and hide from her perse-cutor's view. But she had barely managed to slip behind the wooden wall edged with young stinging nettles when somebody's strong hand came down on her neck and pressed the witch to the ground.

Styopka tried to scratch with both her front and hind paws, but Makar did not release the cat's neck and pressed her spine with his knee as he produced a sack from under his shirt with his left hand.

A bit more and Styoka was in the sack.

Her situation was not an enviable one. Having turned into an animal or a bird, a witch can, as is well known, take on her previous human form after turning three somersaults across leather, nails, needles, or even wooden pegs. Only very few know how to manage without these things. Styopka was deprived of the possibility of turning any somersaults at all, for Makar had wound the top part of the sack around her, in which she was already his prisoner and, more than that, had tied it with a piece of string, just to be sure.

Both youths decided right then and there to go to the forest or a field—to a crossroads—and, after waiting until midnight, to cook in a pot the body of what they thought was a cat.

Rather quickly, Fedka managed to find a pot with a cover somewhere in the neighborhood (probably with Fyokla's cooper-ation). As it turned out, Makar had almost a full box of matches. After grabbing some bread and salt for emergency needs, the friends quickly got ready to head out.

The only thing remaining was to choose in what direction, and where, to go.

It is not so frightening, of course, to go to a field, but it is dangerous in that the kids you know can see you and tease you a long time afterwards about your starting to go out to the meadow where the horses are pastured at night. And in the forest, although there is no danger from people, it is much too frightening.

A decision was made to head out about three versts from the village to the place near the forest where two field-roads intersected. At the crossroads, along the sides of the roads grew alder bushes. It was possible to find a perfect hiding place in them, make a fire, and even cut down small poles for hanging the pot.

Provident Makar took some raw potatoes with him and even some chips of kindling wood for starting the fire.

In about two hours, both of them were already sitting in an alder thicket, awaiting the time when it would be possible to start cooking the cat. The pot with the water from the nearest ditch, attached with wire to a crosspiece of alder wood and hung over the fire, was beginning to boil. In the bundle lying right next to the fire, something was moving weakly at times, making muffled sounds from time to time that sounded like suppressed wailing. A bird, perhaps a woodcock, swooping down toward the fire, circled rather low over it, displaying its light-gray chest, whistled and, soaring above the fire, disappeared in the darkness of night.

"Could it be the unclean force coming to check on us?" Makar said gloomily, testing to see if the potatoes had finished baking.

A rooster started to crow in the village. After him, a second . . . a third . . .

"It's time already. It's the midnight hour," Fedka decided. "Go get the cat, Makar!"

His friend bent over the bundle silently and began to untie the string.

"Only take a look first," Red-Haired added, "to see whether it's a male cat. Otherwise, if it's a female, she'll probably be of no use to us."

"I think that we can cook it even if it turns out to be a female cat. Who knows, perhaps a bone will be found in her?"

Hearing these words and reading her fate in them, Styopka decided that if she could not save herself, at least she could get more for her life.

Makar had barely taken her out of the sack and begun to determine her sex in the light of the fire, when the witch dug her nails into the hand of the youth holding her and, breaking free, jumped on his face. But she had barely managed to jump down to the ground when Red-Haired Fedka's boot hit her painfully on the spine. This new enemy grabbed her by her hind legs with his strong hands, again hit her flattened spine with his shoe, and broke her neck vertebrae. A half-animal cry was heard, gradually turning into a human cry filled with pain, and both frightened youths saw for a moment, and one moment only, that under Fedka's feet something was wriggling—at times shimmering, at times growing dark—and that it resembled a naked woman's body.

Red-Haired Fedka grit his teeth, closed his eyes in fear, and recoiled. And when he looked again, it was dark all around, and only the coals were hissing in the fire on which the pot of boiling water had spilled. Makar, all scratched up and trying to hide and run away, brushed against one of the forked branches which held the pole with the pot on it and knocked it down.

"Makar!" Red-Haired Fedka, who had recovered a bit, yelled out after looking around and making sure there was no one nearby.

But his frightened friend, sitting nearby almost up to his waist in the cold water in the ditch, did not answer him. It was if someone had ordered him to hide and keep quiet.

Only after the cold water brought him around somewhat did Makar finally respond to Fedka's repeated calls and crawl out to dry land.

"Fedka, are you alone?" he asked from behind the bushes.

"Yeah, I'm alone. And who do you need?"

"And the one who changed from the cat?"

"Oh, her! She was, but now is no more!" Red-Haired said, trying not to appear afraid. "She probably died when I, it seems, broke her neck. . . . . She may be an unclean spirit, but she doesn't like it!"

"It turned out this was no devil and no unclean spirit," Makar said pensively, licking the blood running from his hand. "Those beings don't have vertebrae or spines. But this one was alive. Just look at the scratches she's made, that creature with the tail! Can't be anything but a witch. I took a good look: not a male but a female cat. Had it been a devil or a sorcerer, he would have appeared as a male, but this was a witch," Makar repeated with conviction. "There's nothing for us to do here," he continued, picking up the pot that had rolled a small distance away. "Help me find the cover, Fedka. . . . I sure got wet because of this unclean spirit! Never more will I have anything to do with these things! . . ."

"Here it is! I've found it!" Fedka said, bending over and picking up the cover. "Aren't you going to dry off?"

"It's not worth it. I'll dry as I walk," was the answer.

Red-Haired stooped down once more, picked several hot potatoes out of the ashes and, wrapping them in burdock leaves, followed Makar back to the village.

When two days later fellow villagers broke down the door of Styopka's hut, locked from the inside, they saw the contorted corpse of the naked witch with a broken neck and a face that had turned black. The board with the thirteen nails had pierced her spine, but there was no blood visible. They unanimously agreed that the unclean force had strangled Styopka.

Since she had not attended church and the priest refused to read the burial service for her, Styopka was buried beyond the cemetery fence. The peasants nevertheless put a cross on her grave, just in case.

However, even after death she continued to frighten people walking and riding past the cemetery at night by running out in the form of a white dog, black pig, or sheep. It was decided, therefore, to put a stop to the witch's adventures from beyond the grave.

The grave was dug up. Styopka's head was cut off and placed at the feet of the dead but not yet decomposed old woman. Then the corpse's hands and feet were cut off and placed again in the grave but in reverse order. The torso itself was pierced with a sharp stake of aspen wood. This stake was left in the corpse, and only the upper portion was sawed off so that it would not prevent the lid from closing. After all this, Styopka's body was again committed to the earth, and the dead witch no longer prevented anyone from walking near the cemetery at night.

XXII

Again bonfires blazed on enchanted Mount Osiyan. Again young and old witches from everywhere were flying there with screams, howls, and laughter, answering the thundering call of the tambourine. There were many of them, so many that the demons who had gathered there in various forms began to worry that the lustful women, left unsatisfied by the demons' non-human but nonetheless limited passion, would tear them to pieces in the end. There had been such cases earlier. . . . The Fiery Serpent, who had suffered greatly the last time, now did not appear at all for the gathering. The witches, understanding all this, conducted themselves with an air of independence and self-importance, although without any blatant violation of thousand-year practices.

After bowing on her knees like the others before Black Goat, kissing him where he must be kissed, and placing her usual gift— a large bottle of well-distilled vodka—at the feet of the Sovereign of the Night, Aniska got ready to step away to the tables when the muffled and low voice of the Sitting One, completely unexpectedly, said commandingly, "Wait."

The witch stopped as if rooted to the ground. This somewhat hoarse voice sounded not only in her ears but seemingly throughout her whole being, subjecting every vein, every drop of blood, the beating of her heart, and the flow of her thoughts to its will.

"Listen, Aniska. You've fulfilled my behest about vengeance. You were able to be evil and cruel, and you placed in my hands the soul of the one to whom, because of your woman's weakness, you once gave away the secrets we hold in common. With his death, however, you have not made amends for your guilt, about which I knew for a long time, although I didn't show that I knew everything you did with him and everything you said to him. . . . There's no darkness impenetrable to my eyes, there are no whispers I don't hear, and there are no secret thoughts I don't know. . . . You want to say that you meant to turn your lover into a sorcerer? Your justification is pointless. Maksim was too cowardly and not suited for becoming a sorcerer. You know that yourself. . . . But you know how to teach sorcery to others. . . . And so here's what I'm going to say to you. Now listen and fulfill my wishes. Soon a girl will come to you and ask you to teach her how to become a witch. Don't refuse her. Gradually teach her everything that you know yourself. Be sly and affectionate with her; don't frighten your future apprentice, and don't make it difficult for her with hard tests from which her soul could waiver. And when the girl is ready, bring her of her own accord first to the crossroads, and then here as well. Only then will you receive forgiveness and, moreover, a reward . . . . And now go. Don't be afraid to stay until the end of our celebration. I know, you're frightened of the agony of becoming my bride. But women submit to this agony voluntarily. I have too many brides as it is, even without you. . . . And because you brought me good vodka (don't forget to do this henceforth!), I will help you bewitch another lover who is more handsome and younger than Maksim. . . ."

The Devil's promise settled sweetly in Aniska's heart and began to occupy her thoughts. Filled with these thoughts, she observed the ritual—which blasphemously imitated baptism—in which a tall, somewhat thin beauty with splendid, curly braids wound into a knot at the back of her head was accepted and given as a bride to the Goat. Aniska listened apathetically to the sermon of the Sovereign of the Night, observed without any curiosity the frightening faces of the unclean spirits who had come to Osiyan Mountain, and without trepidation felt the cold, pale hands of the dead—brought to life for a short while—touching her. At supper, the witch barely ate, trying to guess who would be sent to her by the Lord of Darkness to be her lover. Aniska's neighbor on the left—a half-gray, half-red-haired sorcerer who had crawled out of his grave for the celebration—time and again stole pieces of cheese, fatback, and sausage from her plate.

These pieces had been placed lovingly before the witch by a stocky and shaggy unclean spirit with a half-bear face, who muttered languidly and sat to her right.

Aniska noticed neither the stealing by her friend on the left nor the persistent attention of her banquet neighbor on the right.

"What are you thinking about, young woman?" the red-haired sorcerer asked her, picking out pieces of cheese from his thick beard. "You haven't come here to think. Thinking makes wrinkles, which women find annoying, appear before their time. . . . You'll have your fill of thinking lying in the grave. . . . And while you're young and strong, think less and have as much fun as you know how. If you're inexperienced, then I'll teach you a few things after dinner. Don't pay attention to the fact that I'm old. Resting in the grave, I have amassed enough strength to exhaust a woman even stronger than you. . . ."

"Leave me alone! I don't feel like talking to you!" Aniska cut him off sternly.

After supper, instead of dancing with the others, she stepped modestly to the side where the bonfire was going out, over which, a short time before, the second face of the Goat of the Night had been bending.

From the bonfire's coals, a thick white smoke was spreading along the ground, which a fat, naked old woman, lying there on her right side, was greedily inhaling. Aniska stepped over her short legs, lay down not far from the fire herself, and began to breathe in strongly and steadily the sweetly cloying smoke. She already knew that this smoke gives you a chance to see, with eyes closed, everything that goes on in this or that town or village, depending on your wishes.

Closing her eyes, Aniska strained her will to invoke the face of the one who had been promised to her by the Master of Darkness.

In the witch's imagination the young, laughing face of the deacon's nephew, Senya, surfaced unexpectedly. Aniska immediately fell in love with the outline of his beautiful, smiling, rosy lips with a little moustache above and with his bright, blue eyes and, as if in answer to the vision, she smiled to herself with an enticing smile full of promise.

The witch, almost to the very end of the demonic sabbath, disturbed by no one and lying by the dying fire, would not let go of this enticing, youthful image which sweetly bewitched her whole being.

Aniska's flight back to her native village, where the happiness of a new and heretofore unexperienced passion now awaited her as the Master of the Celebration had promised, was tranquil and joyous and took place to the sound of roosters crowing in the dissipating predawn gloom.

Her awareness that the eyes of the invisible Goat of the Night were following her all the time, unceasingly, and that each deed was not perceived with indifference but was remembered by him, forced Aniska to adjust her life and actions to the will and wishes of her Master. Knowing that he imposes the obligation on witches to do harm, the enchantress from Zaretskoye zealously and carefully began to "spoil" not only cattle (which she had done at times even earlier) but to affect people as well, something she had avoided doing up to now. At night, in the form of a black dog, she carried away and tore the priest's goose to pieces; she scattered dust to the wind, with the wish that it send swelling and convulsions to where the neighbor's children were playing; she poured out boiled slops—which she had mixed with dog excrement in a garbage pail—into the yard which bordered hers on the other side of the house.

Fear before her Master forced the enchantress to think constantly of how she could please him and, in this way, get rid of all the unpleasantness for being so trusting of Maksim.

In turn, the unclean force began to help her noticeably. Every night Aniska saw in her sleep all those who would to come to her in the course of the day for sorcery or to have their fortunes told. In her sleep she even received instructions on what she must give each visitor in the form of a potion, or what she must foretell. The witch succeeded, by the way, in discovering where the horses stolen from the Gordeyev and Stepanchuk families could be found and in predicting to Feoklista Sedykh that her husband, who had perished without a trace in the war, would soon return to her.

XXIII

It was a very hot summer. There were no downpours for a long time. One might think that the goddesses of rain and dew, because they were angry at the dark, dust-covered Earth for some reason, had decided to leave it without moisture for a long time. Rivers became shallow, streams ran almost completely dry, and the bogs, which had been impassable earlier, now dried up.

The unclean spirits and the living dead of the swamp and water were suffering greatly from this hostility on the part of the invisible but mighty and immortal goddesses. In view of the shortage of dew, the *rusalka*s were wary of going out to the fields at night. Their songs had almost completely fallen silent, their games had stopped, and the silvery radiating laughter of the water beauties was heard no more in areas that had been water-meadows.

The she- and he-demons of the swamp hid during the day in the depths of lakes covered above with half-dry moss, and only in the moonlight did they dare look out from the few muddy, narrow openings which had grown smaller from the sun. But the Bolotnik, who had been fat but now had grown thin from worry, did not feel completely safe even on the bottom of the turbid and muddy bogs. The wise old man knew that misfortune threatened not only from the burning arrows of the sun; he sensed the possibility of even a second, perhaps imminent misfortune. At night, when there was complete silence in the forest and in the muddy bogs, for the frogs were not croaking and the nightjars were not jabbering, the Bolotnik would lie down at the bottom of his lake in the bog and listen keenly to the dull and far-away steps that reached his ears from somewhere below. Because these steps were quickening, the old man sensed that the Lord of the Fire, unhappy with something, was moving angrily through his underground tsardom, and it appeared that he would soon emerge. The master of the bog knew that the greedy demons of flame, the all-consuming fires, would break out on the earth's surface.

And they did break out.

One night, emerging from the rust-colored water of a black opening, the Bolotnik, breathing heavily through his flat nose, inhaled the air which had grown just a little bit fresher since evening, and alarm registered on his wrinkle-covered mug. A fine, barely perceptible smell of smoke could be detected in the air. The next night the smell was already fully discernible. The bog master's keen sense of smell quickly established that the faraway peat bogs were on fire. Raising his wet and dirty claw-like finger, the master of the bog tried to determine the strength and direction of the wind. The wind, barely perceptibly, was nonetheless blowing from the burning peat bogs to the banks of the Yaryn, overgrown with trees.

"It'll be bad," the Bolotnik thought, frowning. "I, of course, will be able to survive this by lying hidden with my wives in the silt of my lake. There probably isn't enough room for everyone there, and the *lozoviks*, who now live under the willow bushes near deep puddles and mud, and those who nest in the sedge, may perish."

Through the swamp demons who served him, the lord of the bog gave an order that under no circumstances, as the fire neared, were any of the little demons and she-demons to run away from here with the rats and rabbits who would follow the departing birds, but they were to dive to the bottom of the underground lake and not come out of there until his, the master's, order.

Slowly but surely misfortune was approaching. The fire was drawing ever nearer. With each day the blanket of fog between the earth and sky which almost hid the sun was becoming thicker and thicker. When you took a breath, you could feel the somewhat bitter smell of the acrid smoke irritating your throat and nose. Soon this smoke began to spread over the ground itself, forcing black grouse, partridges, and lone, pitifully whistling sandpipers and snipes to take wing and fly off into the distance. Small animals that lived in the swamp were making their way to the wet areas which, thanks to underground springs, had not yet dried out, and from time to time made frightened, pitiful cries to each other.

And then the fire, sending out a thick wall of pale yellow smoke, reached the forest which surrounded the demons' swamp as well.

Little fires ran by, twisting and wriggling back and forth along the dry moss and from tree to tree. One after another, tall rose-yellow pines burst into flame like torches and embraced by the flame, sang; fir trees became black and charred; the leaves of the comparatively more moist alder and osier bushes hissed as they curled up. The *drevyanitsa*s, wringing their hands, perished with the trees. The flaming deadwood crackled. Half-monsters, half-spirits of the forest, who usually hid during daylight, jumped out from beneath the deadwood and ran, paying no attention to anyone. Flaming sparks circled like birds and flew above the forest fire.

When she first saw this sight, the Leshachikha called Wart-Face was struck completely dumb and did not know what to do. Her favorite, Brown-Bear, smelling the smoke, also got confused and began to run around the forest in circles. Frightened, the Leshachikha ran behind him, trying to talk him into stopping. But the bear did not listen to her and rushed among the burning bushes as if bees and wasps were chasing him.

The matter came to an end when both found themselves on a knoll surrounded on all sides by flaming moss. In his fright the bear climbed up a high pine tree and, sitting in the top branches where there was almost no smoke, calmed down a bit and took a look around. A sea of flame, above which hung a hazy fog of brown-white smoke, raged around their little island. A red squirrel went "ts-ts-ts-ts" near Brown-Bear, but the bear did not feel like dealing with her.

The crackling of the fire resounded ever louder and closer; sparks flew around the pine tree where the lumbering animal hid. It was becoming unbearably hot. The acrid, hot smoke hid everything below from Brown-Bear's eyes.

For a moment the Leshachikha's drawn and frightened face flashed in the smoke; it flashed and then disappeared. In the same instant, a flame that had greedily licked its way up a pine enveloped the resinous branches and, at the same time, singed the bear's shaggy hide.

The bear let out a roar and, forgetting himself, hurled himself to the ground. Hurting himself badly, he nonetheless jumped to his feet and ran off, burning his paws and not remembering where he was running along the burning forest swamp.

Wart-Face completely lost her head.

Instead of running in the direction of the lake where she had previously come upon Sheep-Mug, Leshachikha began to run around the knoll full of flaming pine trees until the flames enveloped her together with the trees. The resinous sap, which flows in forest spirits instead of blood, burst into flame together with her hard, tree-like body. Her fur, which resembled shaggy moss growing on trees, began to burn quickly. Frightened and waving her long, smoking extremities, Wart-Face began to roll on the ground, listening to her body crackling and hissing. One of the fire demons embraced the Leshachikha and burned the creature—who was seized by fear—with his hot kiss.

The end came quite quickly. After rolling in the smoke among the charred trunks and bushes burning like pillars of fire, Wart-Face suddenly grew motionless. Her contorted body began to resemble a large wooden snag, in some places still black and in other places turned into red-hot coal.

Brown-Bear, with burnt soles and all singed and smoking, reached a small forest lake and, bellowing from mad happiness, jumped into the warm, rust-colored water which billowed under his weight.

He found himself in the company of the swamp she-demons, who were driving Sheep-Mug—just as frightened as Brown-Bear and also burnt in places—from their territory. Sheep-Mug, paying no attention to—probably not even noticing—the *bolotnitsa*s who were disturbed by his appearance, grabbed a willow bush which was growing in one of the tussocks; he would not leave the lake at any cost, no matter how much the beautiful she-demons hit, pinched, or tickled him.

The Leshy sat for three days and three nights in the bog lake until rain falling from the sky put out the forest fire. On the fourth day, he crawled out and went who knows where. No one ever saw Sheep-Mug again in those places where he had formerly lived, quarreled with his red-bearded neighbor, rocked on tree branches, shepherded rabbits and, picking at his bast shoes, sung simple, doleful songs on moonlit nights.

XXIV

"So you've come to ask me to take you on as an apprentice?" Aniska turned to Aksyutka, who stood before her with a somber but resolute look. "But you live with old Praskukha! Why don't you want to study with her?" the witch continued, spooning the honey out of the glass onto a plate, which the taciturn girl had brought as a gift.

"I've gotten all I can from her, Auntie Aniska. She's not going to teach me anything more. I had wanted to apprentice with Styopka earlier, but she, you know yourself, was recently strangled by the unclean force. Other than you, there's no one I can force myself on, Auntie. Praskukha doesn't know that I've come to you, and I don't want her to know," Aksyutka ended in a tone ringing with the will of a girl no longer a child.

"So that she doesn't find out, take this glass and don't forget to wash it out well with ashes before putting it back."

The desire to win over and subject the will of Praskukha's apprentice to herself in secret from Praskukha and by this action spite the old practitioner of magic pleased Aniska very much. Moreover, the command given by the Goat of the Night was still ringing in the witch's ears: "Teach her everything you know yourself. . . . Don't frighten your future apprentice and don't make it difficult for her with hard tests. . . ."

Nevertheless, the witch could not resist putting on airs and showing off a bit before Aksyutka in order to show the young girl her immeasurable superiority over her.

"I can, of course, take you on as an apprentice, but will you be able to manage? Ours is a serious craft. It's not a matter of boiling some herbs that work on aches or removing some warts. This is the kind of learning that not everyone can bear. You're not afraid of devils?"

"Why should I be afraid of them when I'm one myself, the daughter of a demon?" the young girl cut her off curtly.

"So that's the way it is!" Aniska looked at her guest. "And I thought people were lying . . . Why in the world aren't you studying with your mother?"

"If only I knew where she was, that mother of mine!"

"Well, then . . . If you want to, we'll find out, we'll learn this somehow. And if it comes to that, we'll even ask the Main Man Himself. . . . Only that's later. But first you have to cover all the learning."

"It's for the learning that I've come."

"Here's what we'll begin with. There's a moon tonight. This is a most auspicious time . . . As soon as the old woman goes to bed and falls asleep, run over here. We'll go to the grain fields together to learn how to make twists[1] and knots and ruin the harvest."

"I'll be able to manage making a knot, only I don't know the right words."

"I'll teach you," was the answer.

On that very night Aksyutka, after removing her shirt and skirt, was making twists next to the equally naked Aniska and repeating the words of the spell after her teacher:

> The moon is shining, sharp little horns.
> I go from field to field;
> In step behind me seven demons,
> And the eighth—the she-satan with us.
> No one will notice us here:
> Neither black nor fair-haired,
> Neither gray nor bald nor red-haired,
> Neither a top-notch dog nor Granddad Zhiten.[2]
> We're twisting Fedot's rye.
> I twist, the unclean tie,
> The she-satan counts the knots

---

1. a twist *(закрутка)*: a tangled bundle of stalks of uncut grain.
2. Zhiten *(Житень* comes from *жито,* which means "rye" in Ukraine, "barley" in northern Russia, and "spring-sown cereals" in general in eastern Russia. Since Kondratiev's story takes place in the south, *жито* (and forms thereof) will be translated as "rye."

(Five knots per twist),
She casts a spell on every knot.
The first knot—so that it doesn't ripen;
The second—so that rains soak it;
The third—so that hail knocks it down;
The fourth—so that it rots,
The fifth—so that worms eat it.
Whoever undoes our first knot,
His hands will twist in pain;
Whoever unties the second,
Aches will be his due;
And whoever touches the third,
Longing will torment him;
Whoever undoes our fourth knot,
Blindness will be his as long as he shall live;
And whoever decides to touch our fifth,
Must to his loved ones say final good-byes;
Whoever pulls out and throws away the entire twist,
Certain death that year cannot escape.
My spell is stronger than iron.
There is no counter spell to a twist,
Neither wise man nor magic healer—man or woman,
Nor Grandfather Rye himself can remove it.

At first getting cold feet at the mention of the she-satan and
looking all around furtively, Aksyutka, after convincing herself
that there was no third person next to her and Aniska, quickly recovered and at the end of the ritual did not hesitate to ask her
mentor some questions.

"And who is this Zhiten whom we mentioned in the spell,
Auntie Aniska?" the girl asked, when both of them, now dressed,
were walking back to the village along the wet, dewy grass,
which was making their feet grow cold.

Happy with her pupil's ability to quickly take in and memorize the words of the spell thoroughly, the witch willingly satisfied Aksyutka's curiosity.

"This is the grandfather who lives in the grain fields. Not
everyone is permitted to see him. . . . Although I have met this
Zhiten once or twice, I was afraid to come near him. That's why I
don't know if it's true or not that he has three eyes on his forehead. . . . Others call him Goat of the Rye because he's supposed

to have a goat's beard and horns. . . . But I didn't notice any horns. In appearance he is feeble and overgrown with gray hair but, still, he walks about with a club and watches over the growing grain actively and vigilantly. In the fall, when people are sowing, Zhiten walks invisibly along the ploughed fields and tramples the seeds into the damp earth so that birds can't peck them. He guards, it seems, not every field, but only the fields of those owners who plough well and harrow. But I don't believe that. Styopka, when I was still studying with her myself, told me that Grandfather Rye once chased her off the plot of a very bad owner. That owner knew how to please him: after the Great Day[3] he buried the bones of the Easter piglet on the boundary of his field. This Grandfather shows himself not only at night but also in broad daylight, just like the *poludnitsa*.[4] Grandfather Rye usually appears to people in the form of a poor beggar somewhere near the grain fields. If he shakes his finger at the person he meets, that means there'll be misfortune—don't wait for a good harvest then ! . . . But don't you go near him, no matter when you catch sight of him, be it day or night. He doesn't like our kind and can give you a good beating with his club, particularly if he finds you doing your business," the witch finished what she had to say.

"Auntie Aniska, what can the *poludnitsa*s do to us?"

"Although they're not sheep of our flock, they know how to do mischief. For example, the *poludnitsa* leads little children astray who walk in the grain fields and can lead them so far away that they won't make it back home until evening. And she can do harm to adults. . . . I, when I was still a little girl, saw a *poludnitsa* during harvest but was afraid to go near her. . . . All in white, tall, so very tall, walking among the women, stopping, watching them reaping, but they didn't notice her. She walked around, walked around, stopped near one, and touched the crown of her head with her hand. The woman at first sat down and then barely managed to get to the wagon and wet her head with water from a pitcher. . . . Later she kept saying that the sun had been baking hot. Old people say that she doesn't allow women to reap at noon and even can, it seems, twist off their heads. . . . I don't believe

---

3. the Great Day *(Велик День)*, or Easter.
4. *poludnitsa (полудница):* spirit of the fields who appears at noon *(полдень)* as a beautiful maiden dressed all in white. Among other things, she twists the heads of those who work at noon instead of resting.

that. But you, if you ever meet her, bow respectfully and let her pass. You don't have to bow, but don't give her "the fig" either. She's not a demon. . . . Now we'll go our separate ways. You go right. You'll make it to Praskukha's place more quickly through the vegetable gardens. . . . Come see me tomorrow afternoon and don't forget a bit of honey," Aniska finished what she had to say.

The outline of the village buildings already loomed dark against the hazy-bluish night sky.

Aksyutka ran down the path which led along the vegetable gardens and quickly disappeared in the darkness. Only her quick, half-child's legs could be heard stamping in the distance . . .

Aniska's apprentice could not fall asleep the whole night: the harm which they did to Fedot's grain field disturbed her so much. Praskukha, looking at her in the morning, even gasped when she saw the alarmingly pinched face of her adopted daughter.

"What's wrong, my little girl? You haven't gotten ill, have you?! Has somebody put the evil eye on you?"

"No, grandma, I'm well and for the time being there isn't anyone who could have put the evil eye on me. My face has changed because my heart is not at peace. Last night Aniska and I made twists in Fedot's field."

"What's wrong with you, my child? How did you get to know her?! How did she entice you? And what is the pleasure of doing harm to people?!"

"Aniska didn't entice me. I went to her myself. And although there's no pleasure in doing harm to people, sorcery attracts me like a fire draws a moth. Evidently, I'm truly born for it. . . . And I begged Aniska to teach me witchcraft because you, grandma, refused to teach me how to summon unclean spirits and have power over them."

"But Aksyutochka, my poor little one, the unclean won't do anything for you for free. You have to pay them for everything . . . oh, how you have to pay them—with evil deeds! Just think what harm you brought yesterday to Fedot!"

"Why am I telling you this, grandma, if not so that you can prepare for what has been done? Fedot and his wife will come to no one else but you today. . ."

"Yes, that's true. . . . And what kind of a spell was it?"

"A spell with a counter spell. With seven demons and a she-satan."

"Aha . . . I know it. Thanks for telling me . . . I don't understand you, however. Perhaps you really are born for it, since sorcery attracts you. . . . However, you do have a conscience. Neither demons nor those born to sorcery have a conscience. I'm just sorry for you, Aksyutochka. You'll perish for nothing. The unclean force will be your undoing!"

"I'd only like to find out about my parents, grandma. To see what they were like, their names and their sins. And then I'll go to a monastery and pray for my sins and theirs."

"It's good if it's only that, but 'they' won't let you near a monastery, my little girl. 'They' don't like it when their game gets away from them. . . . I see you going to your ruin. Is it really preordained for you?"

"I don't understand myself, grandma. Sorcery just keeps attracting me. But most of all, I want to see my mother."

"Here's what I'm going to say to you, Aksyutka. If you ever do any harm to anyone with Aniska, always tell me about it. I'll try to straighten it out as best I can. Don't decide to do anything terribly frightening or sinful and don't give your consent. And as for the unclean spirits, no matter what kind of gentlemen they might be dressed in their best clothing, don't let them near you. Say that you're afraid and that's that. They'll leave you alone, you'll see, and you'll be able to find out something about your parents from them in the meantime. And as for the rest, whatever God wills."

"Grandma, I took a glass of honey from you yesterday, and I'll take one today. I promised her . . ."

"Take it today, but don't bring her any more. Say that I guessed and am locking it away from you. Don't bring it to her for any reason whatsoever! . . . If it were gratitude for a good deed, but this, may the Lord forgive you, is for demonic pranks. . . ."

Seeing that Aksyutka was willingly learning sorcery and without any hesitation, helping not only with fortune-telling but the personal affairs of her mentor as well, Aniska lost all inhibition with her. She not only taught her various spells, including spells for attracting affection, but she also showed the young girl how to milk other people's cows without leaving her yard. Moreover, the witch promised her apprentice to teach her to fly on a broomstick and to turn into an owl, frog, or cat.

"Only in these matters, my dear, you cannot do without the unclean force. And you have to please this force," Aniska said to the young girl, who was listening to her attentively.

"And how do you please it?"

"By doing everything to make it happy. The first thing is to renounce the cross and the One to whom the priests pray and everything to which the church bows."

"I don't have a cross. I had one, but I lost it when I was still very small, and since my mother was a swamp demon, then it means there's nothing for me to renounce," Aksyutka objected.

"You've already said that to me. But nonetheless you'll still have to renounce it, if in words only. And you'll also have to bow to the new Master."

"What master exactly?"

"The one from whom you'll receive your power over the unclean spirits."

"I don't even need any power... If I could just see my mother..."

"If you don't receive power over the unclean spirits of the swamp and water, better not stick your head in there. They won't let you."

"Well, if I can't do without that, then I can even bow," the young girl said pensively, remembering her unsuccessful journey to the swamp. "And when and where will I need to bow to him in order to receive the power?"

"That's at night, my dear. When there's a new moon on Thursday, we'll go together beyond the village to the crossroads to see him. . . . But for the time being, you have to win him over in advance. . . ."

At that moment, a knocking was heard on the cottage door, and then a woman from another village walked in and, taking Aniska aside, began to whisper to her.

Aksyutka moved off a small distance away.

Her mentor could be seen listening to the passionate whispering of the woman who had come in, nodding her head sympathetically from time to time and saying pensively, "Yes . . . Yes . . ."

"Why not? It's possible," Aniska finally said calmly and confidently when her guest had finished her story.

With these words, the witch got up from the bench and went to a chest.

After rummaging through it, the sorceress removed a can, took out a piece of paper, and poured three tablespoons of whatever was in the can on it.

"Give it in kvass or in cabbage soup," she said. "And if, by any chance, they find it and ask, tell them that it's for the rats."

After receiving the remedy that she wanted, the woman took out an old silver ruble and gave it to Aniska. When she left, the witch explained to her apprentice:

"She wants to get rid of her father-in-law. She's tired of that old sod and his pestering. . . . Well, you see, I've pleased my master as well. Study, Aksyutka! There's a lot of pleasing him in this can."

"And how much should you give?" the girl asked.

"A pinch at a time so that it won't be very noticeable."

"And if you wanted it to be immediate?"

"Well, then, put half a spoonful . . ."

Without asking about anything else, Aksyutka concentrated on watching Aunt Aniska hide the can in the chest.

XXV

The appropriate full moon on a Thursday occurred only a year later, in the month of August. It had occurred, incidentally, in winter as well, but the weather was very cold, and Aniska could not bring herself to take her apprentice to bow before the Master at such a time.

"She can freeze off her hands or feet and then, for all you know, Praskukha will find out," she thought.

In this space of time, Aksyutka became her own woman in Aniska's hut. She already could help the witch make love potions, she knew the make-up of almost all of the medicinal remedies, and she had a good memory for what roots, herbs, and powders there were and where.

Notwithstanding the quick mind and brightness of her apprentice, however, Aniska could not bring herself either to let the girl know the secret of preparing the ointment for flying or to take her to Mount Osiyan. Aksyutka had not been added yet to the host of sorceresses, and she had not been marked with the Goat of the Night's claw, and uninitiated persons could always run into unpleasant situations when they appeared at the witches' celebration. . . .

They were both waiting with some excitement for the full moon to appear: Aniska, in the hope of ingratiating herself before the Master, and Aksyutka, thinking uneasily of the tests which awaited her.

Finally, the solemnly frightening night on which the witch's initiation of the young girl was to take place arrived.

The roadside cross, to which Aniska told her apprentice to come, stood at a crossroads, behind the cemetery, half a verst from the village. The young moon had already hidden behind the clouds; it was rather dark and the air was relatively fresh.

Whether the cool, autumn night was the reason, or whether it was the fear and emotion, when she came to the designated place before midnight and sat down not far from the cross, near a ditch, Aksyutka felt a chill. Her lower jaw shook noticeably; her teeth chattered from time to time and, as for her heart, what is there to say? . . .

Aniska had not yet come. The wind was rustling in the tree tops. The sky was dark. Something stirred in the bushes. Although she was not afraid of the unclean spirits of the forest or swamp, the young girl was afraid of the Devil, whom she imagined as a person of a higher office. Although earlier she had certainly counted on bargaining with him, now her fear before the unknown almost caused Aksyutka to run away.

Suddenly the voice of Aniska, who approached quietly barefooted, was heard not far away. "Aksyutka, are you here?"

"Here, Auntie Aniska! You're finally here! I began to get scared already and almost went home."

"What is there to be afraid of, you little fool? No one will hurt you. I'm just a little bit late. Soon it'll be midnight. We have to hurry! . . Here's what, my girl. The first thing you have to do is take off your cross and step on it with your foot."

"I don't have a cross. You were told I was the daughter of a demon!"

"What now then? . . I don't have one either, you know. . . . Well, if that's the way it is, then we can manage without a cross around your neck. Here's your cross! See it?" And the witch pointed to the wooden cross by the side of the road which towered near them, to which were affixed wooden implements of "passion": a hammer, pliers, a small almost toy-like ladder, a walking-stick with a handle, and a spear. "Put your left heel on the post, a bit higher . . . And now undress and climb up this cross upside down."

"I probably won't be able to," Aksyutka uttered indecisively.

"What do you mean, you won't be able to?! Watch me! I'm no longer a young girl like you, and I'm heavier than you, and my stomach is bigger than yours, but watch me climb up!"

The witch checked her braids, which she had wound into a bun at the back of her head, and quickly took off her dress. Then jumping on a step of the cross, Aniska grabbed the bottom cross-piece[1] and hung with her head down. She threw her feet up and put them between the middle post and the staffs of the walking-stick and the spear which came up against it. Moving with her hands, Aniska grabbed the transverse ladder, then the walking stick and spear, and pushed herself even higher. The witch's legs were now thrown over the main cross-bar of the cross. Aniska hung there for about a minute, first looking at the bottomless starry sky past her feet, then at the earth which seemed like a low, dark roof with bushes and trees hanging from it. There were no unclean spirits nor even any unclean dead visible for the time being.

The naked body, raised strangely high for anyone looking, loomed white, seemingly shimmering in the darkness of the night. Remembering that she was here for Aksyutka, and that there was very little time left before midnight, the witch mumbled the usual words of a short incantation for such situations and began to come down carefully.

"That's how we do it!" she said sprightly, now standing on the ground and throwing on her blouse. "Now it's your turn. I'll help you. And when you climb up as I did and throw your feet across the cross-piece, hold on tightly so that you don't fall when you see somebody. 'He' will ask you about different things: who you are and what you need, and if you're renouncing this and that. . . . Don't forget to say, 'I renounce' when it's called for!"

Aniska helped Aksyutka take off her dress and slip and half-picked up the young girl's slightly shivering body in her arms.

"Lift your legs up! . . Grab the cross-bar! . . And now pull up using your hands! . . . Don't scratch your behind on the short lad-der! . . . Higher! . . Pull up some more! . . Some more! . . That's the way! . . . Well, all set?. . . . Are you hanging? . . . Hold on tightly now and be quiet! . . . I will call 'Him' and 'He' will come soon."

Aniska began to read an incantation . . . But suddenly the enchantress broke off her reading and said in a quick whisper, "Aksyutka! Get down quickly! Look, some boys are coming! . . Look alive, get down quickly!"

---

1. An Orthodox cross has two cross-pieces. The shorter cross-piece, the one below, is sometimes placed at an angle.

The young girl, whose head was already spinning terribly, became frightened and, with her heart beating hard, tried to lower herself quickly, but since she was unused to doing this, she lost her grip and fell, hitting herself hard against the ground. In turn, the two youths who were passing at that time along the road became frightened themselves and, shouting loudly, took off into a field.

Aniska mumbled a curse in their direction, helped her apprentice get to her feet, although Aksyutka had not yet fully come to her senses, and began to dress her quickly.

"Hurry, Aksyutka, because boys from the whole village will probably come running here!" she said agitated. After checking to see if Aksyutka's dress had gotten torn, leaving a piece of cloth on the ground, Aniska took the dressed Aksyutka by the hand and ran with her through the field along the ditch in the direction of the cemetery. Skirting it, they came out on another road which led to the village. When the vegetable gardens came into view, the witch let the young girl go home while she herself walked unhurriedly into the village and, not meeting anyone, made her way to her hut.

"How annoying!" she thought, walking into the entranceway, "now it'll have to be put off until the next full moon on a Thursday. And then it'll probably be a bit cold for getting stark naked and going to all that trouble. . . . Well, we'll arrange it somehow. . . ."

Closing the door behind her, Aniska lit a small candle for a little while so that neighbors would see that she was at home, then extinguished it, got into bed and, covering herself with a sheepskin coat, fell asleep.

The boys who saw her with Aksyutka at the roadside cross told their friends the next day about how the unclean force near the village had frightened them.

"We were walking, you know, from Kurkovitsy. It was already late and dark. We approach the cross and there, on the cross-bars, naked witches are sitting like crows. And two or three are wandering around under the cross. And when they caught sight of us, they fluttered their white wings and darted into the grass and then toward us! We're trying to get away from them, and they're after us. . . . Barely got away! Those damned things were chasing us, and we thought they would get us any minute. . . . They let us be, however. And we had already started thinking that they'd tear us apart! . . ."

XXVI

Evening was approaching. Aniska was telling Aksyutka, who was sitting in her cottage, what one should do in order to bewitch young men. In the window she saw Senya, who had been promised to her by the Goat of the Night at the sabbath, walking down the street and heading home after a hunt, with a rifle on his back and a satchel on his shoulder.

The witch felt as if something struck her heart. Her face became flushed from a rush of blood. "It's him!" flew through her head. But the enchantress was quickly able to control the emotion that overcame her and with an artificially indifferent voice uttered, "Do you see, let's take for example, that youth? If you like, he'll be here tomorrow." And after a short silence added: "Run out of the hut and bring his footprint. He's wearing boots, and you'll be able to find his footprint easily. Collect the earth it's in and put it in the clean rag which is on the bench next to the trunk, then bring it here. I'll teach you how to do it. At some point it might prove useful to you, too. Take a knife from the table . . ."

Hurriedly grabbing the rag that Aniska had pointed out and the knife, Aksyutka rushed out of the hut. The youth man's shirt was still visible in the distance as he walked away. The witch's apprentice quickly found the impression of Senya's hunting boots, looked around and, hurriedly, partly cut out, partly scraped out the earth where there was the footprint in the half-dry mud. A few minutes later she triumphantly brought the rag full of this earth to Aniska.

"Brought it? . . Oh, my girl, you should have cut it out entirely so that the whole imprint would be visible. . . ."

"Then I'll run out again, Auntie Aniska, and cut out and bring the second footprint as you've told me to do."

"It's probably too late. You have to take the footprint while it's still nice and hot, but now those that are still in the street have probably grown cold. And then, children are playing not far off. They might notice . . . For a start, even the one you brought will do. I'll hang it in this rag in the stove and say a spell so that this same Senya will come here tomorrow evening."

Untying the rag, Aniska started to whisper a spell in which the youth was ordered to "pine away" with love for her, to think of the sorceress day and night, and to seek a meeting with her.

"It's a wonderful thing—the footprint," she said to her apprentice. "If you act quickly and cut it out whole and then put it in the stove with the toe toward you and the heel in the direction from which the man came or where he lives, then he'll come without fail. If you want to be the ruin of somebody, then instead of drying it in the stove, you can bury it in a cemetery. Only make sure again that the toe points towards a grave and the heel, in the direction of his home. . . ."

"If you want him to get sick, then hammer a fresh nail or a sharp piece of glass into the footprint. Then the man will have aches and pains throughout his body. And if you drive a nail into a horse's hoof prints, then the horse will get sick. . . . Some people stick a nail in the person's shadow instead of in his footprint, but that's even more difficult. . . . Remember one thing: while you're doing this, wish with all the power in you, with your whole being, that the thing you're saying comes true. That's the main thing . . . The words in a spell—that's a special matter. You have to know them perfectly, too. And regardless of whatever absurd or unclear word you come across, you can't skip over it!"

"And what are these words, Auntie?"

"You'll find out everything later. . . ." And the witch began to whisper the introductory part of the spell.

Aksyutka watched every motion of her teacher carefully and tried to memorize every word she caught.

Judging by the expression on Aniska's face when she repeated the spell, Aksyutka guessed that the witch was taken with Semen Voloshkevich in earnest and would not rest until he was fully in her power.

Although the witch had not asked her apprentice to come, the next day before sunset the girl appeared under some pretext and noticed that Aniska, all dressed up, with her eyes lightly outlined and with a touch of rouge on her cheeks, was clearly waiting for Senya. When Aksyutka arrived, the witch gave her the task of keeping a lookout and informing her immediately when the young hunter appeared.

"It would be good, for the sake of certainty, to throw a birch twig under his feet so that he'd step over it, and then to put that twig in the stove with the words, 'Dry, Semyon Voloshkevich, out of love for me, Aniska Onopreyeva, as this twig is drying.' But this kind of spell you can do only on Fridays, and today is Wednesday," Aniska uttered pensively, "so, my dear Aksyutochka, watch out for that young fellow for me."

Aksyutka began to watch out for him.

The street which had been empty during the day became alive toward evening. Two women quickly went by, one after the other, carrying greyish linen sacks filled with weeds. Little by little, their wagons screeching, the men who had been working in the fields returned home. Small children appeared at the gate, and young girls with twigs in their hands came to meet and lead away the cows, pigs, and sheep returning from pasture.

Senya appeared, too, a bit late today, this time for some reason wearing not his boots but *porshni*.[1]

It was evident from the hunter's walk that he had gone on a big outing today. The killed game hung on his belt on the left.

"Auntie Aniska!.. He's coming!" appearing in the witch's hut, Aksyutka said, gasping for breath from the excitement.

In the meantime Aniska was pouring something dark from a small glass vial into a large jug containing kvass, which she had just brought from the cellar.

Glancing at the piece of looking-glass hanging on the wall and apparently satisfied with what she saw, the witch tugged at her dress and followed Aksyutka out on the porch.

Voloshkevich was already at Aniska's house. It was evident that the day had not been a waste. Besides a few young ducks, a partridge, a snipe, and a pair of black grouse, there was a colorful woodpecker, shot by the young hunter, which stood out as a bright spot on top of all the greyish-brown wild game.

"Hello, Senichka," Aniska sang more than spoke in a sweet voice. "How many birds you've shot! But why did you kill the

---

1. *porshni* (поршни) are shaped like bast-shoes (which look like closed slippers) but made of leather.

woodpecker? Surely you're not going to eat him? His unhappy life came to an end because of your doing!"

"Why was his life unhappy?" Senya could not stop himself from asking.

"Don't you know yourself? And you're schooled! A woodpecker gouges out trees with his beak. He gets so worn out during the day that he can't sleep at night from his head aching. If you don't believe me, then walk up to a hollow in the tree where he spends the night, and you'll hear how he's moaning, the poor thing. . . . Make a gift of that bird to me, Senichka."

"I can't. I've killed him because I need the wings. I want to take them to town and give them to the person I promised them to. . . ."

"You take the wings for yourself, Senichka, and give the rest to me. As it turns out, I have no need for the woodpecker's wings. . . . Come into my cottage. You'll cut them off there. And I'll treat you to some milk or kvass. Which do you want?"

"I don't feel like milk, for some reason, but if the kvass is cold, then I'll have some. And I'll give you the woodpecker if you don't need the wings, Aniska. I'll just cut them off right now."

Senya untied the woodpecker, which was hanging by its feet from his belt, removed the bright, beautiful wings with his knife, slipped them under his shirt, and the body—which had grown small from this procedure—with its dangling, long-beaked head he passed to the witch smiling pleasantly at him.

"Come into the cottage, Senichka. Try some kvass," she said.

Voloshkevich adjusted the rifle on his back and walked up onto the porch. Passing through the entranceway, he found himself in the witch's hut. It was tidy and clean; the floor had been swept. A pair of white clay mugs and a jug covered with a wooden slab stood on the table. Aniska removed the cover and poured some thick, dark liquid into one of the mugs.

"Drink to your health, Senichka," she said, and when he had emptied the mug, she asked, "Do you want some more?"

"No, thank you."

"Isn't it tasty or cold enough? I just took it off ice . . ."

"It's cold all right. It's just that you can't make out its taste, and it isn't sour enough. There's too much sugar."

"I added some honey to it," the witch explained.

"And what are you going to do with that woodpecker?" Voloshkevich asked.

"Oh, I'll find some use," was the evasive answer. "Birds are good for a lot of things. It's not just for the wings or the meat that knowing people value them. . . . For example, if you wrap the heart of a blackbird in a rag and put it at the head of the bed, a secret will be revealed to you. Or if you ever shoot a lark and bring its little feet here, it'll be good for me too: I won't have to put up with slander, and I'll thank you for it. I know a spell that will make your rifle never miss . . . Just bring them, and I won't delay in carrying out my part of the bargain . . ."

"You know how to do all that?"

"I'll be able to do everything for you. Just don't forget me. Bring and show me the birds you kill, and I'll cast a spell on your rifle and teach you the right words so that animals in the forest move toward you, and birds fly where you are, and fish bite when you're fishing. I won't delay in carrying out my part of the bargain . . ."

"Well, all right. I'll bring you both a blackbird and a lark when I come across them. And for now, goodbye!"

Aniska's guest took the rifle that he had put in a corner, threw it on his shoulder, and walked out of the hut.

"Come by anytime," the enchantress said to him in a melodious voice as he was leaving. "I'll give you some kvass or milk . . ."

But Senya was already out on the street, not feeling the four female eyes following him.

"It's probably not worth drinking milk at her place. People say that devils help her milk other people's cows. . . . But as for the kvass, it's not bad—the kvass is cold and sweet. . . . Even sickly sweet," the young hunter thought as he neared home where the deacon's wife was heating up the remains of dinner for her nephew.

XXVII

More than likely Aniska's magical treatments had their effect. Senya began to drop by her whitewashed cottage, which smelled of herbs for healing and love potions, more and more often.

At first he did this when he was returning from hunting, and then he dropped by even when he did not go hunting, sometimes for a spell over his rifle, sometimes to get advice about a dream or a hunting sign, and sometimes simply to chat with the beautiful and fawningly attentive witch.

At Aniska's the youth also often met Aksyutka, to whose presence the witch at first paid no notice but then began to send home, usually immediately after his arrival.

This seemed insulting to the girl, but she did not show her dissatisfaction and would disappear uncomplainingly at the first command of her mentor.

"I know what you're trying to get from him! Do you think I don't know why you're adding your own blood to the kvass and then mixing in honey so that it won't be noticeable? You're making this effort for your Master or for yourself," the young girl thought, angrily striding home along a narrow path, past vegetables beds with cabbage, onions, and peas.

An ill-will had been ripening in Aksyutka's heart for a long time toward the witch who was bewitching the young man with sorcery and deception, a feeling that was combined perhaps with compassion, perhaps with tenderness, toward him.

Aksyutka thought a lot about Senya and sometimes even saw him in her dreams. But in her waking hours she did not let on that she was not indifferent to him and even avoided looking at him when Aniska was present.

Aksyutka made a firm decision in her heart that, whatever the price, she would not allow the young man she liked to become a plaything for Aniska's love games and whims.

With trepidation in her heart, the witch's apprentice tried to guess when her mentor would want at last to take advantage of the love potions' effect on the youth, potions which were poured in or mixed in powder form, first in kvass and then, when Senya began to drop by more often, in tea.

Aniska, however, was in no hurry. She did not want her lover, promised by the Master, to become a chance victim of her whim and to run away in horror after his first half-involuntary embraces.

The witch tried to arouse in Senya an uncontrollable and unquenchable passion so that he would cling to her, as she put it, " 'til death."

When the effect of the potions poured into him almost daily seemed enough to Aniska, she invited Senya, who was already beginning to be unable to take his eyes off her, to come and spend an evening together, promising to finally reveal a spell to him which knowing hunters use to force the *leshy* to send all kinds of wild game in their direction.

"And besides that, I'll teach you what spells to use to tame the leshy himself if you should happen to meet up with him accidentally in the forest."

"And what if instead of the *leshy* I see the *leshachikha*? Then what? Say the same spell or another one?" Senya jokingly asked of the sorceress.

"I didn't even think about the *leshachikha,* Senichka. Only one herb, Senichka, helps against the *leshachikha* . . . However, I won't give you that herb for nothing in return. . . ."

"And what do you want for that herb?"

"When you come to my place this evening, we'll have a talk and bargain a bit. I won't ask for much, don't be afraid!" the witch said with a honeyed smile in an affectionate, melodious voice.

Senya willingly gave his promise to come, but for the time being went off swimming; after that, he still had to drop by the village priest's on some matter.

Aksyutka, who heard the whole conversation, stayed in the hut; Aniska went out to the porch to see her guest off. The young girl's fine hearing caught the whispering, smacking of kisses, shuffling, and happy, slightly suppressed laughter of the embracing pair in the entranceway. The ears of the witch's apprentice pricked up, and immediately there was a change in her facial expression of which she herself was oblivious; it was the same smile which appeared whenever her mother, Maryska, dragged incautious hunters who found themselves in her embrace to the bottom of the bog. A fatal decision ripened immediately in the heart of the daughter of a demon. . . .

Aniska, who had reentered the cottage, began to make preparations with the help of her apprentice for the evening guest's arrival. The witch fell into such daydreams that she had no desire to attend to the samovar herself or to prepare passion-arousing potions which she intended to add to the decanter of sweet, dark liqueur for her guest. Aksyutka diligently helped her with both of these tasks. Maryska's daughter even managed—something Aniska had not asked her to do at all—to pour unseen, onto a piece of paper, some white powder which was used by the witch not only on rats but sometimes even on people.

"Put more of the potion in the decanter," Aniska commanded, "so that there is enough for both of us. I want to tire myself out and to exhaust him as well. . . ."

"Neither one of you will get tired out. Watch out!" Aksyutka joked, smiling enigmatically.

Seeing that Senya himself was striving to possess the comely witch and seemingly not even noticing her, the young girl decided to punish them both. Taking advantage of the fact that Aniska went off to the ice-cellar, Maryska's daughter quickly poured the powder she had stolen into the decanter and shook the vessel a few times so that it would dissolve. Upon returning, Aniska herself mixed in some honey, burdock syrup, and another passion-arousing essence. Then they both sliced sausage brought from the ice-house and put cow's milk, a loaf of bread made with sifted flour, and herring and onions in hemp oil on the table.

When everything was ready, the witch allowed her helper and apprentice to go home after telling her that she should not come too early the next morning.

Closing the door after the young girl, the sorceress took *obratim*[1]—a root for love potions—from the trunk, put it on a large

---

1. *obratim (обратим):* literally, "the herb which turns" someone to another. Unable to find an English equivalent.

piece of looking-glass and looked into it for a long time, whisper-ing, "Just as I look at myself in the looking-glass and not tire of looking, so may my Senya not tire of looking at me. . . ."

⁓

The supper, which Aniska offered to her guest, ended completely contrary to the way the witch, lost in her daydreams earlier, had wanted it to end. After she and Senya rather quickly emptied the decanter with its special ingredients, Aniska began to wait impa-tiently for the potions she had added to it to take effect, but the effect turned out to be entirely different from the one on which she had placed her hopes. Instead of burning with passion for her, the young man suddenly became pensive and began to sigh somewhat strangely, and then suddenly his pale face took on a look of suffering. Covered in cold sweat and shivering, he finally got up from the stool and, saying that he felt poorly, hastily bade her goodbye, and began to look for his hat.

Aniska (who had drunk less) noticed that he staggered twice, as if drunk.

"From not being used to it, I suppose," she thought and tried to stop him from leaving.

"Senichka, stay! This'll pass. That's the fruit brandy hitting your head. Rest here! Lie down on my bed . . . You'll see, it'll all pass!"

But Senya, mumbling something indistinct in answer, stepped over the threshold, slammed the door behind him and, stagger-ing, walked down the porch steps. He was experiencing dizzi-ness, nausea and, at times, a burning pain in his stomach.

The young man had not yet gotten home when he felt even more weak, a need to vomit, and collapsed like a drunk in the middle of the street. . . .

Some youths who were passing by, thinking that he had had too much to drink, laughed and tried to shake him, but Senya did not answer and did not move, as if dead. The youths left him lying there and went on their way. However, one of them, pass-ing by the house of the deacon, knocked on the window and told the deacon's wife that she should go and pick up her nephew who had had too much to drink and was lying in the middle of the street opposite Ipat Saveliev's hut.

The deacon's wife, afraid to say anything to her husband who had already gone to bed, woke up her woman servant and went out with her to search for Senya. Although it was a dark night, they found the young man, who lay without moving, rather quickly. Accidentally touching his head, the deacon's wife exclaimed "oh" and pulled her hand away. Senya's forehead, wet with sweat, was already cold, like a dead man's.

The two women tried to pick up Senya as he lay in the street, but it was hard for them. The deacon's wife then sent her servant to ask Ipat to help them move her sick nephew. Although Ipat had only recently returned from the forest and was still having supper, he quickly finished eating and went to help. The three of them carried Senya, who showed no signs of life, to a tiny side room in the deacon's house and put him to bed. The deacon's wife and her husband, who had been awakened, tried to bring the nephew round for a long time but without any success.

Only toward morning did they finally become convinced that Senya was no longer breathing.

Aniska, after her young guest had left her table and hut so unexpectedly, could not collect herself for a long time.

"It's true, he really didn't feel quite himself. Aksyutka probably overdid it with the potion. . . . Just look, even my head has started spinning! . . . And nausea is rising in my throat. . . . That's it. The girl put in too much. I'll teach her tomorrow! I'll show her!"

Staggering like Senya, Aniska dragged herself to the bed and lay down. Soon burning pains began in the witch's stomach. A cold sweat covered her whole weakened body, which shivered as if she had a fever. Everything grew dark before her eyes, and she felt giddy; she could hear a noise, similar to the summoning booms of the demonic tambourine, in her ears. A bit more, and it seemed to Aniska—who was losing consciousness—that she was naked, sitting on a broom, and flying to a sabbath. "Why not on a Thursday but on a Tuesday?" went through her head. . . . A cold, damp mist surrounded her. The noise of voices vying with one another nearby and in the distance did not stop ringing in her ears. But then, Satan's horn sounded piercingly, calling her, and drowned them all out.

"And here's the Bride!" someone proclaimed in the darkness (for the candle in Aniska's room had burned down). The voice was hoarse and seemingly familiar. In the darkness of the night a red dot began to take shape in outline, at first far away, then nearer and nearer, then gradually turning into a spot. In the spot appeared the face of the Goat of the Night, illuminated by the fires of the sabbath and full of expectation. The face was not the ceremonial one—not the one with the third horn in the shape of a small torch on his forehead, between the two other horns—but the second face, the one which the worshipers of the Sovereign of the Night kiss while bending under the throne. This mysterious face, as the witch had noticed earlier, was strikingly similar to her own. In the reflection of the flames, the outline of this face seemed even significantly younger, more correct, and more beautiful than Aniska's. With a strange smile, he was drawing near, bending down toward the sorceress lying motionless with her eyes wide-open.

For some reason the witch became frightened. She felt that she must jump off the bed and hide or run away, but she did not have the strength even to stir. . . . The face kept bending towards her. The smiling lips were moving and, as the face drew close, the lips merged with Aniska's lips.

The chilling cold of the kiss penetrated the sorceress' whole body, drowning out the burning pain in the lower part of the stomach of the dying woman. The witch felt as if she were merging with the one who was kissing her. This merging was both terrifying and sharply sweet. A throbbing enjoyment ran through her whole body. The limbs of the Devil's bride stretched out and became motionless again. An instant later, Aniska was already looking down—with the eyes of the phantom who had merged with her—at her wide wooden bed, where on a patched quilt her body was stretched out, which was no longer breathing and which she no longer needed.

XXVIII

Sent home by her mentor, Aksyutka tried not to show in any way the emotions that had taken hold of her. She solicitously helped Praskukha with the household, listened to her instructions attentively, and went to sleep on the stove—where a piece of felt lay spread out for her—at the same time as the old woman.

At first, memories of the day's events would not allow her to fall asleep, but little by little the pictures of those memories became more and more dim; more intimate and pleasant images began to mix in with them. Her thoughts drifted off to someplace far away. And with them, the soul of the daughter of the swamp demon Maryska also flew off into sleepy, far-off places, freeing itself of the distressing feelings brought on by the shocks experienced in one day.

At first she hovered somewhere very far away, in a world of states inexpressible in human language; then she returned little by little to earthly scenes and impressions.

The girl saw herself running quickly through a flowering meadow toward a forest. There, she knew, she was supposed to meet someone who would show her how and where she could find her mother. Without hesitation Aksyutka walked under a canopy of trees, intending to make her way to the swamp along a narrow path. But soon somebody dark and unpleasant appeared on the path, blocking her way. The girl started to run. It occurred to her that she could find out about her mother's birth place only on that roadside cross which Aniska had been forcing her to climb. . . . And there's Aksyutka already beyond the cemetery. The sky has become dark. There is no one near the cross. That means, she can take off her dress and slip and stick them in the bushes near the ditch. . . . It's not as difficult to climb onto the cross as it had seemed at first. Even very easy. Her back slides without any difficulty along the damp wood and brushes against the ladder, walking stick, and spear; she throws her feet, one after the other, over the cross-beam. Her head, thrown back, first looks at the starry sky, then surveys the surrounding area. . . . Someone dark emerges out of the ground very close by.

"Get down, girl," a voice resounded, familiar and not at all frightening.

Aksyutka got down obediently from the cross. Peering at the person who had approached, she saw that this was a bearded man, his face overgrown with red hair; he bore a striking resemblance to one of the local peasants. At the same time the young girl understood that under that very ordinary, village appearance was concealed none other than the devil himself.

"Get dressed, girl," the man said commandingly.

Aksyutka got dressed quickly. One question tormented her: What did this hairy person talking to her—in whose voice she could sense hostility—want from her?

"Let's go," the familiar and decisive voice was heard again.

"Where? Why?" Aksyutka tried to ask timidly.

"The authorities are asking for you!" And the devil with the appearance of a peasant led the young girl down a dark road.

"Where are you taking me, uncle?" Aksyutka continued to ask, walking next to him.

"You'll see," her guide answered darkly.

The girl guessed that her hairy companion wanted to take her as far away as possible from the water where, in the words of the old swamp demon, her mother lived, the only person who could save her and not allow the inhabitant of the flames of hell—who had assumed a human appearance exactly as old Praskukha had described demons doing—to hurt her. "If he's of the fiery type, then he won't go in the water," flashed through Aksyutka's mind. This realization calmed the girl somewhat and gave rise to the hope that she would be saved.

"And if I don't go with you?" she asked in an unexpectedly brave voice.

"I'll take you," was the short answer. And the hand with the long claws reached for the girl and tried to grab her by the shoulder.

Maryska's daughter jumped aside quickly and agilely.

"At first you'll have to catch me!" she shouted in a sharp,

shrill voice and, picking up her skirt, rushed down the road to the village.

Making heavy and frequent stamping sounds with his boots, the devil—in appearance a man—chased her tirelessly and persistently.

"Don't you dare run away! I'll catch you all the same! All the same you'll be ours!" he shouted at Aksyutka, who was moving like a whirlwind through the village.

Aksyutka understood that she had to reach the river before the devil. Her mother would defend her in the Yaryn!

The young girl strained every nerve. Winded from running so quickly, and trampling and splashing, she finally ran into the water up to her knees and turned around to look.

The devil was standing on the river bank, extending his long, ever bigger arms toward her.

"Don't you dare! This isn't your place!" the young girl shouted at him and rushed boldly to the middle of the river.

"Why are you moaning, Aksyutochka, what's wrong?" old Praskukha approached her adopted daughter with the stub of a lit candle in her hand and interrupted the dream.

"I had a frightening dream, grandma. I imagined I was hiding from the devil in the river," Aksyutka answered.

"Have less to do with Aniska and you won't have frightening dreams. You, may the Lord forgive you, hang about her place for days on end. . . . You've entirely forgotten about the vegetable garden! . . . For heaven's sake, you could bring some unclean spirits into our cottage from her! Don't go to her place anymore, Aksyutka!" the old magic healer said, ending her speech.

"All right. I won't go anymore, grandma," replied her adopted child, which surprised Praskukha somewhat.

"It should have happened long ago. But now sleep, Christ be with you! Be sure to say your prayers and you'll have a good dream. Otherwise you'll moan and won't let me sleep."

Soon both the old woman and her adopted daughter were asleep again, and the devil did not come any more to Aksyutka in her dreams.

⁓

The unexpected death of Aniska and Senya stirred up quiet Zaretskoye.

They did not find out about Aniska's death immediately. Men

and women had been crowding around the deacon's house since morning. Some had seen the youth going to the witch's cottage in the evening twilight and decided to demand an explanation from the sorceress of what had happened.

After fruitless knocks on the window, the village policeman and his peasant assistant smashed in the door and, thumping with their boots, walked into the witch's dwelling; she had grown stiff long ago. Flies were crawling on her wide-open eyes and blackened lips. Aniska's face preserved a look of surprise full of suffering.

It was impossible to hide such sudden, suspicious, and simultaneous deaths of a young man and woman from the authorities, who, of course, were notified. The next day the district police officer and a doctor came to the village. The doctor conducted a post-mortem and identified poisoning. The district police officer got busy questioning the inhabitants. After finding out that the day Aniska died Aksyutka happened to have been there, the district police officer gave an order to summon the young girl and bring her to him.

Ever since Aksyutka found out about the death of her mentor in witchcraft and, moreover, the death of Senya, she was not herself from emotion and fear. The young poisoner did not even believe that she was the cause of their deaths. But more and more the fear of punishment began to take possession of Aksyutka's heart.

Sensing something bad, Praskukha tried to question and find out from her adopted child what was troubling her, but she could not get anything out of the girl.

The entire time Aksyutka seemed to be in a fog, offering no answers to the old magic healer's questions; she would sit silently in a corner, then suddenly scream out and, jumping off the bench, move restlessly about the hut and even try to run outside.

But old Praskukha would not let her.

"Cross yourself, Aksyutochka! Calm down! Tell me what happened to you!" the magic healer would say, trying in vain to get an answer out of the girl.

From a corner of the hut she sprinkled water on her adopted child and offered her some water to drink over which a spell had been cast; she even tried to say some half-Christian, half-pagan prayers over Aksyutka, but nothing helped. Praskukha became totally depressed and was close to despair.

On the second day of her adopted daughter's illness, toward evening, there came a knock on the cottage door. Praskukha opened the door and on the threshold appeared the village policeman's assistant with the overgrown red beard, sporting a brass name plate on his chest.

"What do you need, Trofim?" the old woman asked.

"I've come for your young god-given girl. The authorities are asking for her . . . Get dressed, girl," Trofim said in the same voice as that of the devil whom Aksyutka had seen at the road-side cross in her dream.

Aksyutka glanced at his face and grew pale, so much alike were they.

"What's happened to her? . . . Look how frightened she is! Do you really know something? Why are they asking for you?" Praskukha asked carefully.

Not answering the old woman and wanting at the same time to show the policeman's assistant that she was not afraid of him, Aksyutka turned to Trofim:

"And where are you going to take me, uncle?"

"You'll see," the latter answered darkly and meaningfully.

"And if I won't go with you?"

"I'll take you."

Without a word the girl threw on her kerchief and began to walk silently to the porch with the policeman's assistant

At the threshold she half-turned around and, seemingly casually, said to Praskukha, "Farewell, grandma!"

Suddenly, instead of walking with her companion to Aniska's cottage, where the inquiry was taking place, Aksyutka unexpectedly took off running through the village toward the river.

"Don't you dare run away!" Trofim shouted behind her, trying to catch up with her.

With bare heels flashing, the fugitive ran past the mill, crossed the small bridge leading to the dam, and dove silently into the Yaryn.

The village policeman's assistant who had been running after her saw her face from afar, half-covered with hair; her face appeared for an instant above the water and then disappeared again.

When Trofim ran up to the edge of the dam, the circles from Aksinia's dive into the water were already far apart on the surface of the quickly flowing Yaryn.

After looking for some time at these circles, the perplexed and winded peasant spat, unexpectedly for himself, and then remembering something, removed his hat; with hasty businesslike steps he went to inform the authorities about the incident.

The attempts with boat-hooks to find the body of the drowned girl on the deep river bottom did not end in success. It was assumed that Aksyutka's corpse was carried off by the current of the Yaryn.

XXIX

Silence reigned on the somewhat dark, cool, and oozy bottom of the Yaryn. On a slippery snag which was covered with soft, dark-green mold and which substituted for a throne, Maryska was sitting pensively with her elbows resting on her knees and her face in her hands. The look of the tsaritsa of the river bottom, motionless like the idol behind her, was focused on the white, naked (the *rusalka*s had taken off the drowned girl's clothing) body of Aksyutka stretched out at her feet. Maryska was waiting for the time when the round patch of moonlight would slip along the river bottom, moving first over the legs stretched out in a pre-death struggle, then over the maiden's entire body and, resting on the dead girl's face, give the drowned girl a semblance of earthly, even if ghostly, life.

"Well, there'll be one more *rusalka*. At first she'll sigh and be sad, then little by little she'll console herself and begin to sing and run through the rye fields, to laugh with pealing laughter and to gambol with her girlfriends. She'll learn to entice children into the water and to catch fellows having a good time in the fields on moonlit, summer nights. Each one wants to prolong her life here, although not a happy one, at the expense of another, before flying off like vapor into the unknown space of the sky, never to return," Maryska thought.

The monstrous idol of Perun looked at the demon who had become the sovereign of the Yaryn and also thought:

"They didn't bring me girls in sacrifice. . . . And why? It's probably just as pleasant to inhale the vapors emanating from the young blood of girls as it is of boys who have been freshly sacrificed. . . . In earlier times, the beams radiating from the bodies of drowned maidens, which resembled patches of weak moonlight, used to become the property of the master of the waters. But now, when he's no longer here, who will absorb these beams? I don't know how to do it, no matter what efforts Maryska has expended in this matter. Only the vapors from blood please me. . . ."

In the meantime the round patch of light from the full, silvery moon which had penetrated to the river bottom touched Aksyutka's legs. Thin and well-proportioned, they seemed surprisingly white. The idol of Perun became involuntarily lost in admiration.

"Some time long ago, still in those times when I was the sovereign of the sky, one of my wives had a maiden-young girl with the same kind of legs. What was her name? . . . I don't remember. Her mother was called Lieto. . . . Oh, now I remember! Lietnitsa or Dzevana. The young girl was a good archer. . . . What happened to her? What fate befell her? She was a goddess, under various names, of various tribes. Leafy groves and small woods were consecrated to her, as to me. . . . What, however, has happened to Maryska?!"

The sovereign of the Yaryn was no longer sitting on the petrified snag but kneeling near the body illuminated by the moon's radiance and attentively peering at the dark birthmark on the bluish-white left hip. Suddenly the tsaritsa of the river bottom bent over and fitfully began to kiss this birthmark; then she pressed her hands to her chest and threw her head back in despair. . . . Then again, continuing to kneel, she began to scrutinize the parts of the drowned girl's body that were being gradually caressed by the patch of moonlight.

When this patch of light reached Aksyutka's face and illuminated it, Maryska, with tormenting pain in her heart, saw for the first time, after what seemed like fourteen inexpressibly long years, her daughter's features.

The face illuminated by the moonlight now seemed to be coming to life so that its possessor could become an indifferent and cold *rusalka* in the waters of the Yaryn. . . .

Appendix

The descriptions which follow are composite portraits of demonic beings developed from a variety of sources and studies. In general, no attempt has been made to point out regional differences or to speculate about the extent to which these beings are part of the cultural space of Russians and Ukrainians today. However, it is noteworthy that in the 1990s a number of new dictionaries and encyclopedias of magic, superstitions and demonology have appeared, and various 19th century and early 20th century studies of Slavic/Russian folklore have been republished. This suggests that people are, at the very least, interested in rediscovering the folklore beliefs and traditions that were part of village life for centuries.

It is hoped that the descriptions which follow, taking into account the most characteristic and essential features of the most important beings in Russian demonology, will help the student to appreciate Kondratiev's vision and art.

Descriptions of practitioners of magic follow those of popular folk spirits.

A bibliography of sources is given at the end of this listing.

Spirits of Water, Forest, and Field

bolotnik (*болотник*):
From the word for "swamp" (*болото*), the *bolotnik* is the spirit and master of a swamp or marsh who, in folk imagination, is related to the *leshy* and the *vodyanoi*. Many kinds of devils inhabit his territory, but it is not clear to what extent they are subject to

his power. The *bolotnik* enjoys leading travelers to his bog and getting them lost.

There are many folk sayings connected with the bolotnik's territory, such as: "If there's a swamp, there are devils" (*Было бы болото, а черти будут*) and "Devils abound in a quiet swamp" (*В тихом болоте черти водятся*).

bolotnitsa (*болотница*):
The *bolotnitsa* is a female spirit of the swamp, who has many features in common with the *rusalka* (see below). She, too, likes to sing and bewitch men; she enjoys leading people astray who have wandered into her swamp.

domovoi (*домовой*):
From the word for "house, home" (*дом*), a spirit of the house or household who looks after the well-being of its inhabitants. He is never addressed directly as *domovoi*, but as "grandfather" (*дедушка*), "master of the house" (*хозяин*), and "dear neighbor"(*соседко*). The *domovoi* is said to live behind the stove, although sometimes he is described as living in the cattle shed and stables because of his fondness for farm animals. In that capacity he is often referred to as *domovoi-dvorovoi* (*двор* meaning "yard"). He is very territorial and protective of the property of the household master; he engages in fights with neighboring *domovoi*s suspected of stealing hay or oats from the horses and cattle of his master; people with acute hearing are said to be able to hear the sounds of the struggle.

The *domovoi* often resembles the master of the house or one of the family's relatives, which suggests the probable origins of the *domovoi* in ancient ancestor worship. He is rarely seen although he has been pictured as a grand-fatherly old man, covered with hair, and a bit grey from the dust and his status as a distant ancestor.

Although the *domovoi* is generally invisible, he can make himself heard. Pots falling, articles breaking, and creaking and pounding sounds at night are attributed to the *domovoi*'s generally mischievous nature. He likes to pull off bed coverings at night and to tickle people. As many demonic spirits, he can change his form; he likes to turn into a grey cat and jump on a sleeper's chest, giving the latter the sensation of being strangled. In folk belief, if the sleeper senses a soft paw, it is a good omen.

The *domovoi* tends to work: he grooms and feeds the horses of his master and watches over his yard, cattle and household. He is happy when the master of the house is clever and industrious and the household prospers; he loves to see horses and cattle multiply. However, if the master of the house becomes lazy and neglects his household, so will the *domovoi*.

The *domovoi* is associated with other characteristics as well. He is said to be fond of tobacco and likes to be treated to a piece of bread. He is reputed to hate drunks and women with loose, flowing hair; he takes pleasure in braiding a woman's hair at night. If someone in the household is dying, the *domovoi* will make howling noises.

If the household moves, steps are taken to ensure that the *domovoi* moves, too. There are various traditions. One ritual calls for members of the household to collect dirt on the threshold of the old hut and scatter it in the new one; the dirt serves as the medium for the *domovoi*'s passage from the old house into the new. In another ritual, during a house-warming the *domovoi* is offered a bowl of kasha and respectfully invited by the master of the house, "Grandfather *domovoi*, leave the old hut and come into the new. Come live with us!" (*Дедушка домовой, выходи домой. Иди к нам жить.*)

leshy (*леший*); **leshachikha** (*лешачиха*), the *leshy*'s wife:
The *leshy* (from *лес*, meaning "woods, forest") is a spirit that inhabits woods and forests. He is fond of fir and pine trees and rarely leaves his domain for fear of encroaching on the territory of the *polevik* (*полевик*), the spirit of fields and meadows. A combination of man and animal, he looks furry like a sheep; his hair is long, and he has a green beard and burning green eyes; he is often described as not having eyebrows or eyelashes. Some narratives describe him as bluish in color because blue blood courses through his veins. One of his trademarks is to button left to right as opposed to the usual right to left. He also wears his left shoe on his right foot and his right shoe on his left. At times he disguises himself as an old man with a knapsack on his back.

The *leshy* can have a wife, a *leshachikha*, usually a girl who had been damned by her parents and thus turned into a dark spirit. The children of the *leshy* are children who had been damned by their parents, or offspring from his union with the *leshachikha.* As in the case of the *vodyanoi,* descriptions of a *leshy's* dwelling differ, from a big house to a small hut.

The *leshy* can sing without using words: the sounds of a storm in a forest, all the whistling and crackling sounds in a forest, are part of his song. People say that a wind storm in the woods is actually the *leshy* moving in disguise. If there are several *leshies* in the forest, one is the tsar *leshy.*

All animals and birds in the woods are subject to the *leshy.* Rabbits in particular feel his power because he uses them as collateral in card games—a favorite pastime—with fellow *leshies.* If he loses at cards, an agreed upon number of rabbits is sent to the territory of the *leshy* who has won. Some sources claim that the bear is the favorite animal of the *leshy.* Since wolves are subject to his power, the *leshy* can send them out against a peasant's cattle unless an agreement has been reached between himself and the peasant.

It is vital not to stay in the woods after dusk has set in; this is the time when the *leshy* likes to be out and hunt for people foolish enough to invade his territory at that forbidden time of the day. He will not tolerate work at night in the forest; some view this as protecting the woods from people intent on stealing wood.

The *leshy* has his mischievous, playful side, too, just like the *domovoi.* He can lead mushroom pickers astray; he can bring on a fog and hence confuse people as to where they are. People who get lost in the woods and circle endlessly are said to be the victims of the *leshy's* trickery. It is traditional for people about to enter a forest to ask for the *leshy's* permission. Prayer and the sign of the cross are also rituals one must follow to be safe in the woods.

People are warned not to go into the woods on October 14 because that is the day when the *leshy* begins disappearing and quieting down. He reappears with the spring thaws.

As other demonic beings, the *leshy* is a shapeshifter. He can turn into a tree stump or a tussock; he can be as tall as any tree in the forest or as small as the smallest leaf.

Like the *vodyanoi,* the *leshy* does not like people cursing and will punish those who use swear words. A woman giving birth who curses herself or her child because of the pain condemns the child to be taken by the *leshy.* He will take the newborn and place a sickly child from the forest in its place. If the cursed child is christened before the *leshy* has had a chance to steal it, he will wait seven years and then lure that child back into the forest Some people claim that the *leshy* is fond of human women and often kidnaps them.

Since the *leshy* is a demonic sprit, he does not like salt; he is also afraid of fire.

lozovik (*лозовик*):
From the word for "willows" (*лоза*), a *lozovik* is a small demon who lives in low-lying willow bushes and osier-beds.

rusalka (*русалка*):
*Rusalka*s are believed to be the spirits of women who have ended their lives by drowning themselves or female children who have died without being baptized. The women or children are considered to have died an unnatural or premature death and belong, therefore, to the "dark" world, the world of the demonic.

As representatives of the unclean force, *rusalka*s can transform themselves into birds, little wood animals, and even frogs.

Establishing a commonly held view of a *rusalka* is somewhat difficult. In the north of Russia, the *rusalka* is closer to a witch and therefore often referred to as a female devil (*чертовка*). In Russia proper, she is evil, malicious, vengeful, and her image is close to that of a *vodyanoi*; she is often described as having a pale face, and green eyes and hair. In the south of Russia and Ukraine, from where Kondratiev draws his image of Gorpina, the image is quite different. Here, the *rusalka*s are beautiful women, with long, flowing hair (usually associated with witches) that is blonde or light brown. They live in groups or communities in rivers, streams, and lakes and answer to the *vodyanoi*; they come out of the water at night when there is moonlight (the moon being associated with the demonic and the world of the dead). They spend their time entertaining themselves, particularly in the summer when they can swing from trees, gather flowers and make garlands, sing and dance in the woods and fields.

The belief that with Trinity Sunday the *rusalka*s leave the waters and go into the woods to swing from willow and birch trees is connected by some scholars to the old Slavic belief that the souls of the dead resided in the trees. In this respect, the *drevyanitsa*s (from *дерево* or *древо*, meaning "tree") or female tree-dwelling spirits, can be viewed as the predecessors of the *rusalka*s. Some scholars argue that since the *rusalka*s are demonic beings, they go seeking shade in the woods when the sun gets too hot on the water. Rusalnaya Week (*Русальная неделя*) (which begins with Trinity Sunday and is more commonly known as "Zelyonye Sviatki" or Green Yuletide, falling during the seventh or eighth week after Easter) is a particularly dangerous time of the year, and people stay away from the woods and waters. Various rituals of appeasement are practiced in recognition of the danger that the *rusalka*s can pose at this time of the year. Village girls bring ribbons and entwine them in the branches of willow and birch trees that the *rusalka*s like so much; they leave wreaths of flowers on the branches for them. Women bring pieces of linen or linen shirts and hang them on the trees as offerings for the *rusalka*s who died as non-baptized children.

The *rusalka* spends much of her time combing her long, thick hair. The comb has magical properties: as she combs her hair, water flows down her hair and onto the ground, providing moisture and thus contributing to the fertility of the soil. It is also said that where the *rusalka*s have danced and sung the grass is greener and the grain more abundant, further testimony of their fertilizing function.

The *rusalka*s are often viewed as being mischievous. They are accused of entangling fishermen's nets out of boredom. During the harvest season one of their favorite pastimes is to make "twists" and "cuts" in the ripe grain, particularly in fields which belong to people who were unkind to them in their past lives. The *rusalka*s are also characterized as a powerful elemental force: they are capable of bringing storms, rains, and destructive hail. In the popular mind, heavy rain and wind storms at night are associated with the wedding celebrations and dancing of the *rusalka*s.

From the perspective of world mythology, the characteristics associated with the *rusalka*s in the south of Russia and Ukraine bring to mind the Greek sirens, the German Lorelei, and the French Ondine. The *rusalka*s long for the company of men. As beautiful seductresses who sing in bewitching ways, they lure men into the water, only to tickle them to death. Since *rusalka*s are also hostile to women, girls and women who go to the woods when the *rusalka*s are out of the water, arm themselves with wormwood (*полынь*) for protection, often intertwining the herb in their hair. It is believed that if you meet a *rusalka* in the forest and she asks you, "Wormwood or parsley?" (*Полынь или* *петрушка?*), the correct answer is "wormwood." If you answer "parsley," she will respond, "Ah, your soul is mine!" (*Ах, моя душка!*), and tickle you to death. The question and answer rhyme in Russian: *петрушка* (*petrushka*), *душка* (*dushka*).

Scholars point out that the memorial services held during the Green Yuletide for those who have died an early or unnatural death are closely associated with the *rusalka*s. Moreover, other village rites, such as making a straw effigy of a *rusalka* and taking her out of the village in a procession of women, "burning, drowning or tearing to pieces the effigy" (Ivanits, p. 80) at the end, suggests banishing something unclean and dangerous from settled areas at the beginning of the new agricultural season.

vodyanoi (*водяной*):
From the word for "water" (*вода*), the *vodyanoi* is the chief spirit of the water, be it river, lake, or swamp. He lives in deep pools (*омуты*) in a river or other body of water and is especially drawn to mills. Some claim that he has a rich dwelling in the reeds and sedge built of river stone and shells; others claim he has a modest hut. The *vodyanoi* has his own herds of cattle, horses, pigs, and sheep, which are driven from the water to pasture fields at night. He likes to splash on the surface of the water, particularly on a moonlit night, and he also enjoys riding on the back of a large sheat-fish (*сом*), which serves as his horse.

Descriptions of a *vodyanoi*'s appearance vary, from that of a man with shaggy long hair and beard to a fat old man, with tangled green hair, green-skinned, and covered in weeds, slime, and hideous warts, with fish scales covering his body. Some people claim that he has a long fish tail instead of feet and that he also has horns, suggesting the devil in appearance. In fact, the *vodyanoi* is often referred to as the "water devil" (*водяной чёрт*) and considered very dangerous by the peasants: he loves to pull people in the water and have them drown, especially if they are swimming at the wrong time of the year or not wearing a cross.

The *vodyanoi* sometimes likes to go among the people, taking on a human appearance. However, he is easy to spot: water constantly drips off the left flap of his jacket. No matter where he sits, the place becomes wet; should he comb his hair, water streams down his hair, making him akin to the *rusalka*s.

The *vodyanoi* has control over the *rusalka*s in his watery domain; sometimes he is said to have a wife, a *vodyanitsa* (*водяница*), whom people often identify as a *rusalka*; he also has children who get caught in fishermen's nets, which makes him very angry unless they are thrown back in the water. The fish are at his command, and a fisherman's catch is dependent on the good will of the *vodyanoi*. Like the *domovoi*, he enjoys gifts of tobacco. He does not like people making a lot of noise, and he gets angry at people who swear on or near the water.

In winter, when the water is ice-covered, the *vodyanoi* sleeps at the bottom of a deep pool; he emerges in the spring. Because he is hungry and angry, he breaks the cover of ice, raises large waves, and scatters the fish. Peasants bring him various offerings of appeasement: geese, butter, oil, honey, sheeps' heads, and roosters (particularly black ones, black being the *vodyanoi*'s favorite color). Peasants are also careful to make similar sacrificial offerings to the *vodyanoi* whenever a new mill is opened since the deep pools of water near a mill are one of his favorite spots for habitation. These sacrificial gifts are offered with a ritualistic saying, for example, "Here you are, granddad, a gift for your house-warming; love and take pity on our family" (*На тебе, дедушка гостинец на новоселье. Люби и жалуй нашу семью*).

The image that emerges of the *vodyanoi* is that of a powerful and frightening spirit who can be very hostile to people who swim, fish, or engage in any activity near water. Noon, midnight, and the period after sunset to sunrise are considered especially dangerous times of the day.

Practitioners of Magic

As W. E. Ryan, Linda J. Ivanits and others point out, it is difficult to classify people who deal with magic. However, for Kondratiev's reader, an acquaintance with the categories which follow may be helpful.

"knowing man" (*знающий человек*):
Literally a "person who knows" or a person "with knowledge," "knowing man" is a euphemistic term for a sorcerer, witch, or someone believed to possess supernatural powers or secret knowledge.

magic healer (*знахарка* in the Russian text):

Although a magic healer can practice malefic magic, she is more interested in helping people than harming them. Unlike the sorceress, she is viewed more as a healer than a "spoiler." Because of her prime interest in healing, she knows a great deal about magical-medicinal herbs, grasses and roots; folk medicine could be said to be her forte.

A magic healer is very good at spotting "spoiling" and practices various forms of anti-magic to remove "spoiling" from the afflicted person. She is adept at using various charms, spells, and potions, which she usually combines with prayer. She often resorts to sprinkling the afflicted person with holy water.

A magic healer is sometimes referred to as a sorceress, which leads to the difficulty of classification.

Kondratiev usually refers to Praskukha as a magic healer.

sorceress (*колдунья*, from *колдовать* meaning "to practice witchcraft, sorcery, magic;" and *ведунья* from *ведать*, meaning "to know"):
A sorceress practices black as well as white magic, i.e., she is able to perform malefic as well as benevolent magic. Her hut is fragrant with the smell of various herbs and roots because she practices folk magic and folk medicine. She can tell fortunes and interpret dreams. But there is also a more sinister side to a sorceress: she knows countless spells and incantations for "spoiling" (see *witch* below), and she is often feared because people associate her with the evil eye. Since a sorceress is often referred to as a witch (*ведьма*) as well, people attribute her supernatural powers to her close alignment with the devil.

Kondratiev frequently refers to Aniska as a sorceress (*колдунья*), although he calls her a witch as well. He uses *ведунья* a good number of times in reference to Praskukha, and once or twice in reference to Aniska.

witch (*ведьма*):
The Russian word for "witch" is also connected with the verb "to know" (*ведать*) and stands for a female person "who knows, possesses special knowledge." A witch is sometimes called a sorceress (*колдунья*) but usually differentiated from a magic healer (*знахарка*), who is strongly associated with white magic and folk medicine. A witch is thought to have a bad character and a wider knowledge of the occult arts than the magic healer.

A witch lives among the people and may look like other women, young and old, during the day, although it is often claimed that she has a little tail which can give her away. In general, a witch in Russia proper tends to be depicted as an old woman, usually humpbacked, with a hooked nose and disheveled grey hair; sometimes she has a limp. In the south of Russia and in Ukraine, she is depicted more often than not as a young woman with long, flowing hair who is single and lives alone. People come to her for her knowledge of black and white magic.

Witches are generally considered to be "born" or "learned." The born witch is said to be the offspring of a witch or of a woman who has had dealings with the unclean force. The learned witch has acquired her knowledge of witchcraft through an apprenticeship or study with a practicing witch, or she has entered into an agreement with the devil on her own initiative. It is also believed that a woman can become a witch unwittingly; for example, a woman who accepts any object from the hands of a dying witch becomes the unsuspecting recipient of the witch's knowledge of the dark art.

A witch is an agent of the devil and her life inevitably entails dealing with the unclean force. She makes special ointments and potions which allow her to fly out on a broom, mop, or stove fork through the stovepipe or chimney at night and attend witches' sabbaths on Bald Mountain (Lysaya gora) near Kiev. Here, it is relevant to note that the concept of a witches' sabbath is of West European origin, reaching Russians and Ukrainians through West Slavic folklore. It is also believed that a witch flies out of a chimney in the form of a bird, whirlwind, or smoke; she does this when evening has set in or at night. The connection of witches to stoves, stovepipes, and chimneys is very strong.

There are many popular narratives about witches riding on the back of a man whom they have changed into a horse.

In order to turn into another being, such as a crow, black cat, or pig, a witch performs a ritualistic number of somersaults (usually twelve in number).

Witches are particularly adapt at all kinds of "spoiling" or malefic magic. Assuming the form of an animal or rodent, she can bite people and bring on illness; she can cast spells and send illnesses through water, wind, and various other objects. She can "spoil" simply by touching a person or by her look , i.e., by giving the person the evil eye. Moreover, a witch has the power to "spoil" not only people but grain fields as well. She is quite adapt at twisting the grain stalks and pressing the ears of grain to the ground and thus ruining the harvest. She can also make a "cut" or a little path in the field so that the unclean force sends the grain to the witch's bins or storage area. More than that, the witch is thought to have power over nature itself: she can assure a good harvest or a bad one and bring rain or drought.

A witch is particularly adapt at milking other people's cows and turns into a pig, cat, fox or other animal in order to enter a cow shed undetected. A witch can milk a cow literally dry, leading to the ruin and death of the animal. Folk narratives tell of peasants leaving a small aspen tree in the door to the cow shed, scattering flax seeds in the yard, and hanging thistle plants on the cow shed doors as anti-magic against witches and their evil designs.

There are various beliefs as to how you can spot a witch during the day. One belief holds that before Easter witches try to touch a priest during the church services in order to receive magical powers from him. Another belief holds that if during the Easter service you look at a woman who is a witch through a piece of wood from a dead person's coffin, you will see a pail of milk on her head. It is also believed that if at Easter time you have a piece of blessed cheese in your mouth, you can see witches turning their backs to the altar when the priest proclaims, "Christ has risen!"

A witch is believed to die a painful death. One explanation is that the soul is having a difficult time separating itself from the body. Another explanation is that a witch's last torturous days or hours are due to her desire to pass on her special knowledge to someone else; people are warned not to come near lest they become the unwilling recipients of the witch's demonic powers. Yet another popular view is that the witch dies in agony because she is tortured by demons and all the ugliness associated with the demonic that is to be found inside her: worms, snakes, toads, and the like.

A witch can cause trouble after death as well. She is said to persecute her former lovers and those who rejected her love, as well as people who tried to unmask or expose her during her lifetime. She can leave the grave at night and move about, giving people in the area no peace. There are a number of folk narratives which describe digging up the grave of a woman suspected of being a witch and driving an aspen stake through her body to stop her from terrifying people at night.

Kondratiev refers regularly to Aniska and Stepanida as witches; he also refers several times to Aniska as a sorceress.

Bibliography

Source Materials
(for the Appendix as well as the Notes)

Afanas'ev, A. *Поэтические воззрения славян на природу*. 3 тома. 1865–69. Reprint. The Hague: Mouton, 1969–70.

Dal', V. I. *О повериях, суевериях и предрассудках русского народа*. Репринтное издание. Санкт-Петербург: Изд. "Литера," 1994.

———. *Толковый словарь живого великого русского языка*. В четырех томах. Репринтное воспроизведение издания 1903–1909 гг. Москва: Терра, 1998.

Dixon-Kennedy, Mike. *Encyclopedia of Russian & Slavic Myth and Legend*. Santa Barbara, California: ABC-CLIO, 1998.

Gol'tsman, Ye. *Магические знаки и растения. Справочник*. Москва: Изд. центр "ТЕРРА," 1996.

Ivanits, Linda J. *Russian Folk Belief*. Armonk, New York: M. E, Sharpe, Inc., 1992

Korinfskii, A. A. *Народная Русь. Круглый год сказаний, поверий, обычаев и пословиц русского народа*. 1901. Репринтное изд. Смоленск: РУСИЧ, 1995.

Maksimov, S. V. *Нечистая, неведомая и крестная сила*. Текст печатается в современной орфографии по изданию 1903 года. Санкт-Петербург: ТОО "ПОЛИСЕТ," 1994.

Moyle, Natalie K. "Mermaids (*Rusalkas*) and Russian Beliefs about Women," *New Studies in Russian Language and Literature*. Eds. Anna L. Crone and Catherine V. Chvany. Columbus: Slavica Publishers, 1987, pp. 221–237.

Novikova, T. A., автор-составитель. *Русский демонологический словарь*. Санкт-Петербург: Петербургский писатель, 1995.

Pankeev, Ivan, редактор. *Полная знциклопедия быта русского народа*. том I и II. Москва: "ОЛМА-ПРЕСС" 1998.

Petrukhin, V. Ia. et al., научные редакторы. *Энциклопедический словарь. Славянская мифология*. Москва: Эллис Лак, 1995.

Platonova I. and Vysotskii, V., составители. *Энциклопедия русской магии. Приметы и поверья*. Санкт-Петербург: "Респекс," 1999.

———, *Энциклопедия русской магии. Волшебство и чародейство*. Санкт-Петербург: "Респекс," 1999.

Redford, E. and M. A and Minenok, E., составители. *Энциклопедия суеверий*. Москва: "Локид"—"Миф", 1995.

Ryan, W. F. *The Bathhouse at Midnight. An Historical Survey of Magic and Divination in Russia*. University Park, Pennsylvania: The Pennsylvania State University Press, 1999.

Sterlingov, M., ответственный редактор. *Русское колдовство, ведовство, знахарство*. Санкт-Петербург: Изд. "Литера," 1994.

Talalai, M.G., автор-составитель. *День Ангела. Справочная книга по именам и именинам*. Санкт-Петербург: "ТРИАЛ," 1992.

Tokarev, S. A., главный редактор. *Мифы народов мира. Энциклопедия в двух томах*. Второе издание. Москва: "Советская энциклопедия," 1987–1988.

Vagurina, L., редактор. *Славянская мифология. Словарь-справочник*. Москва: Линор & Совершенство, 1998.

Vlasova, M. *Новая АБЕВЕГА русских суеверий. Иллюстрированный словарь*. Санкт-Петербург: Северо-Запад, 1995.

Worobec, Christine D. "Witchcraft Beliefs and Practices in Prerevolutionary and Ukrainian Villages." *The Russian Review*, vol. 54, April 1995: 165–187.

Zabylin, M. *Русский народ. Его обычаи, обряды, предания, суеверия и поззия*. Репринтное воспроизведение издания 1880 года. Москва: Совместное советско-канадское предприятие "Книга Принтшоп," 1990.

Zelenin. D. K. *Избранные труды. Очерки русской мифологии. Умершие неестественною смертью и русалки*. Москва: Изд. "Индрик," 1995.

Middlebury Studies in Russian Language and Literature

Middlebury Studies in Russian Language and Literature seeks to expand our knowledge of the latest developments in linguistics, literary and pedagogical scholarship devoted to Russian language and literature. The series includes analyses of texts and authors, translations of significant literary and scholarly works, and writing on theoretical and applied linguistics with special attention to new methods for the teaching of Russian language and literature.

For additional information about this series or for the submission of manuscripts, please contact:

Thomas R. Beyer, Jr.
c/o Peter Lang Publishing, Inc.
Acquisitions Department
P.O. Box 1246
Bel Air, MD 21014-1246

To order other books in this series, please contact our Customer Service Department:

(800) 770-LANG (within the U.S.)
(212) 647-7706 (outside the U.S.)
(212) 647-7707 FAX

Or browse online by series:

www.peterlangusa.com